of **Massachusetts.**

OUSAND EIGHT HUNDRED AND FIFTY,

N ACT

siological Institute of Boston

epresentatives, in Gene ... led,

Ann M. Kendall, C.E.N.

, Rebecca W Clendly,

rs, are hereby made a cor-

Sadies Physiological In-

for the purpose of promo-

FROM THE PAST

TO THE FUTURE

No. 8528

Commonwealth

Be it Known That whereas

Electa N. L. Walton, Mary Ald...
Kilham, Annie T. Colby, Josep...
Holden, J. Arabella Richard...
Mabel Loomis Todd, Ida Ba...
T. Caroline Kellogg, Caroline...

have associated themselves with th...

name of the

Massachusetts State...

for the purpose of securing m...

case of need, united act...

Massachusetts,

FROM THE PAST

TO THE FUTURE

*A History of the
Massachusetts State Federation
of Women's Clubs: 1893-1988*

By
The History Committee
of the Federation

Published for the
Massachusetts State Federation of Women's Clubs
by
Phoenix Publishing
Canaan, New Hampshire

Library of Congress Cataloging-in-Publication Data

From the past to the future.

Includes index.
1. Massachusetts State Federation of Women's Clubs—
History. I. Massachusetts State Federation of Women's Clubs.
History Committee.
HQ1905.M4F76   1988   305.4'06'0744   88-9844
ISBN 0-914659-32-4

Copyright 1988 by the
Massachusetts State Federation of Womens Clubs

Printed in the United States of America

Contents

Introduction   vii

Foreword   ix

I   The Federation Presidents   1

II   The Federation Story   47

     Beginnings 1893-1918   49

     Growth 1918-1942   83

     Adjustment 1942-1960   116

     Maturity 1960-1988   141

III Member Clubs   187

IV   Chronology   207

List of Illustrations   220

Index   223

Introduction

IN 1932 the first history of the Masssachusetts State Federation of Women's Clubs was written to preserve its achievements since its inception in 1893. *Progress and Achievement* was the title and the contents have proven invaluable over the years.

The second history was written during Marcia Shepard's administration thirty years later in 1962. This book was a revision of the first history with the purpose of bringing dates, personnel, and other data up to date. Again we appreciate this fine piece of work and have used it many times for reference.

In 1986 the incoming president (being somewhat of an historian) wished to have a new history prepared which would encompass all phases of our Federation story. The emphasis is on the heart of our Massachusetts Federation, the local clubs. The worth of everything we do starts with the programs undertaken by the local clubs. It is important that we learn of the past in order to build our future. With this delving into past accomplishments, the future shines brightly for all of us.

The committee chosen for this monumental task was selected with care by the president. Eleanore MacCurdy was named chairman to coordinate the committee's work, and the members were Bernice Ahearn, Anita Jackson, Florence Magrane, Mildred Orlitzki, Jeannette Pauplis, and Rita Revil. Each of these women has worked countless hours preparing and collecting material to be written in the final history.

Accomplishing the researching and writing of this history within two years' time is an incredible feat. The committee should be commended for undertaking and completing such a task. We can be proud of their work and will always be grateful to those dedicated women.

The history of 1988 is written and is everything we hoped it would be. It is readable, interesting, and full of information and anecdotes, and most of all expertly compiled and attractively presented. Our history is one to make all of us proud to belong to the Massachusetts State Federation of Women's Clubs.

Nancy Beatty
President

Upton, Massachusetts
November 16, 1987

Foreword

WHAT A PRIVILEGE we were given two years ago when our president, Nancy Beatty, asked us to compile a new history of the Massachusetts State Federation of Women's Clubs. In appreciation we dedicate this history to Nancy who guided, inspired, and supported us in our endeavor.

As we gathered data from the memorabilia of the Federation, scrapbooks, files, and histories of local clubs, we became aware of the tremendous influence the Federation has had upon our state, our towns, our families, and our own lives. What a world we would live in today if there had been no Federation — no leadership goals — no women of vision — no one to risk implementing new ideas, new programs.

Reading the pages of history you will be proud to be a member of the Federation. We have been the social engineers who established libraries, founded visiting nurse associations, started kindergartens. Long before literacy was a national concern Federation members set up lending libraries like the one established in 1855 by the Ladies' Library Association of Randolph. Good health has also been emphasized since 1847 when the Ladies' Physiological Institute of Boston was formed.

Turning the pages of our history you will read about the tremendous response to the needs of Chelsea when a fire swept that city in 1908 leaving thousands of people homeless. Time and again Federation members have demonstrated that they care and they have the organization which can cope, no matter what the emergency — natural disasters, world wars, the Depression. You, the Federation members, were there giving of yourselves with hours of unselfish volunteer work and the monies that were needed.

Through the years your work continued with your commitment to conservation as seen at the Memorial Forest, now the site of our Headquarters. You have sponsored pioneering educational programs to provide learning opportunities for all, not only the bright students but everyone, no matter their ability or disability.

All work and no play would indeed be a disaster. Remember the first POPS Night in 1959, international trips, many cultural programs, trips to the United Nations, and entertainment at our annual conventions.

It is a story to instill pride, for the Federation has made a difference for all of us. As you read about the vision of our state leaders and the accomplishments of the local clubs you will achieve new concepts, new directions your club can take, from our Federation past to your future.

Teamwork has been our answer to the challenge. We are also deeply indebted to Harriet Weston, who guided us through the maze of memorabilia.

From the past we gain insight to our Federation. It is a heritage to cherish and a foundation on which we shall build our future.

Bernice Ahearn, *Eastern Region*
Anita Jackson, *Southeastern Region*
Florence Magrane, *Northeastern Region*
Mildred Orlitzki, *Western Region*
Jeannette Pauplis, *Central Region*
Rita Revil, *Southern Region*
Eleanore MacCurdy, *Chairman*

The History Committee

FROM THE PAST

TO THE FUTURE

I

THE
FEDERATION
PRESIDENTS

The Federation Presidents

3

Julia Ward Howe, Boston
(Mrs. Samuel G.)
1893-1898

Mrs. Samuel G. Howe, founder and first president of the Massachusetts State Federation of Women's Clubs, brought to the position faith, wit, concern, and friendship. She was fortunate to have been well-educated and broadened by travel. She felt the ideal aim of life was "To learn, to teach, to serve, and to enjoy."

The Federation's first problem was "organization." Business was transacted by the Executive Board, and no record is found of any public meeting between June of 1893 and June 1894. In January 1894, it was voted at a board meeting to join the General Federation of Women's Clubs. It was also voted to hold three public meetings of the Federation each year.

The only committee appointed by Mrs. Howe was "legislative." Prior to the organization of Federation, delegates from all women's organizations in Boston had united to watch legislative proceedings of the Boston City Council, to cooperate in community betterment efforts, and create public opinion for good legislation.

In 1894 also, a Federation committee was appointed to determine the number of women's clubs in the state and bring them into Federation membership. Of the 166 women's clubs, 58 belonged to GFWC, and 23 to the state because GFWC had been formed before MSFWC, and clubs had that direct membership. In 1898 the Conference of Presidents was held for local leaders and found so valuable that yearly sessions were held until 1928.

For most people Julia Ward Howe had established her own memorial in 1861 by composing the stirring and patriotic anthem, "Battle Hymn of the Republic." Mrs. Howe was a brilliant leader and her administration provided the opportunity for service by Massachusetts women. At the end of her administration, she was unanimously elected to the office of Honorary President of the Massachusetts State Federation of Women's Clubs, an office which she held until her death in 1910.

4

Olive M. E. Rowe, Boston
1898-1901

Miss Rowe came to the presidency with a thorough knowledge of the Federation, a great insight into social welfare work, social service and health measures as a result of living with her brother for many years at the Boston City Hospital where he served as superintendent.

During these years, administrative changes were made to give better service and coordinate the club activities and the first listing of clubs, officers and Federation directors was published in 1898, and in 1899 became the first "Federation Manual." In 1900, the manual was enlarged to include reports of standing committees, and also, the Federation was incorporated in order to hold property and administer trust funds. A "Directory of Club Speakers" was prepared to help clubs locate lecturers and programs.

Several Massachusetts women served on the bylaws reorganization committee of GFWC considering sectarianism, non-partisanship, requirements for membership and representation, and final changes were voted at the GFWC Biennial Convention in 1902.

In its first five years, the Federation had grown from 22 clubs to 129. Six standing committees were appointed — education, social service, household science, library committee on home talent days, music publication, and arts and crafts, followed by three additional in 1900 — civil service reform, legislation, and finance.

In 1901 the state federations of the other New England states were invited to be guests — 400 attended the gala evening at Symphony Hall and business sessions the following day at Malden Auditorium. The New England Women's Club members were hostesses before the gala and the Malden club members served luncheon.

The Federation had made progress by establishing departments of work for greater service for Massachusetts clubwomen. In memory of Miss Rowe, a social service scholarship was awarded in 1955.

May Alden Ward,
Cambridge
(Mrs. William G.)
1901-1904

5

Mrs. Ward had great experience in Federation organization, serving under two presidents, and had extensive knowledge of world affairs. As the organization grew, new committees were appointed — press committee, forestry committee, and "reciprocity bureau" instead of "library committee on home talent days." In 1902 a subcommittee of education was formed — the library extension committee. Clubwomen donated books which were put into libraries and sent throughout Massachusetts and beyond wherever the need existed.

In 1902 the Conference Committee of Federated Clubs and the Association of Collegiate Alumnae were created to demand better elementary schools, secure efficient teachers, and eradicate politics from the schools. " A Syllabus for the Study of Civil Service Reform" was printed and distributed, and requests for it came from many other states.

Administrative changes came with growth at a delegate session, per capita dues were raised from four to five cents, with a minimum of two dollars for any one club. Delegate sessions were planned in various locations to benefit local clubs. Representation of clubs was defined, and delegate seats were provided at sessions.

Mrs. Ward was descended from Pilgrim ancestry, and lived most of her married life in Cambridge with her husband, a professor of Ohio Wesleyan University. Her committee work in the Massachusetts Federation totalled forty years. She was a president of many Massachusetts organizations. She was also a noted lecturer on current events, "History in the Making." She was killed in an automobile accident in 1918. Three thousand six hundred and seventy-seven dollars were raised for a scholarship fund at Simmons College in her name.

Helen A. Whittier, Lowell
1904-1907

Helen A. Whittier had been active in Massachusetts club life for many years, and published, with Miss Helen Winslow, the first magazine, *The Club Woman*. In addition to her journalism talents, she was an art critic, a teacher of art, and became an executive at the Whittier Mills in Lowell when her father died.

A few new committees were added *i.e.*, a subcommittee on household economics to study food values, sanitary conditions, and the need for greater efficiency in the home, and extend these through public schools, libraries, and lectures. In 1905 the Social Service Committee became the Civics Committee and one of its first crusades was against tuberculosis by distributing valuable information via a traveling library. A subcommittee of education to promote teaching of citizenship and civic responsibility in the schools, and another on industrial and social conditions was called Consumers League to secure better working conditions for women and children. The Finance Committee's first report showed Federation income of $1,600, with estimated expenses of $1,200 and $355 for contingencies.

In 1906 the Education Committee held a bazaar to raise funds to help finance a new building to replace one that had burned at the Georgia model school, and netted $6,000. Some money was sent, and the rest placed in a separate fund for emergencies and philanthropy.

Clothing and funds of $1,650 were raised to help victims of the San Francisco earthquake. Mrs. Sarah Platt Decker, GFWC President, came to Massachusetts in the spring of 1905, and GFWC accepted the invitation to hold the 1908 biennial in Boston. Miss Georgie A. Bacon declined the nomination to be president as she was chairman of the Biennial Board so Mrs. May Alden Ward accepted the office of president for one year to complete the task of entertaining GFWC.

A scholarship in "Art as Applied to Living" was presented by the Federation to the University of Massachusetts in Miss Whittier's name.

May Alden Ward, Boston
(Mrs. William G.)
1907-1908

Mrs. William G. Ward, the only president to serve a second term, was faced with the preparation for the General Federation Biennial as the primary concern. A Committee of Literature was added, and the subcommittee of School City was changed to Committee on Moral and Civic Training.

The Federation, with the Women's Educational and Industrial Union, hired an expert to inspect manufacturing concerns where women and children were employed and to report back to the Federation. This survey resulted in the improvement of working conditions.

The Federation decided to finance the Biennial instead of asking other organizations to help, and clubs contributed over $11,000 while 2,000 women accepted positions on committees. Many social functions were hosted by clubs and individual clubwomen in honor of the visiting delegates.

Mrs. Ward was nominated by the General Federation Nominating Committee for president, but Mrs. Philip North Moore of St. Louis was nominated from the floor and elected.

The inspiration gained by Massachusetts clubwomen from contact with women from all parts of the United States at the General Federation Biennial meeting gave a new impetus to local club work.

8

Georgie A. Bacon, Worcester
1908-1911

The great fire in the city of Chelsea, leaving thousands homeless, also affected more than one hundred clubwomen directly. A letter was sent by Miss Bacon to all clubs asking for money, clothing, and food. Nearly every club sent to the Federation Special Fund, to the Massachusetts General Relief Fund, or the Chelsea Woman's Club to help.

After fifteen years of extensive growth in the Federation, changes needed to be made, and Miss Bacon suggested committees and departments should conform to the General Federation. Some new committees were formed, others were combined.

In 1909, first rules of the Executive Board were adopted. Vice presidents were designated, i.e., first, second, third and fourth, and duties and scope of the committees were prescribed. The first affiliated organizations were admitted to the Federation in 1910. The *General Federation Bulletin* was successor to the *Massachusetts Federation Bulletin*.

In February 1910 twenty-seven delegates (officers and standing committee chairmen) of other New England states came to meet in Massachusetts. It was voted to hold yearly meetings, to work for the general good of New England, and adopt cooperative efforts in pure food, forestry, health and child care. Thus the New England Conference came into being.

The General Federation found dues from clubs inadequate to meet its financial needs so it was decided in 1911 to create an endowment fund through voluntary contributions from clubs, the income to be used to finance work of the departments of the General Federation.

Because of her recognized executive ability and efficiency, Miss Bacon held many positions in the General Federation. The title Honorary Vice President was conferred upon her by GFWC in 1922. A total of 241 clubs with a membership of over 30,000 in Massachusetts was the count at the close of her administration.

Minna Rawson Mulligan, Natick

(Mrs. Henry Coolidge)

1911-1913

Mrs. Mulligan's administration marked the close of the first twenty years of the Federation during which the membership increased, activities diversified, and its public usefulness became even more effective than it had been hoped for by the most optimistic. First efforts went to raising the Massachusetts quota for the GF Endowment Fund — $10,000, one-tenth of the full amount, which meant a fifty cents per capita obligation.

Mrs. Mulligan and Mrs. Emmons Crocker, first vice president, visited all but one of the clubs in the western part of the state in 1912, and then the clubs in the southeastern section.

To recognize clubs in the middle and western part of the state the number of conferences in those areas were increased, sectional meetings were held, and the 1912 annual meeting was held in Templeton, and the fall meeting in Warren.

In February 1913 a mass meeting of men and women was held by the Federation in the interest of International Peace and Arbitration, due to the generosity of Mrs. J. Malcolm Forbes of Milton, an ardent advocate of settling international disputes by law rather than by war.

The twentieth anniversary of the Federation in 1913 was hosted by The New England Women's Club, and all past presidents, with the exception of Mrs. Howe, gave addresses. Mrs. Percy Pennybacker, General Federation President, also attended and brought greetings.

Service to the community had become the predominant purpose of organized women's clubs, formed originally for self-culture, as a result of the inspirational leadership of the Federation department chairmen. Indeed, the cultural departments expanded their programming to include community projects.

Mrs. Mulligan, after two years of harmony and cooperation, declined the third year, thus setting a precedent which is now the constitutional limit of service. Federation now numbered 260 clubs, two city federations, with a combined membership of 57,246.

10

Florence T. Perkins,
Roxbury
(Mrs. George Winslow)
1913-1916

One of the first successes of this administration was the completion of the General Federation Endowment Fund. Massachusetts clubwomen contributed $11,802, more than their quota of $10,000. Next the state organization turned to the task of obtaining additional income — proceeds of the 1914 Pure Food Exposition with the Boston Retail Grocers' Association at Mechanics Building netted $2,195 for the State Federation Endowment Fund.

Two emergency calls were answered promptly and generously by the Federation for victims of the disastrous Salem fire, and needy hospitals in northern France. Materials and money amounting to 36 cases consisting of 234,706 pieces of dressings, sponges, bandages, absorbent cotton, old linen, chloroform, antiseptics, and surgical instruments were sent.

Recognizing the need for increased communication between the state organization and the clubs, it was determined that the monthly *Bulletin*, first issued in February 1915, would include messages from the chairmen and the president and would be sent to each club.

In May 1916 to obtain a closer liaison with the local clubs, the following recommendations, prepared by the chairmen and approved by the Council, were voted at the annual meeting: the state to be districted into not more than ten areas, with a representative from each, that the state appoint a Federation Secretary from each district to receive all communications and report, that a director be appointed from the Board for each district, that the slogan for 1916-1917 be "Know Your Own Community," and that at least one program a year be devoted to Federation work.

The New England Conference of State Federations of Women's Clubs was held in Boston in 1916 — addresses presented were "Prison Reform," "Baby Week," and "The Problem of the Feeble Minded."

Claire H. Gurney,
Wollaston
(Mrs. Herbert J.)
1916-1919

Mrs. Gurney, referred to affectionately and appreciatively as the "War President," turned the attention of Massachusetts clubwomen to the unusual conditions of the time.

At the October 1916 Federation meeting it was voted to increase per capita dues from five to seven cents. The task of districting the state and the appointment of directors ensued, and two definite aims of "Know Your Own Community" and "A Study of Latin America" were relegated to the background as the great needs of Red Cross activities and the growing menace of World War I became of pressing interest.

All state women's organizations coordinated activities under the Women's Council of National Defense. Clubs involved in war work supplied money, Liberty Loans, necessary supplies, and knitted items. Clubs increased food production and provided comfort and entertainment for the soldiers. The War Victory Commission of the General Federation was to provide funds for soldiers' recreation overseas. Massachusetts raised $23,000 (second in the states).

The epidemic of influenza was responded to by Massachusetts clubwomen. Clubhouses were turned into hospitals and clubwomen became volunteer nurses. In December 1917 the collision of two vessels, one loaded with munitions, in Halifax, Nova Scotia harbor, led to clubhouses again becoming receiving stations for clothing and other necessities for victims.

Even though it had been feared that war activities would weaken the Federation, women who had formed relief units merged into regular club work or formed new clubs, and in 1919 there were 301 clubs, 4 city federations, 6 affiliated organizations, and a combined membership of 110,577 in the Federation.

A scholarship was awarded in memory of Mrs. Gurney in the field of international affairs and historical writing.

12

Marion Chase Baker,
Concord
(Mrs. George Minot)
1919-1922

Following the period of club projects that would help the war effort, this administration looked to the spiritual side of life, urging "it is to the practical things we must direct our best thoughts and energy . . . each club can do so much to help better its own community. The circle of service is ever widening."

Once again departments of the Federation were rearranged to correspond more closely with that of the General Federation. In 1920 the four Massachusetts girls who had served in cantonments with the GFWC War Victory Commission returned home, the unit was demobilized, and the service flag was placed among the cherished possessions of the Federation.

The Public Health Committee created great support for the Children's Hospital in Brookline, endowing two beds (more than $2,000) in the name of the Federation. Local clubs endowed several beds, and provided hospital facilities for underprivileged children.

A redistricting plan creating fifteen districts was voted to go into effect the following year. Past presidents of the state federation were given delegate privileges in 1921. At the fall meeting, "America, the Beautiful," written by Katherine Lee Bates was adopted as the state song of the Massachusetts Federation.

Again the number of clubs increased from 308 in 1919 with a membership of 47,231 to 355 in 1922 with a membership of 67,235. Four city federations and four affiliated organizations brought the member total to 143,963.

She was founder and honorary vice president of the Massachusetts Presidents' Club, very active in the DAR, and a Marion Chase Baker Fellowship was established at MacDowell Colony in Peterboro, New Hampshire, from a trust fund of $3,000, to benefit an art-gifted student in her name.

Grace Poole Reynolds, Brockton
(Mrs. H. G. Reynolds)
1922-1924

In 1922 the objective of $25,000 for the Endowment Fund was reached with an excess and the decision was made then to establish a permanent headquarters. The first was a single room at 585 Boylston Street, Boston, open five half-days with volunteers. Equipment and furnishings were donated by clubs and clubwomen — 685 visitors registered the first year.

Then monies were also raised to contribute to GFWC Headquarters in Washington, and Massachusetts gave $6,956 for the furnishings of the Julia Ward Howe Room. *Federation Topics* grew to 3,810 subscribers, and became self-supporting. A Press and Publicity Committee was appointed, and the Board of Directors was enlarged.

Resolutions adopted were varied; support rehabilitation of refugees in the Near East, oppose any change in the salute to the flag, uphold law in regard to games of chance. The Federation was active in legislation, and presented both sides of every question before final action was taken by delegates. The Federation was instrumental in obtaining favorable action providing for educational films in schools and colleges, and was successful in putting forth an initiative petition for the examination and classification of prisoners in county jails.

In September the New England Conference was entertained at the New Ocean House in Swampscott, and in May the annual meeting was held there, a tradition that continued for many years.

The State Federation continued to grow — from 335 clubs with a membership of 57,870 to 358 clubs with 63,828 members. Mrs. Poole was elected to fill the unexpired term of Mrs. Baker as GFWC Director, later was elected corresponding secretary, recording secretary, vice president, and GFWC President in 1932. Following her presidency, she became Dean of Stoneleigh College for one year, then married Dr. H. G. Reynolds, and moved to Kentucky.

14

Mabel Johnson Smith,
Somerville
(Mrs. Frederick Glazier)
1924-1926

Federation Headquarters, now at 687 Boylston Street, Boston, proved so valuable, this administration decided to add another room and employ a paid secretary.

Administrative changes, too, included in 1924 all sessions of the Federation to be business meetings, department names and committees were conformed to those of GFWC, and in January, 1926, a regular weekly radio service was inaugurated. WNAC and other stations offered facilities from time to time. Conferences were limited to five each year in various districts where all chairmen could present their programming, in addition to a legislative conference for each.

The General Federation Music Committee asked state federations to schedule contests for "music memory" and compete later at Atlantic City. This was designed to encourage young people to become better acquainted with good music and many Massachusetts cities and towns became so enthusiastic about it, the music competition became a part of school work. The Arlington "team," co-financed by the Arlington Woman's Club and the MSFWC, had one of its contestants, a girl, sixteen years old, win the top prize of a radio victrola and one hundred dollars worth of records. The Federation Choral Society, organized by the State Federation Music Committee, gave its first concert with 100 voices on April 22, 1927. In a contest for state songs, the top selection was "Massachusetts, Old Bay State."

Interest in Junior Membership developed during this administration, and at the 1924 annual meeting Juniors brought a message, and past presidents gave greetings linking past, present, and future.

The number of clubs in the Federation had now increased to 372, and membership to 65,353. Mrs. Smith was elected GFWC Director as she retired from the Massachusetts presidency.

Mary Pratt Potter,
Greenfield
(Mrs. Arthur Devens)
1926-1928

15

Mrs. Potter was the first president of the MSFWC to come from the "west." During this administration round table meetings were established at conferences, and Club Institutes at the Vendome, Boston.

At the fall meeting in 1926, the following legislation policy was discussed. The modified policy adopted at midwinter meeting, 1928, was "that legislative matters be presented to the clubs for consideration and study and that the Federation reserve the right at all times to action on the principle of any measure recommended for consideration by the Legislative Department and the Executive Board."

In February 1927 an exciting achievement of the Art Department together with the Boston Society of Sculptors and the Boston Society of Landscape Architects was an exhibition of sculpture and settings. The Federation contributed one hundred dollars to help organize the Boston Women's Symphony Orchestra of seventy women with a woman conductor.

Outside organizations recognized the Federation with participation in the (all-male) New England Council, the State Advisory Board of the Department of Education, and the Americanization Exhibit at the Eastern States Exposition at Springfield.

In May 1927 the Convention Hall at the New Ocean House was dedicated to the MSFWC, and at its annual meeting, "the MSFWC was ready to cooperate with the plan of GFWC trustees to raise a Foundation Fund, if it were approved by the majority of state federations."

Mrs. Potter wrote beautiful invocations, and Junior Membership still uses the one written for them at the beginning of all their meetings. A landscape in oils by Marie Day Alexander, given in honor of Mrs. Potter, still hangs in Headquarters. Two fellowships were given in her name in 1950 at the University of Wisconsin.

16

Isabel Packard Westfall,
Springfield
(Mrs. John V.)

1928-1930

During this administration, much Federation activity was increasingly directed through committees. GFWC urged other federations to appoint Mothercraft and Child Welfare divisions. The Community Service Division efforts were directed at raising standards of moving pictures; the Americanization Division prepared "racial background exhibits" to be displayed in many cities; and committees continued to cooperate with state agencies outside the Federation, i.e., American Opera, Chicago Civic Opera Company, Art Week in Boston with the Retail Trade Board.

Once again department names changed, and new committees were formed. Junior Membership, formerly a special department, became a committee. For the funding of the GFWC Endowment Fund, it was hoped each member would contribute $2.50 – half of which would revert back to the State Federation for its work.

Although work was completed for the 14th and 15th Districts Forest, it became necessary to abandon the plan to maintain it, and the land was sold. The money realized was given to the Conservation Division for the purchase of 150 acres in Petersham which was later presented as a gift to the Commonwealth, "as a tribute to the heroic women who have preceded us during three hundred years since the founding of the Massachusetts Bay Colony – a recognition of the Tercentenary in 1930."

A two-day Youth Conference providing features of special interest to young clubwomen was one of the most gratifying projects of this administration. At the fall meeting in November 1928 the Federation was presented with a gavel made of white oak taken from *Old Ironsides*, the head of which was from a piece of the keel that had been underwater for more than 130 years.

The New England Conference again met at New Ocean House in 1928, as well as the GFWC Council two-day meeting in 1929.

Maude Wallace Schrader, Belmont
(Mrs. Carl L.)

1930-1932

P receding her election to the presidency of the Federation, Mrs. Schrader was called the "Book Lady" because of her many book reviews given before organizations and on the radio.

Plans were made for months throughout the country for the "George Washington Bicentennial." Thirty-one women's organizations — political, patriotic, fraternal, and civic — sponsored the event with speeches, presentation of fourteen tableaux, and music. A special performance was given in the morning for school children.

Mrs. Schrader was also appointed by the governor to the Massachusetts Commission for the Blind. As a result of the increased interest in consulting the Headquarters secretary for ideas for club programs, a service was inaugurated whereby names of recommended entertainers and lecturers could be obtained.

Mrs. Schrader became chairman of the committee to conduct the national campaign to present Mrs. Grace Poole Reynolds as candidate for GFWC President in 1932, and a huge bazaar was held at the Copley Plaza, Boston. Card parties, luncheons, and a POPS concert were held — all socially and financially successful.

The Federation's outstanding work for the unemployed in 1930-1931 was the "Welfare Chest," with Mrs. Schrader serving as chairman. Clothing for more than 10,000 was collected at Headquarters in John Hancock Hall, Boston, and local clubs carried on the same work in their communities, reporting weekly to the Federation president. In this way bonds were strengthened between individual clubs and the Federation, and the satisfaction experienced by all in helping the unfortunate brought about a unity of purpose and interest.

18

Irene Willard Bennett,
Cliftondale
(Mrs. Frank P.)
1932-1934

Mrs. Bennett had already served in many important capacities before becoming MSFWC President. She had been on the George Washington Commission, Unemployment Commission, chairman of the Commonwealth Chest and the Commission for the Blind.

During her administration two outstanding projects were developed — the state beautification program and the purchase and presentation of the Federation State Forest to the Commonwealth. Town and city commons, churches, highways, schools, homes, and river banks were beautified. Eighty dumps were cleared, old trees and buildings were removed.

It was necessary to raise $5,000 to purchase the 150 acres in Petersham, and "Play Day" at Petersham opened each club season until the hurricane of 1938 which caused great damage to the area.

The President's interest in the juniors' welfare and progress never lessened, and in this eighth year of junior membership, forty-four clubs flourished. Another youth project Mrs. Bennett was interested in was the Greater Boston Information Service Center for Girls.

On May 10 the Federation Headquarters was moved to 115 Newbury Street, in a new building. Again, money and gifts of furnishings added much to the efficient and gracious decor of the new office. Thirty-one meetings were held there the first year with 835 visitors registered.

The following resolve depicts Mrs. Bennett's outlook on life:
"To keep youthful at heart, and yet grow in wisdom;
To cherish friendships great and small,
To gain in life by retrospection;
To be honest with self and others;
To think well, to work well, to lose well,
As step by step we climb each rung
On the ladder of life!"

Viola White Walker,
Whitinsville
(Mrs. Thomas J.)
1934-1936

M rs. Walker's experience in the Federation as organizer of the Club
Institute before she became president made her initiate changes in her administration to improve the machinery of the Federation to benefit the
clubs. Deans of Directors and Deans of Chairmen were appointed, and
vice presidents assumed particular duties of responsibilities such as editor
of *Federation Topics,* and subscription manager.

She felt annual meetings and conferences should be relieved of the
tedium of too many and too lengthy reports so they were shortened.
Chairmen were divided into two groups so that some were assigned to
speak at the even-numbered districts, the others at the odd-numbered ones.
More time was given for round table discussions, group meetings, and
question periods. She contended officers and chairmen should be granted
the opportunity to hear experts in their various fields. She felt those attending the meetings and receiving the full benefit should help finance them
so her suggestion of a registration fee was begun at the midwinter meeting.
Also, a Federation traveling expense fund was begun to pay for the expenses of a Federation speaker going to the local club.

The Junior Department was reorganized to an all-Junior Department
with a subcommittee of senior members. Mrs. Walker suggested Junior
Membership have a pre-convention meeting at the next MSFWC annual
meeting. Fifteen new clubs joined the Federation, averaging one to a
district.

A heart ailment had made it impossible for Mrs. Walker to accept all
invitations or to attend some meetings before her term as president was
over. She passed away a few years later. She will be remembered for many
improvements in the Federation structure as well as for Club Institute which
she founded.

20

Maria Grey Kimball, Boston
(Mrs. John H.)

1936-1938

Mrs. Kimball was a dynamic president who charged "each club and club member to dare to be different and to do some definite work for peace." Peace was the keynote of her term. She urged that clubwomen cooperate with other individuals and groups doing similar work, banish fear and show courage to accept truth, to understand cases that lead to war, and to do something to build for peace.

Innovations in the annual meeting program were made. Juniors had a pre-convention meeting on Saturday which permitted more to attend, Sunday vesper service for clubwomen and families was held, and the Presidents' Recessional was followed by a reception.

The Legislation Department planned programs on current state and federal legislation, and engaged speakers from both sides of the State House. The International Relations Department conducted six conferences. The evening group included business and professional men.

The "Talking Book for the Blind" became the main project of Junior Membership which had gained nine new clubs. Club Institute gained in attendance and meetings were held in Springfield and Worcester in addition to Boston.

At the end of her administration, Mrs. Kimball urged continuing community surveys of local clubs "to gain a better understanding of each community, and find within ourselves that Spirit which is God Himself and which alone will make for Peace." She hoped a signpost marking the pathway which Federation would travel in coming days would be found in the words "Straightforward and Unafraid."

The Maria Grey Kimball Peace Fund was established as an honor and testimonial to her brave and patriotic spirit.

Harriet C. S. Hildreth,   21
Winchester
(Mrs. Henry W.)
1938-1940

Mrs. Hildreth's two reports show a marked contrast in the world affairs during her administration. Referring to the watchword "Peace" of the previous administration, she urged "to further a continuation of that peace, we take as our slogan 'Good Citizenship,' for without good citizens, there can be no peace." In her final report, she said, "The atmosphere about us today is full of forebodings. We are saddened by the ruin, chaos, and wanton destruction across the sea. We American women are sisters to these others who once were happy like ourselves. Our hearts go out to them, but it is still our firm resolve that we do not join that chaos."

"Good Citizenship" was carried out by each department in this administration, including Good Citizenship Sundays, Club Institute programs, and establishment of community centers for underprivileged youth.

In 1938 the Federation joined with other New England states and the New England Council to bring visitors to New England with proper and dignified advertising, financed by contributions of a penny per person. The chairman for Massachusetts reported a total of $1,602.37 raised, which indicated 160,237 contributors. Another project was to clear away and replace trees felled in the 1938 hurricane, and much was donated for this through the Arbor Day program of the Conservation Department.

The juniors' outstanding project was Health Camp Scholarships for Underprivileged Children, which received $800 from the Juniors' 1939 Charity Ball. The following year the project was "Work with Cardiac Children" for which $1,000 was raised. The Cardiac Summer School in Cambridge was the first of its kind in the country.

Women's clubs held birthday parties honoring their own local pioneer women to solicit funds for the Golden Jubilee of the General Federation of Women's Clubs, and the GFWC Foundation Fund which was in need of more monies.

22

Luella P. Westcott,
Dorchester
(Mrs. David A.)
1940-1942

This administration carried on during a critical period in our national
history, a time of great anxiety, sacrifice, and generosity. Even before our
country was at war, a war relief committee was organized and a "Rolling
Kitchen" was sent to the women of England, in addition to bales of
clothing, and homes were opened to receive British children.

Over $25,000 was received from clubs, and workers were in daily at-
tendance at the Little Building in Boston after March 1941 to receive and
donate items.

A Hobby and Treasure Show was held by the Department of Press to
exhibit valuable and unique collectibles. Jubilee Americanism parties in
recognition of the GFWC Golden Jubilee were held by many clubs and
almost $2,400 was given to add to the GFWC Foundation Fund and to
initiate a national program for defense.

In June 1941 a Home Defense Committee was formed to coordinate
all defense efforts and promote the purchase of defense stamps and bonds.
Almost $100,000 in defense bonds was purchased by clubs.

Even though so much effort was occupied with war relief activities,
reports indicated that work for local charities, hospitals, disabled veterans,
and scholarships had increased. Each yearly conference which dealt with
conditions beyond our borders and the preservation of our own democracy
was attended by over 1,000 women. War gardens, salvaging essential
materials, and community improvement projects were an important part
of the Conservation Department programming.

Mrs. Westcott's final report observed, ". . . wisdom and strength come
with acceptance of responsibility, and there is unbounded satisfaction in
serving through days when the need is great."

Edith French Anderson,
Braintree
(Mrs. George L.)
1942-1944

During this time of World War II, clubwomen gave of themselves in service to their country as non-essential programs were suspended, and efforts for the war relief took precedence over all other activities. Chairs, day rooms, and sun rooms at Camp Edwards, Westover Field, Camp Framingham, and Fort Devens were provided for by women's clubs. At War Relief Headquarters in the Little Building (later the Berkeley Building), volunteers worked. British and Chinese babies were "adopted," weekly cases of clothing were sent to England, and money was sent to China, Norway, Greece, Poland, and France. The Federation worked with service officials to aid in the recruitment of WACS, WAVES, SPARS, and raised $4,091 to finance training for nurses.

The sale of war savings bonds and stamps totalled $133,017 during the first year. The West Roxbury Woman's Club reported sales of $64,500, and $75,000 in Series E Bonds were sold in two days at the annual meeting in Swampscott to entitle the Federation to name a bomber for combat duty. Another campaign in 1943 to buy an ambulance plane was so successful, twenty-six planes could be purchased. A total of almost eight million dollars was sold by the MSFWC.

At the 1943 annual meeting a resolution was adopted for a conference of the United Nations to formulate plans for the enforcement of world peace by a Federation of Nations.

The Golden Anniversary in February 1943 was outstanding as past presidents helped to re-evaluate the past, appraise the present, and plan the future. The Pan American Fellowship Fund drive was successful, providing a scholarship here and a reciprocal one in a South or Central American University, with money remaining given to the Federation to serve as the nucleus for a Memorial Scholarship Fund to be administered by the Federation in memory of past state presidents.

24

Ethel M. Troland, Malden
(Mrs. Edwin)

1944-1946

As president during the end of the war and the following post-war readjustment, Mrs. Troland urged "Reconstruction, Rehabilitation, and Readjustment." Because of war travel restrictions, no midwinter or annual convention was held. Conferences were held in various parts of the state, and club membership began to increase noticeably, as women looked to local clubs for guidance, inspiration, and relaxation from the strains of war.

Headquarters was renovated and 214 meetings were held there with a registration of 2,103 visitors. The next year a midwinter meeting was held at the Shubert Theatre, Boston, with a news forum of world affairs where speakers were supplied by the *Boston Globe, Herald Traveler,* and the *Christian Science Monitor.*

The sale of war bonds and stamps continued to grow — the total sale for the Seventh War Loan was $4,060,515, and the final total of war bonds sold during the year was $11,000,000.

During this administration a Memorial Education Fund of $50,000 was proposed by Mrs. Herbert F. French, immediate past president, who was then made chairman.

The Memorial Forest Fund was also conceived during this administration, and now the Memorial Forest in Sudbury is a living memorial to the men and women of World War II who gave their lives for their country.

Mrs. Troland's final report closed with, "Another chapter in the history of the Massachusetts State Federation of Women's Clubs has been written — written amid global war with its tragedy and heartache, with its insidious destructive force. . . . We close this chapter with hearts torn by the sorrow and tragedy which came to many among us, with thanksgiving that the war in Europe has been won, with a prayer that the Pacific war may be won speedily, and with determination to use all our strength to help bring enduring peace to the world."

Edna T. Greenwood,
Newton Centre
(Mrs. Harvey E.)
1946-1948

25

"The Responsibility of the American Home" was the over-all theme of Mrs. Greenwood's administration because she was confident American mothers would accept the responsibility so necessary to happy homes, and that the future generation would do its part to keep faith with the ideals of our pioneer American forebears.

One of the highlights of this administration was a two-day midwinter meeting at which Press Forums were given with leading newspaper speakers covering subjects such as politics, veterans, youth, drama, literature, national and international affairs. The registration was 3,480. Economic rehabilitation and various philanthropic projects within the United States and other lands were supported with funds of $283,927 during these two years.

The Division of Music raised by a "letter appeal" an amount of $547 making possible four $100 awards to students for the New England Conservatory of Music. The new projects of the Memorial Education Fund and the Memorial Forest Fund continued to grow.

The Council of twelve members met twice a month, and the Executive Board once a month on the afternoon of Club Institute. Club members were dedicated to expend every effort in relief work, and work towards the betterment of their communities.

After a three year lapse, the Junior Department sponsored a Charity Ball to aid its Cardiac Fund, and raised $1,200. CARE was introduced by the GFWC Division of Foreign Service and received immediate and generous support. The Mothercraft Committee organized classes in clubs, schools, Girl Scout troops, and young mothers' clubs.

Hortense S. York, Medford
(Mrs. A. Chesley)
1948-1950

Before Mrs. York became president of the Federation she had served in two presidencies, of the Medford Women's Club, and of the Daughters of Vermont, the first "daughter club" accepted into the Federation. She also organized the Medford Junior Women's Club, and was particularly fond of her experiences with the juniors, locally and with the Federation.

She chose for her administration theme, "Education for Citizenship." Once again, the Federation was hostess to the New England Conference at the New Ocean House in Swampscott at the time of the Federation's fall meeting.

As she realized the juniors who had reached the age limit to attend the mother club's afternoon meetings were unable to do so because of professional or family responsibilities, Mrs. York proposed that the senior clubs invite evening groups into active membership as "evening divisions."

The final acquisition of the Memorial Forest and Wild Life Sanctuary of land formerly owned by Henry Ford in Sudbury was accomplished during this administration. In 1948 only $1,000 had been raised but an accelerated drive, the response of the clubwomen, and the liberal donations of a devotee of wild life protection, made the purchase possible. On January 18, 1950, 277 acres of woodland plus a small house and building became the property of the MSFWC, and it was dedicated on April 29, 1950, with Mrs. York saying, "This will indeed be a living memorial which will keep forever green not only the loving memory of those who served in the war, but also the responsibility which is ours to maintain that for which they fought and died."

Following her presidency, Mrs. York became Literature and Poetry Division Chairman of the GFWC fine arts committee. In 1954 she was appointed MSFWC historian, a position she held for many years.

Lillian S. Stevens,
Worcester
(Mrs. Lewis C.)
1950-1952

During this administration twenty district conferences were held and and nine chairmen conducted statewide meetings as well as a General Federation state meeting to which the New England state federations were invited. Five directors of education in New England and Miss Chloe Gifford, GFWC Department of Education Chairman, were the principal speakers.

Club Institute programs continued to be well attended, and one half hour each time was given to a course in parliamentary procedure.

Legislation interest was high also, and resolutions were passed pertaining to price control, reduction of government spending, preventing the sale of alcoholic beverages to minors, asking officials to stop waste of public funds to agencies not essential to the security of our national life, top priority for school building materials and equipment after major military needs were met, and urging the United States to take action to roll back the price of food and other essentials as of July 1, 1950. Five thousand letters were written to legislators regarding this last resolution. During these two years, membership in General Federation became mandatory, and this was accepted at the midwinter meeting of 1952.

Scholarships continued to be of prime interest in the Federation. Classes in leadership training were given in all districts. A new long-range project, "A Crusade for Freedom" incorporating all departments and chairmen, was initiated.

An Evening Division report appeared in the Manual and the first convention of Evening Divisions was held at Swampscott in May.

Later, Mrs. Stevens served as president of the New England Conference but suffered a fatal illness and passed away in October 1958. She will be remembered for requesting every club meeting be opened with an invocation, and God's blessing be asked at every meal.

28

Ada W. Swain, Brockton
(Mrs. Ralph G.)
1952-1954

"The Preservation of Our Heritage in a Free World" as the theme of Mrs. Swain's administration was a twelve-point program, involving each department of the Federation in some way to "strengthen the ideals and freedoms on which the American way of life was founded."

The first step was to "Get Out the Vote" which resulted in 95 percent of the electorate voting. Evening Division clubs surveyed radio and television programs which led to improved programming. ESO, a General Federation program for promoting reading of fine books, was established by the literature committee.

Through a hospital service committee appointed to recognize and coordinate the work done by clubwomen volunteers, an incomplete report showed more than 71,600 hours in hospital service.

The Junior Department, after twenty-one years, had progressed so well that it was accepted as an affiliate organization — Junior Membership, with its own bylaws, and the right to elect its own officers. Miss Barbara E. Shaw, first junior president, became the successful candidate for GFWC Junior Director. Evening Divisions, begun in Brockton in 1944, and now numbering sixteen groups, were formally included in the bylaws in May 1953.

The Sixtieth Anniversary of the MSFWC in January 1953 was observed as Founders' Day, depicting highlights of Federation history. Announcement was made of the first fellowship in honor of a past president by the Memorial Education Fund trustees. The Federation had raised more than $7,500 by selling place mats to help replace trees destroyed in the Worcester tornado in June 1953.

Tax exemption was obtained for the Federation and the Memorial Forest, by changing the charter of the Federation, establishing the Federation as an educational organization in 1953.

Esther Z. Small, Allston
(Mrs. David M.)
1954-1956

Mrs. Small chose "Enlightened and Responsible Citizenship" as the theme to be incorporated into each department's work in this administration.

She placed great emphasis upon the development of a keener appreciation of the great documents which form the foundation of our democracy, stressed great attention to the home as a means to build character, a more thorough acquaintance with teachers' colleges, campaigns to eliminate comic books, promotion of better human relations, and a more responsible attitude to the nation's Civil Defense.

The continued widespread participation in Veteran's Service with hours of service, articles, televisions, and radios, amounted to a monetary value of over $35,000 in each of the two years.

A committee on Membership Extension was established to help the clubs develop interest in club work to retain members and gain new ones.

The Federation extended its own immediate program by participation with The Massachusetts Council for Public Schools, Massachusetts Public Health Council, Massachusetts Roadside Council, and the Massachusetts Conference on Education.

The Federation was also represented on the Massachusetts Citizens' Committee for Education Television, the Legislation Clearing House meetings, the Conference on Probation held by the Massachusetts League of Women Voters, and the Conference on Nutrition sponsored by several agencies. Mrs. Small also participated in the meetings of the Women's Advisory Council of the University of Massachusetts.

In planning delegate meetings, Mrs. Small carried out a theme related to the overall theme of the administration — "Women of Achievement, Our Country and Our World, Youth — Its Aspirations and Its Needs, Our Homes Are Our Citadels, Education — Cornerstone of Democracy, and The Blessings of Liberty."

30

Florence Alexander, Orange
(Mrs. Kirke L.)

1956-1958

Mrs. Alexander as president of the Federation had the unique position of having her daughter serving as president of her own home club, and also serving as the president's page.

In announcing the emphasis of "Community Improvement" and her theme, "Knowledge is Power," Mrs. Alexander said "without knowledge — precise, accurate, realistic knowledge — our dedication to Community Improvement and our every goal would end in frustration."

A special project was the establishment of a maintenance fund to redecorate and replace furnishings at Federation Headquarters. In 1958 a total of 1,726 visitors signed the guest book.

General Federation and Sears Roebuck Foundation announced the co-sponsorship of a community service, two-year competitive project. The Woman's Club of Shelburne Falls won the first and sweepstakes prize in Massachusetts.

Local clubs supported national organization projects such as blood drives, cancer and polio clinics, sales of tuberculosis seals, and gave many hours of hospital service. The Veterans' Service Committee reported $96,107 in money given in Massachusetts which was the top state in both service and money given, and was so cited by GFWC in Los Angeles, California, in 1959.

Mrs. Alexander was appointed by Governor Furcolo as a member of the Women's Division of the Massachusetts Department of Commerce, and at the end of her term as president, she was then appointed to serve as a representative to the department from the western part of the state.

At the 1956 fall meeting held in Quincy, the Federation was presented with a beautiful rosewood gavel by the Quincy Chamber of Commerce president.

Natalie B. Weidner, Malden
(Mrs. Earl R.)

1958-1960

The theme, "Better Citizens, Better Communities, A Better Country, and a Better World," was chosen by Mrs. Weidner to have the clubwomen "hope to preserve the beauties and values of the life for which the world is struggling," because she felt the importance of club life should not be minimized in spite of everyone facing many tests in an uncertain world.

Federation Night at POPS in May was a financial and social success, and Station WORL provided the Federation time for a five-minute broadcast each weekday morning when club presidents told of their club's outstanding accomplishments.

The fall meeting in Franklin challenged clubwomen to greater service in mental health, local government, safety, and the beauty of the highways. The midwinter meeting featured speakers on the blind, youth fitness, and the great need in the Philippines for support of the self-help plan. A resolution was passed to support the policies and objectives of the President's Council on Youth Fitness, and Mrs. Weidner was appointed by Governor Furcolo as a member of the Governor's Committee on Youth Fitness.

In 1959 at the fall meeting, the permanent resolutions were amended to strengthen the stand of the Federation against pornographic literature and for more support of educational television programming. A fellowship of $1,500 from the Memorial Education Fund was established in memory of Mrs. Lewis C. Stevens who passed away during this administration.

Sixty-five members of the Evening Division monitored nine Boston radio stations to survey the day and evening programming. Massachusetts won the first-place award from GFWC for Veterans' work, and fifth for contributions to CARE. During her administration Mrs. Weidner visited most of the smaller clubs, many of whom had never had a state president visit. She will also be remembered as a talented organist.

32

Marcia E. Shepard, Warren
(Mrs. Charles E.)

1960-1962

Her administration theme, "Building Firm Foundations for the Future," demonstrated her belief that benefits were to be gained in the community through the organized efforts of women, and she also hoped that this theme would improve the organizational structure of the Federation. A coordinated summary of the chairmen's plans and projects was sent to each club president, and in 1961 a Program Outline Handbook was prepared which contained the purpose, aims, programs, and resource material for each division.

Bylaw changes were adopted to have junior members, formerly associate members, become active members of the Federation.

Fall and midwinter meetings covered United Nations' Day, Prospects for the Future, and followed the legislative format of former years. The 1961 annual meeting theme, "With Liberty and Justice for All," featured education and international affairs. Again, the Federation was hostess at the New Ocean House in Swampscott for the 1961 New England Conference.

Federation Headquarters was most attractively renovated, the bylaws were completely revised. Local club interest in community service showed a 100 percent increase in club participation, and the legislative committee supported expansion of services for public higher education, highway safety, conservation of natural resources, and vigorously opposed legalized gambling.

In the fall of 1961 a substantial sum was raised to rebuild the education TV channel destroyed by fire, "$10,000 for 2 in '62," and the second edition of *Progress and Achievement*, incorporating a revision of the previous 1932 edition, was produced.

Lillian A. Porter, Holden
(Mrs. Thomas L.)
1962-1963

L illian Porter fell gravely ill during the first year of her two-year administration, carrying the theme, "Horizons Unlimited," and her duties were carried out during 1963 by the first vice president, Mary Wood.

Clubs contributed record numbers of hours of service to hospitals, veterans, and their communities — 1,070,348, and a grand total of $245,434.91 in philanthropies. Federation clubs responded so generously with contributions to art, music, drama, and international projects that twelve scholarships were given in those fields in addition to the $1,500 fellowship given in honor of Julia Ward Howe. Though the Federation fell short of its fund-raising goal of $10,000 — $9,785.26 for "Channel 2 in '62," most of the funds were matched by the Ford Foundation, thus nearly doubling the clubwomen's contributions to support educational television.

The outstanding new project of this administration was raising funds to create the garden area and furnishings for the historic Clough-Langdon House adjacent to Boston's Old North Church. Funds this year totalled $2,106.70 from the proceeds of a Christmas musicale held at the Old North in December.

To meet the financial responsibilities of the administration, the much-needed twenty-five cents per capita increase in dues was presented and adopted at the midwinter meeting, to go into effect the following year.

34

Mary H. Wood, Newton
(Mrs. Frederick J.)
1963-1965

Believing that the Federation can build on seventy years of education, service and accomplishment to even greater achievement, Mary Wood chose "Our Heritage — To Dream, to Dare, to Do," as her theme.

In addition to staggering totals again in the area of volunteer service hours and reported philanthropies of our federated clubwomen, the Federation gave $500 from the income of the MSFWC Shannon Fund for Youth to the Careers Program in Mental Health as a memorial to President John F. Kennedy, and $300 to the Girls' Club of Boston Building Fund.

This year a second international scholarship of $750 was awarded to a foreign student for study in this country, made possible by special donations in memory of Lillian Porter. More than $2,000 was given to the GFWC Dimes for Liberty project, $1,400 for the Memorial Bell Tower in Rindge, New Hampshire, and $8,060 for Clough-Langdon restoration. The Evening Division cooperated on a project and gave $1,000 to the John F. Kennedy Memorial for the Performing Arts to be built in Washington, D.C.

A portable public address system was donated by Mrs. William Munroe in honor of Mrs. Edmund I. Wilson, the forest's first chairman. A President's Handbook was prepared for each club president in addition to a free-programs booklet from the American Home Committee, and prayers and meditations from the Religion Committee.

Legislative action was stimulated and two bills, "Library Aid and a Consumer Study" were filed by the Federation with 1,000 clubwomen at the Federation Day on February 12.

The Memorial Education and Endowment funds were placed in investment trusts. A two-day Fine Arts Festival, co-sponsored by Sears Roebuck and the city of Worcester, was held in that city, and a two-day conservation conference at the University of Massachusetts.

35

Irene B. Chaves, Arlington
(Mrs. Americo)
1965-1967

With the theme, "Cherish the Past — Challenge the Future," district directors in Mrs. Chaves' administration held six regional conferences, and chairmen presented programming at three publicity workshops, three membership seminars, an education conference at Brandeis University, and the Federation had three winners in the GFWC Shell Oil Scholarship competition. With renewed interest in legislative activity, legislation round tables were conducted in various districts in addition to the annual Day at the State House in March. The main thrust was for the bill to regulate retail installment sales to enable consumers to "shop" for credit. Three hundred women passed the driver improvement course, and 40,000 clubwomen supported the "no-fix ticket" law, signed in November by the governor.

Department scholarship and programming continued in all fields, well-supported by the clubwomen. The top Massachusetts Hallmark art contest winner became the national winner. Forty-five clubwomen journeyed with the international affairs chairman to the United Nations for a special seminar. The music committee scheduled a delightful spring musicale and tea at the Isabella Gardner Museum. The literature committee sponsored the writers' contest, and worked to eliminate pornographic material from newsstands, in addition to collecting three truck loads of books for the Merchant Marine Library.

Clubs throughout the state celebrated the GFWC Diamond Jubilee with special birthday parties, the Federation drama committee prepared and presented a skit, and a special commemorative stamp was issued in recognition of GFWC's 75th anniversary.

Well-planned conferences in community improvement, international, conservation and garden, safety, public health, and music as well as a series of "Days at the State House" attracted good attendance.

36

Frances M. Clark,
Sunderland
(Mrs. Clarence F.)
1967-1969

A busy administration with the theme, "Today's Best is Tomorrow's Beginning," was involved with the extra tasks of hosting the New England Conference at the Yankee Drummer Inn in Auburn, the 75th Birthday Party for the Massachusetts State Federation, and the GFWC convention at the Statler Hilton, Boston. The 75th gala was attended by 1,300 clubwomen.

The February Club Institute was omitted, and three legislative workshops, combining several districts, were held in March. A very successful Artists' Tea and Exhibit was held in North Easton, and Pennies for Art donations to the Music Division were so generous, eight $200 scholarships were awarded.

A special note card project brought profits to the Federation of $4,235.68 which were used to defray expenses of the GFWC convention. Two hundred sixty-nine clubs that participated gained $21,178.40 for their interest.

Federation clubwomen generously donated a desk for the Federation Headquarters secretary, and a picture of our first president, Julia Ward Howe. Also, a new typewriter, curtains, and bathroom accessories were provided from the Headquarters maintenance fund.

Massachusetts gave $2,232.66 to CARE, and was the third highest ranking state. Nine hundred dollars was given to the Clough-Langdon House plus $500 contributed by Art Linkletter on behalf of the Crown Cola Company — a total of $1,400. Two Memorial Education scholarships were granted in the names of Mrs. Edwin Troland and Mrs. Harvey Greenwood, past state presidents.

A very successful Conservation Conference was held at the Drumlin Farms Wildlife Sanctuary in Lincoln, and a large group of directors attended a CIP Seminar at Rutgers University in Brunswick, New Jersey, co-sponsored by Sears-Roebuck Foundation and GFWC.

Beatrice A. Peterson, 37
Franklin
(Mrs. Raymond N.)
1969-1971

Mrs. Peterson selected the theme, "Rise Up and Build," to coordinate with the GFWC theme, "A Better Environment." Successful conferences were conducted by department and division chairmen in conservation, international affairs, and community improvement in addition to an Artists' Tea and exhibit, and an international musicale.

October and April Club Institute meetings were held in Worcester to stimulate attendance in that area. Monetary donations of $1,162 were added to the Clough-Langdon restoration fund, and a beautiful old maple slant desk was purchased as a valuable addition for the room's furnishings. The Division of Religion and Ethics sponsored prayer breakfasts to pray for the 1,500 POWs, and thousands of letters were mailed to the president of North Viet Nam requesting treatment and release of our servicemen. The Justice and Rehabilitation Division was formed, with a meeting held at Norfolk Prison to learn more about the penal system.

Four new junior clubs joined the Federation. The Memorial Forest clubhouse and cottage were painted, and a new trail was cut near the old windmill and to the second bridge.

The special survey committee completed its evaluation and a copy of *Blueprint for Action* was given to each Executive Board member and club president for study. Proposed bylaw changes as a result of this study were acted upon at the annual convention.

An additional state project was the "Save Our Shores" campaign, an effort to preserve the shores and waterways of historic Dorchester Bay and the beautiful islands in Boston Harbor.

The Norwood Woman's club had one of its talented members design and produce a "bee pin" in honor of Mrs. Peterson. Profits from the sale of the pins were given as a music scholarship at the end of Mrs. Peterson's presidency.

38

Eleanor B. Ross,
Mattapoisett
(Mrs. Marshall W.)
1971-1972

Mrs. Ross' one-year administration with the theme of "Freedom and Responsibility" was indeed an "era of change." A year-long, in-depth study of practices, procedures and policies called *Blueprint for Action* resulted in recommendations for many changes. The third vice president and clerk positions were eliminated, their duties to be delegated to other Federation personnel; and to line up with GFWC biennial elections, officers were to serve concurrently with the national officers. Thus, to effect the transition, Mrs. Ross became the first president to voluntarily serve only one year.

Each club member was asked to contribute one dollar to the President's Fund, one-half to go to the Massachusetts Council on Crime and Correction to its mass media education program for crime prevention and criminal justice, and one-half to the maintenance fund of the Memorial Forest. Total funds collected were $6,040.

For the first time, Junior and Evening Division memberships appointed legislation chairmen, and there was a strong emphasis in all departments of the Federation on legislation activity. The Federation cooperated with the State Environmental Protection Agency in the Governor's Spring Cleanup Program, and the Massachusetts Safety Council for legislation to better control alcoholic drivers.

A record attendance of 951 clubwomen came to the midwinter meeting at the Chateau de Ville, Framingham. A Federation packet named "Operation Stop-Gap" covering programming was produced to improve communication between the Federation and its member clubs.

A "lighthouse" pin was sold in honor of Mrs. Ross, and profits went to the Massachusetts Council on Crime and Correction media program.

Helen C. Congdon,
Springfield
(Mrs. Paul E.)
1972-1974

39

Mrs. Congdon chose her theme of "Bridge the Gap" to indicate a bridge of understanding and closer relationship with the General, Junior and Evening division memberships in the State Federation.

Three conservation divisions all supported the main project of this administration with the Massachusetts Association for the Blind and the Perkins School in Watertown for the establishment of the "Touch and See Trail" in Hampden, the home of Thornton W. Burgess, built in 1742. The trail at "Laughing Brook," developed from monetary donations of $2,583.60 from the Federation clubwomen, was dedicated for the unsighted.

Through the Division of Health of the Federation, the General, Junior and Evening Division memberships worked for education, legislation, and fund-raising projects for the mentally retarded, called "Special Help for Special People." The State Department of Mental Health and Governor Sargent instituted plans to move qualified retarded citizens out of institutions into half-way houses in local communities. Efforts to oppose legislation that would legalize marijuana, distribute drug information to schools because of the downward trend age-wise for drug and alcohol abuse, and establish "Hot Lines" and youth centers were pursued by the Federation.

To promote the Federation a professionally-prepared "There's Something for Everyone in the MSFWC" profile was produced and thousands given to prospective members, libraries, and other community organizations. Conferences were held in all districts, incorporating this title as the theme by a Federation "traveling team" emphasizing public relations, leadership-membership, and volunteerism.

The State Federation was hostess to the New England Conference at Sea Crest, North Falmouth, and during this administration there was a gala celebration of the Junior Membership's 50th anniversary.

40

Catherine M. Faucher,
Newton
(Mrs. Eugene G.)
1974-1976

Mrs. Faucher selected "Improve the Quality of Life" for the theme of her administration to be implemented through four avenues of service — education, legislation, opportunities for women, and the Bicentennial.

The Federation accepted the challenge of the Massachusetts Department of Education to become involved in Chapter 766 and Mass/Pacts, citizen participation in education decision making. Mrs. Faucher's major emphasis program, "Help for Children," was supported by $5,000 in donations from clubwomen by the purchase of $1 Shareholder's Certificates.

The Legislation Committee published three issues of "Federation Focus," and the Federation was again represented on Beacon Hill at meetings and hearings. Federation members served on the Governor's Commission on the Status of Women helping to set standards and evaluate needs of women in the Commonwealth, and also served on the Governor's Highway Safety Committee. Issues of primary concern to the clubwomen were opposition to off-track betting, sports pool betting, uniform product code, gun-control laws, and the Massachusetts bottle bill. Clubwomen were involved in initiative petitions and 95 percent of the clubs responded, helping to collect the needed 56,000 signatures.

Bicentennial programming featured Clough House hosting, the Heritage Ball in addition to the Fine Arts Festival with music, art, crafts, and drama at the Framingham Chateau de Ville, which drew an attendance of 934 women.

Family Day opened the club season at the Memorial Forest, and April Club Institute became the Special Awards Day. Congresswoman Margaret M. Heckler and MSFWC sponsored essay contests in recognition of the International Woman's Year on the subject, "Women in Transition — Past, Present, and Future."

41

Ann L. Holland, Falmouth
(Mrs. John W., Jr.)

1976-1978

Mrs. Holland's theme, "Concern, Courage, Commitment — A Better World for All," with emphasis on conservation, was directed not only to energy and natural resources but also to all six departments of programming of the Federation.

Investment scrolls on which clubwomen pledged their signatures for one dollar raised $18,000 in two years which was returned to the Children's Protective Services districts in which the individual clubs functioned, to help battered and abused children as well as those who had an insufficient diet or poor nutrition.

Family Day opened the club year at the Memorial Forest, a GFWC "Hands Up" Syncon was held to exchange ideas and thoughts with leaders in the crime reduction field and the judiciary. A successful Conference "By the sea" at Woods Hole by the Conservation and International Affairs Committees was followed by the Education Department's Conference at Tabor Academy. The "Tulip Time Ball" raised an additional $1,300 for CPS, while the sale of the "windmill" pin amassed further profits.

Fifteen district conferences featured Great Decisions Program of GFWC American Policy Association and the Division of Continuing Education at the University of Massachusetts. A "Community Organization for Action" kit was developed for each clubwoman to use and this effort resulted in the establishment of forty new Great Decisions groups in the state. There were "Green Thumb" and "Three R's" (recycled, recoverable, and reusable) contests at the conferences.

On January 14, 1978, the Panama Government Access Forum was sponsored by the MSFWC, World Affairs Council, and the Massachusetts State Coordinator for Great Decisions which gave MSFWC members involvement in foreign policy decision making.

42

Mary E. Warner, Sunderland
(Mrs. Edward C.)
1978-1980

The theme, "Invest in the Future," chosen by Mrs. Warner for this administration was to benefit the Federation, schoolchildren in Peru, CARE recipients, as well as MSFWC leaders.

Through a grant from the Frank Stanley Beveridge Foundation (Stanley Home Products) it was possible for the Leadership-Membership Committee members and Executive Board members to participate in a leadership seminar at Wheaton College.

Fall meeting was held at the newly-restored Mechanics Hall in Worcester, and because of the MSFWC participation in the Great Decisions Program, Mrs. Warner represented the Federation at a State Department briefing on the Strategic Arms Limitation Treaty (SALT).

Through the purchase of "souvenir stock," it was possible to build a school in Huacho, Peru for 250 youngsters, and benefit the MSFWC Endowment Fund. Also, a four-room addition to an elementary school in Caso Urbano, Province of Santa, Peru, was made possible.

One thousand copies of a leadership-membership packet, prepared by the MSFWC committee, were printed by the John Hancock Insurance Company for distribution to each club president and leadership committee member, the balance sold to club individuals.

The Exxon Corporation and MSFWC sponsored a two-day seminar on energy for women leaders in Massachusetts. A pilot project of the Massachusetts Department of Public Works to install $183,000 of highway reflective markers came about from the urging of MSFWC.

Gasoline prices soared anew so Club Institute and midwinter meeting were combined. Mrs. Warner attempted to highlight all the programs of the Federation in a seven-minute dialogue on the Sharon King TV Show, on Channel 4, Boston.

Annette M. Keessen,
Whitinsville
(Mrs. Garry R.)
1980-1982

43

The theme selected by Mrs. Keessen, "Reach Out," was carried out by the six departments of the Federation in programs to help the elderly, the youth, the handicapped, the underprivileged.

Six regional conferences dealt with adolescent suicide, leadership-membership and parliamentary law. "Families are Forever" was the title of the Colonial Family Holiday held at Christmas in the Old North Church and the Clough House — a grand finale to Boston's 350th birthday celebration.

A combined President's Project of the Talking Information Center (TIC) and the MSFWC Endowment Fund was proposed by Mrs. Keessen. TIC, a radio reading service for the print handicapped, was generously supported as thirty-six special closed circuit receivers were purchased by MSFWC clubs and given to worthy recipients. In addition, an initial down payment of $3,500 was raised for the first microwave installation at the TIC station.

The sale of the "gold key" pins' profits added to the President's Project and the Endowment Fund, as did the honor roll contributions.

Proposition 2½ made its debut in Massachusetts, but Massachusetts clubwomen quietly contributed by diligently raising funds to offset some of the projected cutbacks.

The Federation combined efforts with the American Cancer Society to enable thousands of Massachusetts residents to participate in a screening day for the detection of colo-rectal cancer.

Contributions to the MSFWC/CARE Chile School/Family Garden exceeded the $5,000 goal. MSFWC was also recognized for its support of the veterans at the Disabled American Veterans' Convention in June 1980 at Chicopee.

44

Bernice E. Ahearn, Milton
(Mrs. F. William)
1984-1986

Choosing "For the Common Good" as the theme of this administration, Mrs. Ahearn challenged the MSFWC clubwomen to continue to dedicate themselves to service for others, seeking neither remuneration nor recognition.

The Talking Information Center and the Endowment Fund continued as the combined President's Project. Thirty-two receivers were purchased by clubs in one year, forty in the next. Additional donations were given for two taping rooms and renovations to the station's reception area. The "whirling sun" or "sunburst" pins, depicting six departments and six regions of the Federation, were sold, with profits going to TIC and the Endowment Fund.

To counteract the inflation in our economy and its effect on the Federation's general fund, "Federation Station" was begun as a special project — a "store" for the Federation. Gift items from GFWC affiliated suppliers were sold at state meetings and Club Institutes and gained $5,000 for the MSFWC.

The emphasis on public relations to improve communication within and beyond the Federation resulted in the compilation of a public relations handbook, "Tell the Federation Story," and the production of 6,000 new profiles for distribution to libraries, and as a tool for membership recruitment. A souvenir booklet on the Clough House was made available in the Old North Church gift shop and at the Clough House for visitors. Also, a unique "all-time ad" for use in any club's local paper for prospective members' inquiries was supplied by a Cape Cod newspaper for the Federation.

Mrs. Ahearn represented the Federation as MSFWC was awarded a "Good Neighbor" award from Boston's Channel 7 WNEV-TV-Priority One program for community involvement in the area of crime awareness and crime reduction.

Penny Billias, Nahant
(Mrs. Theodore)
1984-1986

With Malice Toward None" was the theme selected by Mrs. Billias to be implemented by the Federation family for this administration. Education was the main thrust, and was emphasized and supported by the General, Junior, and Evening Division memberships.

A Federation trip to Greece enriched the Headquarters Building Fund by $3,500, and the Talking Information Center, the continuing President's Project and the MSFWC Endowment Fund, profited from the sale of the pewter "penny" pin. On June 25, 1986, at the State House, Mrs. Billias presented a check in the amount of $14,000 to Ron Bersani, executive director of the Talking Information Center, for installation of the microwave tower at the station's new location in Marshfield.

Planning continued for the future permanent home of the Federation at the Memorial Forest, so also were fund-raising efforts. A successful fashion show added $3,550 to the coffers for the Headquarters Building. An MSFWC charm and Headquarters button were sold, in addition to a fund-raising silent auction at the annual meeting.

A Home Life Festival on nutrition, community and consumer relations, learning with elder hostel, with the theme, "Family: Be in It!" was held. Christmas Vespers again took place at Old North, and Evening Division and Junior Membership joined to have a combined *Federation Topics Previews*. Once again, the MSFWC was hostess for the New England Conference at Sea Crest, North Falmouth, with an attendance of 563.

The study committees reported, Redistricting was requested to continue working, and the Nominating and Elections completed its work and submitted its report to the bylaws committee.

Three outstanding women, outside the Federation, in the fields of art, communications, and human services were honored in the "Celebrate Women" program of GFWC and MSFWC.

46

Nancy Beatty, West Upton
(Mrs. Royce E.)
1986-1988

The new Headquarters facility was completed at the Memorial Forest during this administration after years of dedicated planning. Mrs. Beatty chose for the President's Project, the "Garden in the Glade," a plan to conserve the beloved Forest in Sudbury in its natural state, and add to it species of shrubs and plants to enhance its beauty. The building was dedicated in August 1987, noted by Mrs. Beatty on that day, as "a monument to our membership's foresight and ingenuity."

The garden project was implemented by the Conservation Department and the Memorial Forest Committee, and in the first year, 2,500 bulbs, all donated by clubwomen or purchased from funds given for the project, were planted.

Mrs. Beatty's theme, "Sharing is Caring," and the conservation emphasis, were carried out in all departments of MSFWC — whether in communication with others, or programming as it was transmitted to the local clubs.

The pin for this term combined the chickadee, the elm, and the daisy, resurrecting the symbols chosen many years ago to represent the Federation. These were also used in the cup plate designed to raise funds for the Headquarters building.

Innovations were the production and distribution to each club president of a "white notebook" with periodic inserts for additional information for improved communication from the Federation chairmen for departments and GFWC programming for club participation, and the printing of a new "profile" for public relations and membership recruitment. The legislation chairman position was reactivated, and a hard-working committee completed in two years a "history" of the Massachusetts State Federation from 1893 to 1988. A unique "Heritage Craft Fair" at the Museum of Our National Heritage in Lexington drew a large attendance in April 1988.

II

THE
FEDERATION
STORY

BEGINNINGS

1893-1918

HISTORICALLY, it has been said, "the hand that rocks the cradle rules the world." As we study the roles women play, we realize women are the social architects of our world. Women have realized the power of the several over the one and the values inherent in unity and diversity. Church circles, quilting bees of the early days in our country grew into the organization we call a woman's club.

In the United States clubs did not emerge until early in 1880 when the "Ladies Association of the First Parish Church of Brighton" was chartered by the Commonwealth of Massachusetts to provide religious education and to do community work. The club loaned sick room equipment to anyone needing it and during the sewing meetings books were read aloud and discussed.

In 1847 the Ladies' Physiological Institute of Boston was formed to study and discuss health problems of women and children. Eight years later the Ladies' Library Association of Randolph was organized to furnish library books to women in the town.

The New England Women's Club organized in 1868 was the first to call itself a "women's club." Also it was the first to sponsor a diverse program including social, literary, philanthropic, reformatory, and educational projects. Then as more and more clubs were organized throughout the Commonwealth for social, educational, and humanitarian purposes, women emerged as social architects.

Our history of the Massachusetts State Federation of Women's Clubs will reflect the impact women's clubs have had on the growth, the progress, and achievements of our Commonwealth, as well as the cities, towns, and villages of Massachusetts.

Decades of development have been established that encompass the administrations of several state presidents. In the beginning there was our first state president, Mrs. Julia Ward Howe, who had a keen wit, a deeply religious nature, and gave freely of her friendship. Her definition of life was, "To learn, to teach, to serve, and to enjoy." Her philosophy provided a firm foundation and high ideals for the Massachusetts State Federation of Women's Clubs. From 1893 to June 1898 Mrs. Howe served as president and then was unanimously elected Honorary President of the Massachusetts State Federation of Women's Clubs, which office she held until her death.

Miss O. M. E. Rowe, our elected second president, served from 1898 to 1901. She had been first vice president during the last two years of Mrs. Howe's administration and possessed a thorough knowledge of the Federation. Her long residence at Boston City Hospital, while her brother was its superintendent, contributed to her emphasis on welfare work, social service, and health measures.

Mrs. May Alden Ward accentuated libraries, child labor, and world affairs during her presidency (1901-1904). While she was in office the application of the Era Club of Boston, which had colored members, created a controversy over membership requirements of the General Federation of Women's Clubs. In 1902 the delegates voted to add the following section to the bylaws: "Section 2, Article II, From a state where a club is a member of the State Federation it would also be eligible to the General Federation if recommended to its Executive Board by the Executive Board of the State Federation."

Today our eligibility clause reads, "All applications must show that the organization requires no sectarian or political test for membership; that it is not a secret society; that no one of its members is affiliated with any organization which tolerates, either by practice or teaching, violation of national or state laws, and it agrees with the constitution and bylaws of the General Federation."

"Unity in Diversity," was introduced in Miss Helen A. Whittier's first report when she said, "We ask the clubs for this one thing — a widely diffused interest in Federation work." Miss Whittier served as president from 1904 to 1907.

In 1906 the *Federation Bulletin* became the *official* organ of the Massachusetts State Federation and a new Federation pin was designed by Miss Whittier, an art critic and art teacher by profession. The pin has been used as the official badge ever since.

During Mrs. May Alden Ward's second term (1907-1908) the Federa-

50

tion hosted the biennial convention of the General Federation of Women's Clubs, a time consuming activity for the membership. Growth of programming for the Federation continued and added to the agenda were the establishment of a traveling library and an investigation of working conditions for women and children.

Hosting the biennial convention of the General Federation increased the awareness of the members of the Massachusetts State Federation of the interrelationship of the state and national organizations. The inspiration gained from contact with women from all parts of the United States furnished a new impetus for club work.

As Georgie A. Bacon assumed the presidency in 1908, a catastrophe occurred in Chelsea when a great fire swept the city leaving thousands of people homeless. Immediately Miss Bacon called on Federation members for contributions of money, clothing, and food. The response was tremendous! The clubwomen proved the value of organized womanhood, ready to act in times of emergency as well as to cooperate in assisting with community projects.

In 1910 at Miss Bacon's invitation representatives of the other New England states met and adopted a cooperative program. It was voted to hold yearly meetings of the New England Federations and nine years later the New England Conference was established.

"Service to others," was Mrs. Henry Coolidge Mulligan's theme when she was elected president in 1911. Mrs. Mulligan, accompanied by Mrs. Emmons Crocker, first vice president, visited almost all the clubs in the Federation, in an effort to impress upon the outlying clubs that the Federation was equally interested in them as in the clubs organized in Boston and its suburbs. She reminded them that they were a vital part of the Federation upon whose loyalty and efficiency the power and influence of the state organization depended.

The criticism had been made that nearly all Federation meetings were held in the eastern part of the state. To correct this situation more conferences were scheduled to be held in different parts of Massachusetts.

Thoroughly versed in Federation organization and philosophy, Mrs. George Winslow Perkins picked up the presidential reins in 1913. With the growth of the organization membership, power, and influence, additional income and improved lines of communication became necessary. The 1916 annual meeting appointed a committee to propose a program to raise $25,000 for a permanent fund. These monies would be restricted and the interest earned used for expenses and programs voted by the Council and the Federation.

In February 1915 the first "Bulletin of the Massachusetts State Federation of Women's Clubs" was issued and our monthly magazine was begun. It has continued uninterrupted, under a variety of names, to the present time.

At the 1915 annual meeting the delegates endorsed the following resolution: "Whereas, the question of political equality of men and women is today a vital problem, under discussion throughout the civilized world, therefore, be it resolved, that we record our belief in the principle of political equality regardless of sex."

Reviewing the histories of the member clubs of the Federation we perceive how they reflected the leadership in their programs of self-improvement, service to communities, and friendship.

Southeastern Region

Like their sister clubs throughout the state, the clubs of the Southeastern Region of MSFWC were comprised of women who felt the urge to come together and help meet the needs that arose in their respective communities. Again, doing something worthwhile was accomplished.

It is the opinion of the history committee that the Ladies' Library Association of Randolph can lay claim to being the second oldest, if not the oldest club in the MSFWC ranks, as it was the second formed and the first to join the Federation. Founded in 1855 and federated in 1895, the club established a library with about fifty volumes, purchased books and lent them out to any member of the community for a fee. Books were kept in a local bonnet shop where they were accessible to all. In 1857 classes were formed—physiology was the first subject. In 1861 they worked for Civil War soldiers, sending money to aid the "Sanitary Commission" for work among the sick and wounded.

The Ladies' Library Association, the first of the Southeastern Region's clubs to be organized in 1855, was followed by the Wareham Monday Club, 1889; The Tuesday Club of Assonet, 1893; and The Cabot Club of Middleboro, 1897. In 1898, the New Bedford Woman's Club, Edgartown Woman's Club, Abington Woman's Club, and the Woman's Club of Brockton were formed. The Philergians of Braintree was founded in 1899 and the Sippican Woman's Club of Marion along with the Falmouth

Woman's Club followed in 1904. In 1905 the Quincy Women's Club was formed and the ranks of the Federation swelled with the founding of the Nautilus Club of Provincetown in 1907, and the establishment and admission of the Whitman Woman's Club that same year. In 1910 the Taunton Woman's Club was founded and federated and in 1911 both the Old Colony Union Women's Club of Bourne and the Brewster Woman's Club had formed. The Plymouth Woman's Club was organized in 1912, and the Chatham Woman's Club was the last to join during this era, in 1915.

In the early 1900s The Cabot Club, Wareham, Whitman, Sippican, Abington, and Quincy clubs were all responsible for organizing the Visiting Nurse Association in their respective towns. The various clubs showed their pride in their communities by supporting them in many ways. One of the first community services performed by The Tuesday Club of Assonet was to raise funds to repair and wind the town clock. The Wareham Monday Club, in 1889 financed the installation of lamplights throughout the town, and paid for the oil and the lamplighters' services for twenty-five years; and in 1905 provided the first town rubbish barrels, as did the Nautilus Club of Provincetown. The Whitman Club established a drinking fountain in the town park, and the Nautilus Club also provided its town with a large drinking fountain, benches, trees, and a cleaning cart for the streets. In 1901 the New Bedford Woman's Club financed and established summer playgrounds for children. In 1913 The Cabot Club also created playgrounds in their community. In the early 1900s many of the clubs established scholarship funds, stamp savings programs and domestic science classes — among them were The Cabot Club, Whitman, The Philergians, and Quincy. Abington, Quincy, and the Ladies' Library Association were also responsible for establishing lunch-rooms in their respective schools. A great many of the Southeastern Region's clubs sponsored children's gardens. Quincy alone distributed 10,000 packets of seeds to local school children, and the Ladies' Library Association also contributed their share.

The early town libraries were amply endowed, with Quincy starting the first two branches of a library. The Tuesday Club of Assonet and the Edgartown club made contributions, and Wareham established a "Free Library" in their town. Upon the outbreak of World War I, the Abington club knitted and rolled bandages; Whitman organized a Red Cross Auxiliary and sold War Savings Stamps, for which they won an award; and The Tuesday Club of Assonet undertook sewing for various hospitals. The Ladies' Library Association also participated in this effort.

The Quincy Women's Club was given their clubhouse in 1905 by Dr.

54

The historic Jonathan Belcher House on North Main Street in Randolph was built in 1806.

Jeffrey R. Brackett, and in 1907 sponsored a "Young Women's Community Club." In 1913-1917 the Quincy club began Americanization classes, and paid the teacher. The Ladies' Library Association held their early meetings in church halls, and in 1911 the Jonathan Belcher Homestead was presented to the Association for their use as a clubhouse. The Old Colony Union Women's Club of Bourne's clubhouse was built in 1911 and contained a tea-room, meeting-room, sales-room, and a small classroom to teach various handicrafts. Products were sold on site and provided income to sponsor their various projects. A silver vase was inscribed each year with the name of the person doing the best work. In 1917 members of the Taunton Woman's Club purchased the old Simeon Daggett House for $7,000.

In 1900 The Cabot Club provided financial help to a model school in Georgia, sent several hundred books to the Tennessee mountain area, gifts to Boston Floating Hospital, and later furnished a dormitory at the YMCA. In 1902 the Abington Woman's Club printed their first program book and charged members five cents. In 1902 The Tuesday Club of Assonet formed a Doctors' Aid and Calling Committee. In 1912 the Wareham Monday Club dispersed leaflets with information on how to get rid of the "Pesky House-fly."

It is interesting to note that the New Bedford Woman's Club in 1896 was a Parliamentary Law Class consisting of four women, but on February

Today with its basic structure unchanged it serves as the Ladies' Library Association Clubhouse.

17, 1898, became known as the New Bedford Woman's Club. Members met rent free in a home on County Street where they held classes in literature and current events. In 1898 on October 19, the Executive Board of the MSFWC held its meeting at the New Bedford club and luncheon was served at the North Christian Church for twenty-five cents per plate. In March 1902 members of the New Bedford club made a motion that all ladies remove their hats during club meetings — the motion was voted down. In 1908 the club began to take an interest in child labor laws, women's suffrage, and a tuberculosis sanitarium. On May 24, 25, 26, 1911, Mrs. Philip N. Moore, of St. Louis, President of the GFWC attended the nineteenth annual meeting of the MSFWC which was held by invitation of the New Bedford Woman's Club at the First Baptist Church in New Bedford. The Levi Standish House, homestead for three generations of the lineal descendants of Myles Standish, was purchased by the club in February of 1916.

The first annual report of the treasurer of the Sippican Club of Marion read: "Receipts $21.25 — Expenditures $21.25." A Christmas tea was served for the magnificent sum of sixty-five cents! In 1915 the Sippican Club hosted the MSFWC annual meeting, for which 600 gathered at the Congregational Church. Federation President Mrs. Herbert Gurney presented

Standish House, home of the New Bedford Woman's Club, is entered in the National Register, and was built about 1830 by Levi Standish, seventh generation descendant of Myles Standish. The Woman's Club acquired the property in 1916 and sold it to the YWCA in 1979, retaining the privilege of holding meetings there.

a resolution on women's suffrage. The vote for equal suffrage was 203-99 and this was considered the hottest session in Federation history! Headquarters for visitors were at the Hotel Sippican — rates $4.00 a day. Transportation was provided by special car for the visitors on the train from Boston for two days, round trip fare was $1.21!

Speakers taking the lecture stage at the various clubs in the Southeastern Region were Booker T. Washington, Fannie Farmer, William Howard Taft, President Woodrow Wilson's daughter Jessie, Judge Jennie Loctman Barron, Julia Ward Howe's daughter Maude Howe Elliot, Edgar Guest, Helen Keller, and many others.

Southern Region

In the year 1893 a train belched smoke and cinders as it sped through the suburbs on its way to Boston's South Station. On arrival the conductor placed a stool on the platform at the foot of the steps and assisted the ladies from many clubs off the train. Dressed with hats, gloves and ankle length dresses with bustles, they then traveled by horse and buggy over dirt roads to the Hyde Park Thought Club where they had been invited to a tea. This club, the fifth oldest in Massachusetts, was organized in 1881, the year James Garfield became the twentieth president of the United States. Membership was limited to thirty as meetings were and still are held in members' homes. Programs resembled a liberal arts college and included Shakespeare, history, philosophy, music, literature, science and travel. Theodore Weld, age eighty, guide and philosopher to the club, was made an honorary member. Members discussed what women could do even without the ballot to elevate moral standards of government and politics and voted to send a delegate to the ratification meeting of the Union of the Massachusetts Women's Clubs. Julia Ward Howe was President and their delegate was named one of fifteen directors.

A club named for the first published female author in America was Hannah Adams Women's Club of Medfield. In 1904 the membership urged selectmen to paint white lines on the edges of the road for safety as motor cars were beginning to appear. Some of the early cars included the Duryea, Ford, Packard, and Oldsmobile.

In 1895 the Walpole Women's Club declined an invitation by the Francis Bird Lyceum to debate women's suffrage. Poetry was a safer subject for a club to discuss since its principal interest was English literature.

Community Club of Canton answered a great need of immigrants by conducting English classes and providing medicine, food, castor oil, and orange juice to undernourished children. The descendants of those who came seeking a better world are now the moving force of many of our women's clubs today.

The Ashland Women's Club numbering fifteen members showed how much a few women can accomplish. In 1890 they formed what is now the Village Improvement Society and held field days to raise money for trees and shrubs. The club's historical committee collected information and memorabilia which would otherwise be lost. Eventually the Ashland Historical Society was formed and is still very active.

In 1899 the Milton Woman's Club furnished volunteer aid to what became a local branch of the Red Cross and developed a Social Service League which is now the Visiting Nurse Association. They launched a hot lunch program in the school and this dedicated group gave $3,000 toward a free bed at the Milton Hospital and $500 to a tuberculosis clinic, a disease which was quite prevalent at that time.

The Walpole Woman's Club started a free kindergarten; furnished a living room at Pond Home, which was a cancer hospital; established the Walpole Health Center which had a well baby clinic; and furnished milk to undernourished children in the schools.

Ousamequin is the name Massasoit took when he became chieftain of the Wampanoag Indian Tribe. A friend to the Pilgrims, he sold land that included Bridgewater for seven coats, nine hatchets, eight hoes, twenty knives, four moose skins, and ten and a half yards of cotton cloth. Just as he was a leader of his people the Ousamequin Club has been a leading force in the community. The members called a meeting in 1901 to consider the appearance of the village and this led to the formation of the Bridgewater Improvement Association. Proceeds from the production of eighteen yearly plays were given as subscriptions to purchase a fountain at the head of the common. A five-day art and craft exhibition, the largest of any outside Boston, was held in Bridgewater. The club also started a Visiting Nurse Association.

Kalmia Club of North Attleboro, which grew from twenty-one members in 1895 to one hundred and fifty members, derived its name from a North America mountain laurel denoting perpetual life, vigor, and endurance, thus inspiring members to achieve excellence. Members undertook projects to improve the town's schoolhouses, clean yards, correct unsanitary toilet conditions, paint classroom walls, and donate pictures. These were the days of two-room schoolhouses. During these early years thrift was taught in school along with discipline, respect, and prayer. Penny saving stamps were started by Kalmia, Ousamequin, Norwood, and Framingham clubs.

The four-leaf clover is the emblem of The Clover Club of Eaton. Membership was limited to twenty-five, all elected by ballot. One blackball meant rejection by those ladies who met for improvement and amusement in the homes of members according to the alphabetical order of their last names. The lady of the house presided and the attendance fee was five cents, while an additional five cents was levied if late or absent (unless ill). Early subjects were: "Ethics of Household," "Is Club Work a Menace to the Home?" and "Good and Evil Effects of Club Life."

In 1906 San Francisco was devastated by earthquake and fire, leaving two hundred and fifty thousand people homeless. Milton, Norwood, and the New Century Club of Mansfield rose to the occasion by sending money and clothing.

Friendship Circle for the Blind was aided by the Roslindale Women's Club which also presented the first large print book to the library and continued such giving as an annual event.

In 1911 when Mrs. Henry Mulligan of the Natick Women's Club became a state president, the club membership rose from 52 to 250.

The Newton Centre Woman's Club, organized in 1888 for the purpose of mutual improvement and service, contributed most of the monies raised to charity. The club's first civic project was to buy land for a park and playground. As soon as this was accomplished the park and playground were turned over to the city of Newton and the city had its first playground. Monies were raised in 1900 for the Newton Cottage Hospital (later to become the Newton-Wellesley Hospital) and this has remained on the club's list of philanthropies to the present day. At the time of the devastating Chelsea fire, money, clothing, and volunteers were donated — "a gesture of compassion to those in need."

Eastern Region

The West Concord club was formed in 1890 as a social group with music, reading studies in literature and art to broaden the women's minds. The social and educational emphasis continued until 1917. The first year of World War I, funds were raised for children of the soldiers and members offered their services at Fort Devens and knitted hundreds of socks and other garments. At the end of the war, money was raised for many local causes.

The first regular meeting of the Waltham Woman's Club was held on November 3, 1893, at Asbury Temple, and Julia Ward Howe was the first speaker for a fee of $15. She was accompanied by her daughter, Maud Elliott. After battling with the town for sixteen years, the club finally admitted defeat and appropriated $45 from the treasury to buy the first waste barrels for the streets of Waltham. In 1898, largely through the efforts of the Waltham Woman's Club, a curfew bell was to be heard each evening at ten minutes of nine which was a signal for children to scurry homeward.

The Watertown Woman's Club was founded on March 20, 1894, by Mrs. Alice M. Silsbee, a woman very active in women's suffrage. She served on the school committee and her name is in Constitution Hall in Washington, D. C. as the founder and first president of the Daughters of the American Revolution in Watertown in 1898. When the motor cars came, she was one of the first woman drivers in the state and continued to drive until her late seventies.

In 1903 the club entertained one thousand members of the Massachusetts State Federation and Julia Ward Howe was the guest of honor. It was in 1903 that the club took over District Nursing from the Waltham district and supported it until it was able to support itself. It was also during this period that a petition was sent to the police commissioners asking that a prescribed limit of the Watertown line be revoked and that they remove nine saloons in the district that were within less than two thousand feet of the Watertown line. It was also proposed that the club help other clubs in the vicinity to close a notorious resort in Boston; the treasurer said that it would cost the club "forty-six dollars."

These were the days of great uncertainty — World War I was declared and the dreadful influenza epidemic was raging. The woman's club responded to all demands from the community; there were women in railroad offices, factories, munitions plants, for the women "over here" had replaced the men "over there." During World War I, the women of the Watertown Woman's Club opened a public canning kitchen, there were talks on food conservation and economy, war bonds were sold and many other relief activities were supported as other clubs were also doing.

There are three clubs in Arlington: the Arlington Heights Study Club organized in 1907, joined the State Federation in 1913, and the General in 1926; the Arlington Woman's Club formed in 1895, and joined the State and General Federation in 1896; and the Kensington Park Study Club which was organized in 1911, joined the State Federation in 1921, but did not join the General Federation until 1954.

The Arlington Heights Study Club started with the thoughts of "social intercourse, self improvement, and promotion of efficiency." From this auspicious start grew an important organization that has sponsored or founded a number of still active groups in the community such as the Garden Club, the Friends of the Drama, the Philharmonic Society, the Visiting Nurses, the Girl Scouts Council, the Evening Adult Education Center, the Arlington Chapter of Friends of the New England Home for Little Wanderers.

Over the years the club has supported longer library hours, the position of the tree warden, better elevated car service, summer school and playgrounds. Local schools received slides of Arlington history from the club.

The Boston City Federation of Organizations, Inc. was formed in 1912 by a group of civic-minded women, their object to bring together for united service and action the various organizations in the city of Boston. They met in homes, various clubs, churches, and the public library. Finally, the Women's Educational and Industrial Union became their regular meeting place and later, at the New England Women's Club. In the early twenties, the club moved to the Young Women's Christian Association. Its early projects were the first paint and clean-up of Boston, women's suffrage, and juvenile court proposed by Judge Ben Lindsey of Denver who was Speaker of the House at the time. Factory owners were persuaded to place screens over the tops of their big chimneys to counteract smoke (nuisance) from some of the factories. These members were responsible for the baby week clinics, lectures, and promoting better health for babies. The club women sat at booths in many of the large stores, distributing literature and buttons which resulted in many donations enabling them to give substantial gifts to various hospitals and homes for the care of babies. The project received the support of the governor's wife, Mrs. Samuel McCall. During the war years they took an active part in the establishment, on Boston Common, of an Army Recreation Tent.

The Ladies' Physiological Institute of Boston and vicinity, organized in 1848 but had its origin in 1843. The club was dedicated to the courageous and far-sighted clubwomen of over a century ago whose prophetic vision of women's wider sphere of influence in the world has come to realization in the present and gives even greater promise for the future.

In the year 1843 a small, earnest group of fact-seeking women persuaded Harriet K. Hunt, later one of Boston's first women physicians, to instruct them in matter pertaining to the physiology of their bodies. After five years of meeting, the ladies assembled in Tremont Temple on April 5, 1848, in response to an announcement by Professor Charles P. Bronson of Harvard of a course of lectures to ladies "who should form themselves into a society for the promotion of useful knowledge among their own sex," proposing to present them with his apparatus valued at $700, provided $1,000 was raised.

The club adopted a constitution, earned $1,000 at a bazaar and serving business men's luncheons, and on May 2, 1848, Professor Bronson presented the full-size model of a woman, manufactured in Paris, a skeleton, and several organic models.

Despite its rapid growth as an organization, the cause was decidedly unpopular. It was considered most immodest for women to talk about matters pertaining to the human body. They met with ridicule and abuse and generally wore thick veils to meetings in order not to be recognized.

Only one minister could be found in all Boston to deliver an opening prayer for them at the first annual meeting, the Rev. Dr. Jenks.

The club was incorporated under the laws of Massachusetts on May 6, 1850. Eunice H. Cobb, (Mother Cobb) became the first woman president and remained a staunch supporter during her life. The club chose for its motto "Know Thyself" and, its aim "To teach women the laws of life and health and how to apply such knowledge in the home and community." For many years lectures at the meetings dwelt upon physiology, hygiene, etc., but the scope gradually broadened changing with the growth of women's interests and opportunities. LPIs continued interest in matters of health including enthusiastic support of the day nursery for underprivileged children at Morgan Memorial; Dr. Albert Schweitzer medical work in Africa; Massachusetts State Federation Veterans' work; Red Cross; and in 1960 the club received a citation from CARE for the largest contribution from a club of its size.

Dr. Salome Merritt, president from 1888 until her death in 1900, was one of the first women members of the Boston School Committee. She instituted sanitation in the schools and was instrumental in having seats placed behind the counters of department stores. Two years of intense effort finally resulted in the Massachusetts legislature passing a bill providing for segregation of persons in public institutions of Boston. This law was enacted in May 1897, establishing separated unpaid boards of trustees composed of both men and women in four departments, separating prisoners, paupers, children, and insane persons. The Institute has furnished a room at Llewsac Lodge, Bedford, Massachusetts, "In memory of its founders, Dr. Harriet K. Hunt and Mrs. Eunice Cobb."

To date, six current members have also been state presidents: Mrs. Americo Chaves; Mrs. F. William Ahearn; Mrs. Clarence Clark; Mrs. Eugene Faucher; Mrs. John Holland, and Mrs. Marshall Ross.

The Brookline Woman's Club was formed in 1917 and joined the Massachusetts State Federation in the same year. It gives four scholarships to the Brookline High School each year. As other clubs in its district this club knits for the veterans, gives contributions to the Little Wanderers, Perkins Institute for the Blind, the Salvation Army and many other charitable organizations.

The Dorchester club was formed because of the glowing report of Mrs. Clara May Ripley on her visit to the home club of Boston, and they, the Dorchester women, thought that this is what they needed. The first regular meeting was at the Harvard Street Church on March 22, 1892 — and they were presented a gavel by the Harvard Improvement Society. The club was a charter member of the MSFWC in 1893 and joined the General Federation in 1892.

In 1893 it was voted to use a seal, the Shield of the Seal of the Corporate Town of Dorchester. The background is the Blue Hills which served as a landmark to pilot early settlers to the mouth of the Charles River. The rising sun is shining on a colony seeking religious liberty. The castle on top of the shield is in respectful memory of Dorchester in Old England. The motto signifies that piety, learning, and industry were the virtues the early settler coveted.

Then came the application to the Secretary of State for a charter who, on inquiry, was satisfied the club was not organized for gambling, sale of liquor, or other unlawful purpose and on payment of five dollars granted the charter.

On a cold spring day in 1898, ground was broken for their so-called "Air Castle," many members witnessed the turning of the first sod, a piece of which was enclosed in a frame and hung in the office for many years. The new hall was opened November 8, 1898, with each member paying sixty-nine cents for her own chair. By 1900 the club was settled in its new building and the serious work started — meeting the needs of the community, visiting hospitals, and making numerous donations. In 1906 the club organized "the helpers" who made clothes for expectant mothers and needy school graduates.

In 1913 musical instruments were given to the Dorchester High School Regiment, consisting of ten bugles and fourteen snare drums inscribed with the name of the club. On retirement from her presidency in 1915, President Merritt presented the club with a substantial sum as a nucleus of a scholarship fund. In later years the fund exceeded the goal of $10,000 and by a unanimous vote on October 14, 1930, the fund became known as The Merritt Scholarship Fund.

In March 1917 a company of cadets from the Drum and Bugle Corps of the High School Regiment presented the club with an American flag and a beautiful state flag was given to the club. But dark clouds of World War I were gathering. Liberty bonds and sewing machines were purchased and the clubhouse became a beehive of activity and industry.

After the end of World War I, an Honor Roll of ninety-eight names of sons of members serving their country was hung in the reception hall.

During the term of Mrs. Alice Taylor Jacobs, the club was privileged to have a visit from former U. S. President William Howard Taft. It was a community affair and the Second Church offered the use of its building.

The New England Women's Club was really the brainchild of Mrs.

64

Whiton Hall, home of the Dorchester Woman's Club, was dedicated in October 1898 and named for Mrs. Ella Whiton who was instrumental in the purchase of the land and construction of the building. The first meeting of the club in Whiton Hall, also fondly known as the "Air Castle," was held on November 8, 1898, at which each member paid sixty-nine cents for her own chair.

Caroline Severance, who from her work with organized women became knows as "The Mother of Clubs." She succeeded with the help of a few like-minded women in organizing the first women to call themselves a women's club. Previous groups had been known as associations. The first slate of officers was an imposing one, many names that are honored in Boston's history. Mrs. Severance was president, other officers included: Julia Ward Howe, wife of Dr. Samuel Gridley Howe, revered for his work

The Dorchester Club seal incorporates the town shield, a castle in memory of Dorchester in England, the dates of town and club incorporation, and the motto "piety, learning and industry," all virtues revered by the early settlers.

1892

with the blind; two of the Peabody sisters of Salem, educators; Miss Lucy Goddard; Mrs. James Freeman Clarke; and many others. Two women doctors, Dr. Harriet K. Hunt and Dr. Marie Zakrzewska from Poland, were early members and are credited with establishing the New England Hospital for Women and Children with an all-woman staff.

The club became part of the State and General Federation in 1893, and in 1912, at the New England Women's Club rooms, the Federation of City Organizations was established.

The New England Women's Club was the first to succeed in having women elected to the school boards and to the boards of all public institutions. Women superintendents were put in prisons for women as well as police matrons in large cities. The first women's exchange and the first employment agency for women were started. The club supported the suffrage movement, the first horticultural school for women, and the kindergarten system was begun by Elizabeth Peabody, one of the early members.

The higher education of women has always been of deep interest to the New England Women's Club. From its beginning the club supported the Massachusetts Society for the University Education of Women and through that organization gave a scholarship beginning in 1899 which is still being used to help young women get a college degree.

The Norumbega Club was organized in 1893 in Charlestown, and was so named in hopes that the club would possess the qualities of that race of men who were known for its strength, force, and determination. At the first meeting, Mrs. Julia Ward Howe reminded the ladies that when women come together they find they can contribute something to each other. Mrs. Mary Livermore made the remark that "it was not possible for men to do all there was to do, that they must be assisted in the struggle by women, who have ever been in the main when any philanthropic project was to be undertaken, and by their example have proved an incentive to those less ambitious." One appreciates the remark "that a man is known by the umbrella he carries, but a woman is known by the club she belongs to."

The club made contributions to local organizations: The Bunker Hill Boys' Club, Hunt Asylum for Children, Nursing Association, and the Winchester Home for the Aged. A generous donation was made in 1910 to the Boston Floating Hospital and in another year one was sent to Dr. Emily Ryder for her work among the widows of India.

It is interesting to note that the club had the same speakers that were lecturing in all districts — Fannie Farmer who received eleven dollars, and

Dorothy Dix only five dollars. After each meeting the refreshment table cloth was laundered at a charge of twenty-five cents.

The Women's Italian Club of Boston Inc. was founded May 28, 1916, with the same principles that have been observed in all of the clubs in the Federation, that of mutual improvement in literature, music, art, and science plus the companionship of other women and the good of the town or city where they lived.

The Presidents' Club of Massachusetts was founded on April 13, 1916. The records of this associate club prior to 1970 have disappeared, and so little information has been given about the club's work. We do know that it does more than its share in supporting the state federation as do the following associated clubs: Boston Parliamentary Law – 1913, Council Club – 1958, Massachusetts Maine Daughters – 1918, the Professional Women's Club Inc. – 1907, The Women's Service Club of Boston (organized in 1919 joined the Federation in 1959), the Evening Division Past Presidents' Club – 1964, the Junior Past Presidents' Club – 1969, and the Past Junior Officers Club – 1982.

Northeastern Region

It was the undercurrent feeling throughout the formation of the clubs, that the women felt there was a need for them to get together and see if they could not do something about some of the conditions in the town or city where they lived. They also wanted to be with other women for congeniality, for doing something worthwhile, and for the lasting friendships that were formed.

Very few clubs owned their own meeting places, most met in various churches of the towns or cities where they were organized. The majority of the clubs in districts 8, 9, and 10 were founded in 1895 or later, the exceptions were: Old and New of Malden, 1878; Winchester Fortnightly, 1881; Danvers, 1882; Beverly, 1890; Medford, 1892; Reading, Old Melrose Club and Woburn, 1893; and Revere, 1894.

The Winchester Fortnightly and the Woburn Woman's Club were two of the original charter members of the General Federation of Women's Clubs when it was organized in 1890. Woburn attended the first Federation convention representing eighteen states. There were twenty clubs from Massachusetts.

It is interesting to note that many of the clubs instigated the organization of visiting nurse associations, among them being Reading, Stoneham, Wakefield, Winchester, Wilmington, and Manchester. The work of the clubwomen in disaster areas was remarkable during the 1908-1917 era. Within three weeks Reading raised almost $450 for material, finished 1,811 pieces for the Red Cross and French Relief, and 834 layettes for French babies. The Winchester Club collected and sent 900 garments to the Chelsea victims of the 1908 fire. It is noted that all clubs outdid themselves in volunteer work for World War I relief. Rockport was responsible for starting the group of Red Cross workers that was organized in 1914. Littleton, Groton, and Lawrence supported the Red Cross and war relief work, and Littleton also put on benefits for the Italian sufferers.

In public service to their town or city, club work was again outstanding. The Beverly Lothrop clubwomen furnished the grade school with reading material; until then the school had little or none. This club was also responsible for the "Little Libraries" in schools. In grade schools there was very little or no supplementary reading material, so the education committee of the club earned money for the above project, furnishing material from the first grade up to when the public library took over for the high schools. The Littleton Club's conservation group planted a mile of trees and beautified the Common, sponsored cooking and dressmaking classes for the schools, and pushed for the acceptance of a policewoman for the town; Groton, Lawrence, and Wilmington promoted hot lunches for the schools. Wilmington was instrumental in establishing three parks for the town, started a school dental clinic and a public health department, and also furnished a domestic science room in the high school. In 1901 the Revere Club sold soap and peanuts, its members walking through the town dressed in quaint costumes and carrying hand organs to raise money for a free library, realizing $1,300. Through the efforts of Mrs. Sparhawk (their first president) and Ernest H. Puerce (editor of *The Revere Journal*), an appeal sent to Andrew Carnegie realized the sum of $20,000 for a new library which was dedicated on March 18, 1903. The Pepperell Woman's Club planted trees along the main highway and placed trash barrels and settees throughout the town. Reading Woman's Club was instrumental in planning and donating the Memorial Park to the town. The Stoneham Woman's Club during the early 1900s secured free postal delivery for the town, cooperated with the town in placing electrical and telephone wires underground, and was responsible for starting the garbage and trash collections, after which they were to be the town's responsibility. They also started a public savings bank program for the school children and helped to form a Girl Scout troop. The Kosmos Club of Wakefield also began a stamp savings program for school children and established a student loan program.

68

The Lothrop Club of Beverly was named for Captain Thomas Lothrop, who commanded the *Flower of Essex* in King Philip's War and was killed in an Indian ambush. Their flower is the daisy due to the fact that Governor Endicott's china was packed in dry sprigs and seeds of this plant. He was responsible for their being scattered over the fields from Beverly to Danvers and they still grow profusely throughout Essex County.

The Rockport Woman's Club had two meetings per month either in the Baptist Church or in what is now the American Legion Hall, it being necessary to transport dishes and food to and from each meeting. Many of the clubwomen came to the meetings in horse and buggy, but the Amesbury-Elizabeth Whittier Club more so than others, because their town was known as the carriage center of the world. The Amesbury Club was named after the sister of the famous poet, John Greenleaf Whittier, who made his home there.

In 1917 the Lawrence Woman's Club welcomed into their midst Mrs. Malcolm Peabody, mother of the former governor of Massachusetts, Endicott Peabody. From 1893-1918 only women from Lawrence were admitted to the club, but starting in 1919 ladies from the neighboring town of Methuen could join.

A heated discussion at a Woburn Woman's Club meeting in 1890 was: "Are Women of Today [1890] Less Strong in Essential Characteristics than the Women of the American Revolution?" Another discussion that was enjoyed: "Is Harvard University Justified in Refusing to Extend Its Advantages to Women?" A heated debate arose in the Nahant Woman's Club on April 3, 1897, when a resolution was introduced that "A College Unfits a Woman for Practical Life." Another resolution made on March 18, 1898, stated "Women Should be Obliged, by Law, to Remove Their Millinery in Public Places."

It is interesting to note that ever since 1898 the Woburn Woman's Club has been listed in *The Women's Musical Clubs in the United States*.

Early clubs all seemed to have the same speakers who included Julia Ward Howe, Booker T. Washington, Fanny Farmer, and other famous people.

And so the first era ends — new friends have been made, a door has been opened and now the women throughout the state realize there is much to be done. They know they are the ones who can do it and there is no stopping them now.

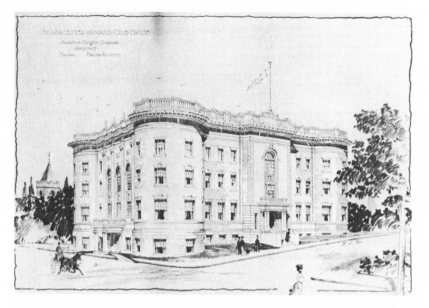

The impressive clubhouse of the Worcester Woman's Club was designed by Josephine Wright Chapman and built in 1902 on land donated by Stephen Salisbury, husband of a club member.

Central Region

The majority of clubs in the Central Region were founded in the 1890s. This was a time when women sensed the beginnings of a new era for them, wanted to improve themselves, and expand their world. It was a great thing for our nation that these feelings were aroused. In their pursuit of intellectual growth, their vision expanded to wider horizons, and the desire grew to share their knowledge with others in the community and use new skills to improve the lives of those around them. They sought the means to provide more liberal opportunities for women and a freedom from their limited participation in government and the so-called "business of the nation." But they did not neglect the importance of fellowship and the need for sociability and friendship while seeking these goals. Most clubs included the following in their aims or objects: intellectual growth, sociability, and the betterment of mankind. This has certainly been demonstrated by clubs in the Central Region, consisting of the 11th and 13th Districts.

The oldest club in the region is the Worcester Woman's Club, founded in 1880 with a charter membership of twenty-two women, and if we may quote from their preamble:

70

"We, women of Worcester and Vicinity, feeling the necessity which the present and prospective status of women imposes on us of informing ourselves more fully, not only upon subjects of present general interest, but also upon the more important special questions which are now pressing upon all peoples, everywhere, for a just solution, because involving the welfare of humanity, do agree to form ourselves into an Association for the prosecution and accomplishment of the above named purpose."

From 1880 to 1918 twenty-eight clubs were formed in this region. Different circumstances led to the formation of clubs. A talk by the president of the Worcester Woman's Club on club accomplishments was responsible for Millbury organizing its club in 1894. In 1898 a few ladies interest in hearing a paper on the "Use and Work of Women's Clubs" founded the Berlin Tuesday Club. The same year several women who attended art classes in Hudson decided to start a club so others could share the fellowship and knowledge they were acquiring. The Templeton Woman's Club founded in 1899 was brought about by a local woman reading in *Madam Demarest's Fashion Magazine* about the Sorosis Club of New York and wanting to take part in the widespread advancement believed coming to women.

In 1905 the Clio Club of Ashburnham began as a literary club to fill the gap between graduating from Cushing Academy and belonging to an older women's reading club. Membership was limited to young women over eighteen and unmarried.

Aid to others was also responsible for banding women together. In 1914 two hundred women joined the Southbridge Woman's Club. Southbridge had a population of varied ethnic backgrounds brought to the area by local industries. They saw the need to assist the women with learning the language, customs, and the beginning of Americanization classes. Polish women were taught English, Greeks and Albanians were taught to can vegetables. This was in spite of a picture of women as "homebodies, tea drinkers and wearers of the latest in millinery." They were called "foolish fools" to take on so much and make efforts in so many directions.

The constitution of the Northborough Woman's Club, organized in 1894, provided that "meetings should be held every second and fourth Saturday from October to April from 2:45 P.M. to 4:15 P.M." Following was a clarification: "It may be seen that this schedule would not interfere with the daily household duties during the week and would allow plenty of time for arriving home before the supper hour, to say nothing of providing time for enjoying the usual hearty noonday family dinner and its extensive cleaning up chores." Obviously, it was pointed out that attendance at meetings must not interfere with womanly duties!

The Spencer Monday Club, organized in 1892, was formed as a social club and in early years had evening meetings at the Massasoit Hotel with men invited for the programs and refreshments.

Most of the clubs founded in this era were very concerned with learning the history, both of their local areas and the United States, and thus were often responsible for sponsoring historical societies and the preservation of local memorabilia for future generations.

The Lancaster Current Topics Club, organized in 1897, had programs on "What Women Have Done" and "Early Settlements and the Naming of the Town." The Fortnightly Club of Leominster, founded the same year, considered "A Study of American History" their first important subject for presentation. In 1908 the Berlin Tuesday Club had farsighted members who proposed that the club "Receive and care for articles of historic interest to the town, until some future time when they should have a room for such articles." The Westborough Woman's Club, organized in 1916 (proud of their town, called "The Hundredth Town" because in 1717 it was the hundredth town to be established in Massachusetts) became very active in historical drama and musical presentations.

One common trend among the clubs was to have the meetings consist of their own talent — because they usually lacked funds to obtain professional speakers and there were transportation problems. But the main thrust of this era was that the women did prepare and present papers on literary works and historical and current events. The seriousness of these papers was demonstrated by the Leicester Woman's Club, which presented as many as four papers for discussion at one meeting and had a slogan that read "No fines, no fees and no food." (However, by the tenth year in operation they were serving lemonade and had fees of $1 per year.)

Food, of course, was always served, with the exception of the above. Copious quantities of ice cream were consumed and, in some clubs, lines had to be drawn to prevent a "friendly" outdoing by the more culinary-creative members. Members of the Hudson Woman's Club were admonished for serving cherries on top of vanilla ice cream to dress it up for a guest night because a "Woman's club should stand for better things." This was too frivolous, especially for a club that, during its year of programming in 1899, studied the following topics: Greek and Roman architecture; the problem of the unemployed and the results of strikes; the Peace Congress and the principles of arbitration; homes for consumptives; prisons; and "our opportunities in the home." In 1915 they held a series of public lectures and joined in bringing Chautauqua to the town.

Music played a most important part in programming and many clubs such as Westborough formed glee clubs and choral groups from their own members as well as others from the community. Plays and skits were widely produced and used as fund-raisers as well as for cultural development.

Stressing spiritual, moral, and patriotic values was always uppermost in club activities. Meetings opened with the Pledge of Allegiance, singing an anthem or hymn, an invocation, and usually closed with a "thought for the day."

It is most interesting to read the topics discussed from 1900 to 1918 by various clubs. Templeton Woman's Club had speakers on the "High Cost of Living" (things never change!) and "Pure Food"; Harvard Woman's Club on the woman's suffrage movement; Worcester Woman's Club on "Co-Operative Housekeeping," "How Not to Get Sick," and "Mortuary Art." Marlborough Tuesday Club presented papers on "The Effect on the Home of the Widening Sphere of Woman's Work" and "Will the Home Influence of a Child Counteract the Association of School." An ambitious program attended by thirty-five members of the Clinton Women's Club in 1914 consisted of fourteen sessions on "Labor and Capital as Reflected in Contemporary Literature." An international aspect was also introduced by the Leicester Woman's Club which heard Mrs. Chenowith speak. Her husband was United States consul in a Chinese port and had been captured. She then became consul and lectured afterwards in the United States. In 1895, the Fitchburg Woman's Club began a women's edition of the evening newspaper and the next year featured the MSFWC founder Julia Ward Howe as a speaker. Our founder was also honored at a reception given by the Worcester Woman's Club, as was Mrs. Custer, wife of General Custer.

Interest and concern for community betterment was an important area of club activity even in the early days of the century and became more so with the threat of war.

Conservation, which today we describe as a current topic, was advocated as early as 1899 by the Lancaster Current Topics Club which gave funds to destroy a thousand caterpillar nests in trees. In 1900 the Fitchburg Woman's Club supported tree planting and upgraded unused land in their town. In 1909 the Clinton Women's Club raised funds to plant

Meetings of yesteryear.

trees on Greeley Street. In 1913 the Berlin Tuesday Club asked selectmen to appoint a tree warden to save the town trees. That same year Lunenburg Women's Club planted a rock maple tree on Arbor Day. (Perhaps to compensate for the fact that the gavel the club used was cut from an historic buttonwood tree on the Common. It was believed this was done surreptitiously by lantern light as no one would dare touch a tree planted by the Lunenburg Militia when they went to join Washington at Cambridge.) In 1916 the Southbridge Women's Club lobbied to have Massachusetts plant trees on the highway between Southbridge and Sturbridge, and Harvard was one of many clubs which erected bird fountains and planted trees and flower gardens on town property. The Hudson Woman's Club

74

donated an urn which they kept filled with flowers at a downtown intersection and in 1916 planted ivy around the town hall and supplied rubbish barrels for Main Street. The Upton Woman's Club planted flowers on the Common and gave funds to fight the elm tree beetles.

Libraries benefited greatly from club sponsorship. In 1899 the Clinton Women's Club started a public library with a financial donation and a book from each member. The Berlin Tuesday Club started a fund to erect a library. In 1914 the Millbury Woman's Club formed a fund to aid the library and started the "Library Extension." Book donations were an ongoing part of club activities.

Community projects were not only supported but instituted. In the early 1900s the Berlin Tuesday Club formed a Village Improvement Association. The Fitchburg Woman's Club furnished a parlor in Hastings Hall, a residence for young working women. In 1907 the Hudson Woman's Club was foremost among the organizers of the district nursing association, which became the Hudson Community Health Association. The club still helps support the expanded Assabet Valley Home Health Association, as it is called today. In 1911 the Fortnightly Club of Leominster started the first public playground. Two years later the Winchendon Woman's Club approached the town and proposed establishing a Visiting Nurse Association. The expenses involved the costs of car, salary, etc., and were supported by this club until 1963. Between 1916 and 1918 two more clubs, Clinton and Northborough, established district nurse associations in their towns. The Worcester Woman's Club, with great determination, were responsible for the first isolation hospital, establishing a boys' and girls' trade school, kindergartens, and vocational schools, out of which grew the playground movement. They also launched a penny savings program in twenty-five public schools, and worked for the hiring of the first police woman.

Young people were perhaps the most direct benefactors of club projects. It is a proud fact to report that all clubs within a few years of founding started scholarships for students. Many, such as Gardner in 1914, set up funds that have grown through the years to the point that interest alone fulfills yearly commitments.

In the 1900s the Upton Woman's Club established courses in manual training for boys in public schools by supplying sixteen benches completely equipped with working tools, as well as a room for the study of household arts, with two sewing machines and a flatiron. The Clinton Women's Club instituted the school stamp savings plan and founded a girls' health league for high schoolers. In 1915 the Harvard Woman's Club sponsored manual training for twelve boys in a summer school. In 1912 the Hudson Woman's Club started sewing classes in the public school and in 1915 sponsored the Camp Fire Girls. The Holden Woman's Club urged selectmen to arrange for domestic service classes for girls in schools.

In 1901 the membership of the Worcester Woman's Club had grown to 600 and land was given to them to build a clubhouse. One fundraising project during a weeklong carnival they held, was publishing a Worcester Woman's Club edition of the *Evening Gazette*, through the generosity of George F. Booth. The sum of $7,150 was raised to pay off the final mortgage and in 1914 they burned the mortgage of a building planned, designed, and paid for by women! What an achievement!

Reaching out to other states, in 1907 the Lancaster Current Topics Club, after hearing a speaker named Hindeman praise a settlement school in Kentucky, donated five dollars, the first outside help given to this school.

Most of these clubs also joined the MSFWC and were influenced by their aims and projects. In 1912 Templeton hosted the MSFWC annual meeting, many arriving by horse and buggy.

World War I was the first major upheaval for the nation that involved clubwomen across the state in a common goal. Countless hours were devoted to rolling bandages, classes on first aid and home nursing and knitting scarfs and socks. Liberty Loans, War Bonds and Stamps were sold by all clubs. Tremendous support was given to the Red Cross. The Fortnightly Club of Leominster donated $2,500 in 1917 — a princely sum in those days! Berlin Tuesday Club ran a war group called Aid. Templeton members did military relief work at Camp Devens along with many other clubs. Afghans, helmets, socks were knitted in abundance with one seventy-year-old woman in Lancaster alone knitting over 100 helmets. Harvard Woman's Club was one of the clubs sending boxes to servicemen for Christmas and bought a five-hundred dollar liberty bond. Hospital visits became a duty for clubwomen. Southbridge Woman's Club also helped the needy at home by filling thirty-six boxes with food. They also helped to organize a visiting nurse association and promoted a series of baby weeks. In 1917 they adopted a French war orphan, as did the clubs in Clinton and Holden. The Tatnuck Woman's Club of Worcester, which during the early years of the war had adopted an isolationist policy as they felt this was "a European affair," changed their stand after the United States entered the war, and joined many clubs in sending clothing and donations to relief funds in Belgium and France.

Several clubs followed the pattern of Shrewsbury Woman's Club which voted to omit five meetings in 1917-18 and devote that time to serving and knitting for the Red Cross and for the American Fund for the French Wounded.

In 1917-18 the influenza epidemic hit the nation. The Hudson Woman's Club was active in establishing and operating a temporary hospital to cope with the ill. Many clubs were forced to cancel meetings through this crisis.

Western Region

Agawam Women's Club

Joined the Massachusetts State Federation in 1926 and the General Federation in 1929.

The Agawam Women's Club was organized in 1926 by twenty women whose objective was the "mutual helpfulness, the advancement of public welfare and the promotion of the civic and cultural interests" of the women of Agawam.

In earlier days when membership was over 200, there were many activities such as garden parties, lending cupboard (sick room supplies), an organized dental clinic, dancing classes for the town teens, and a mothercraft group to teach and train girls in the care of young children.

This club was also instrumental in forming two other groups which are very active today. They are the Historical Association and the Agawam Garden Club.

Amherst Woman's Club

Member of the General Federation since the founding of the club in 1893.

The Amherst Woman's Club was conceived on May 18, 1893, and officially inaugurated on October 4, 1893, as the "Ramona Club." The Ramona Club as such was short lived, for in only a few months the name was changed to "The Amherst Woman's Club" and it has been known by this name now for the past ninety-four years.

During the years 1901-1903, the list of speakers at the club included the President of Wellesley, the President of Amherst, the Dean of Barnard, the Dean of the Women's College of Brown, the President of Mount Holyoke, and the Dean of Radcliffe. Shortly later we find the names of Alice Freeman Palmer, Gerald Stanley Lee, John M. Tyler, B. K. Emerson, and others.

From its beginning the club has been civic-minded and eager to enhance the beauty of the town and welfare of its citizens. Perhaps an occasional item in the club record may be read with a smile — as for instance, in 1897 a committee of three was appointed to confer with the proper authorities in regard to the practice of spitting on the streets. A little later we find the club preparing a float for the Fourth of July parade. The sections were represented by ladies dressed in white with yellow parasols on which were the names of the various club sections.

During the first five years, $115 was given for the Boys' Club and reading room. A reading room for women was opened in the town hall. The Audubon Club for the study and observation of birds was organized by members of the Science Section. In 1897 twenty-five dollars was appropriated toward the expense of introducing sewing into the public schools. Shortly later one hundred dollars was designated to support a summer cooking school for girls in the three lower grades and a teacher came from Springfield for this purpose. The lessons were held in the Amity Street Building with fifty-six pupils attending. Dismayed by some evening rowdyism, the club petitioned the town meeting that a curfew bell be introduced. As early as 1896 there was active agitation among club members for establishing an old ladies home.

In 1893 the pressing needs of the town as enumerated by the club were felt to be a new high school building, a town library, a waiting room for trolley passengers and a district nurse. With characteristic energy, eager women set about agitating these matters before proper authorities.

Chicopee Falls Woman's Club

Joined the Massachusetts State Federation in 1897 and the General Federation in 1916.

The Chicopee Falls Woman's Club was founded in August 1894, chartered with twelve members. Its main purpose was the study of "Parliamentary Drill, the Constitution of the United States, and American History." The club expanded and enveloped the fields of nature study, the social services, conservation and national forests, and in 1904 women's suffrage.

The study of domestic science was started early for one of the Home Programs in 1898. The first subject was "The need for keeping the Cellar clean." (This was really starting at the bottom.) This was the origin of the American Home Day Program which to this day is an Annual Program Day of the club.

During the years 1909-1910, household economics was studied with lectures on health building. The year 1911 was epoch-making to the club, for this was the year the club voted to deposit twenty-five dollars as a nucleus for a scholarship fund to be used as a loan for students of Chicopee High School desiring a college education. This scholarship program is still in effect today.

Granby Woman's Club

Joined the Massachusetts State Federation in 1909 and the General Federation in 1916.

On April 30, 1908, at the invitation of Mrs. Maud C. Eastman, thirteen ladies assembled at her home for the purpose of organizing a Woman's Literary Club.

Mrs. Ada Warner Gray was elected the club's first president and the purpose of the club was to encourage study in all possible departments of literature; to secure all possible social and intellectual advantages for its members; and to consider vital questions in a practical way.

Members were responsible for the programs at each meeting. A member would be responsible for discussing current events; another would be responsible for research and presenting a paper on a subject such as important people of that time, international trade relations, history of witchcraft, history of different cities in the area, garden hints, problems of the homemaker, etc. If a poet or writer was to be honored, the members might have to respond to a roll call with a short verse or line from his works. It was not unusual in the early days of the club for a member to present a recipe or quote a famous saying when answering the roll call. It is interesting to note that the club still takes roll call.

Southampton Woman's Club

Joined the Massachusetts State Federation in 1923 and the General Federation in 1926.

On September 26, 1917, a group of twenty-five women gathered to form a Home Economics Club. They voted to meet at various members' homes on the 4th Tuesday of each month with a meeting format that would include debates, contests, readings, and demonstrations. This was the start of what would later be known as the Southampton Woman's Club.

Some of the programs selected for that first year 1917-18 dealt with women's health, labor saving devices, household accounts, school lunches, household sanitation, and most significantly, community improvement. This area of community improvement became the focal point around which the club would work and grow throughout the coming years.

The Home Economics Club soon began to make its mark on the community by beautifying homes and roadsides, establishing well-child clinics, sponsoring 4-H Clubs and scout troops, providing hot lunches to school children, and by contributing significantly to the cultural growth of the town.

Tuesday Club of Warren

Joined the Massachusetts State Federation in 1898 and the General Federation in 1951.

The Tuesday Afternoon Club was organized in 1888 by nine ladies, who met to form a society for mutual improvement. Mrs. Edgar J. Buck served as president for twenty years from 1888 to 1908.

Dues at that time were twenty-five cents a year and membership was limited to fifteen. A new member could be admitted by a unanimous vote of the members, and if three consecutive meetings were not attended, she was dropped from membership. Women whose husbands were involved in church or school positions were given associate membership status, however, when the husband's position ended, so did the wife's membership.

In these early years members delivered papers on current events. Some other topics covered were "Evidences of an Ancient Civilization in America," "Early Roman History," "Ancient Forms of Religion," "Folk Lore," and "Life of Washington."

By 1917 interest began to develop in women's rights and legislation.

The Hampden County Women's Club

Admitted to the Massachusetts State Federation in 1914 and the General Federation in 1923.

In 1912 during the political campaign of Theodore Roosevelt, a group of women banded together to form the Hampden County Progressive Club. They worked diligently during the campaign and after the election of Theodore Roosevelt these women decided to organize. Mrs. William Towne, Mrs. William Dwight of Holyoke, Mrs. Ernest Bagg of West Springfield, and Mrs. Eleanor Hale of Chicopee invited women in the area to join them and from this group "The Hampden County Women's Club" came into being; Mrs. Ernest Bagg serving as its first president. The object of the club was to broaden the horizons of thinking, and all programs stressed education for women interested in human advancement.

Since its beginning the club adopted a motto which has remained the same throughout the years: "There is a solution for every problem and soul's highest duty is to be of good cheer." (Emerson)

The Ladies Mission Club (Wilbraham Women's Club)

Joined the Massachusetts State Federation in 1910 and the General Federation in 1928.

On January 27, 1905, sixteen women formed "The Ladies Mission Club." Six months later under the name of "World Wide Study Club," a constitution and bylaws were adopted. Meeting in their homes, the members presented papers on various countries, literature, and local history.

In the early years of the club, projects for civic improvement were undertaken which included: cleaner streets, rubbish removal, the Schick Test for school children, hot lunch programs, a dental clinic, PTA, Outdoor Laboratory, the Planning Board and Finance Committee, sponsorship of 4H Clubs, scholarships, and service to veterans.

Athol Woman's Club

Joined the Massachusetts State Federation in 1901.

"To promote intellectual improvement, and social intercourse, and to improve all movements for the betterment of society." With these purposeful words as a challenge, on April 7, 1900, a group of fifty-three women banded together in the old GAR Hall at the "Highlands." Under the guidance of the MSFWC President, Miss O. M. E. Rowe, and Miss Mary L. Epps, an Athol school teacher, the Athol Woman's Club was founded.

In a short time the membership soared from the original 53 to 112 charter members. Within two years the membership climbed to 300 and then there was a waiting list. The club's dreams of community aid began to bear fruit as they engaged the first visiting nurse, sponsored a Girl's Club numbering 250, and organized the first PTA In World War I, the club served with town committees and the Red Cross. Much sewing for French war orphans, bandage rolling, and knitting was done.

The first May Breakfast was held in 1908, an occasion of such popularity that it became an annual custom. Now known as the Annual Meeting and May Luncheon, it is the day of days for the Woman's Club for the members have worked faithfully to carry out the far-seeing desires of the founders.

The Charlemont Study Club (Charlemont Woman's Club)

Joined the Massachusetts State Federation in 1923.

The Charlemont Woman's Club began as the Charlemont Study Club in 1898. Afternoon meetings were held at the homes of members; programs were arranged by the members and included art, music and literature; and current events were an important feature. Men's Night was a yearly event as were picnics.

The following four articles of the original constitution of the Charlemont Study Club are of interest: "The object of this club shall be to promote the intellectual and social life of its members, and to contribute to the welfare of the community," "If a member fails to give a current event, she must be fined five cents," "If any member is absent three meetings in succession without giving reasonable excuse, her name shall be crossed off from the Constitution," "The number of members shall be limited to twenty."

The Woman's Club of Greenfield   81

Joined the Massachusetts State Federation in 1917.

The Woman's Club of Greenfield was established in March 1911 with seventeen charter members. By the Fall of 1911, membership had risen to 143 and was still climbing.

A crisis arose in May 1911 when a piece of land of fifty-six acres was destined to be cut down for lumber. The newly established woman's club asked for ten days to raise the $8,000 required to purchase the land. Stipulations were enforced to keep the land in its natural beauty for the enjoyment of the town's people. Holding the land required the club to incorporate, which they did in June 1911 with their same officers.

In 1911 there was no radio or television, and movies were in their infancy. Women did not work outside the home, and anything of an entertaining or instructive nature was a live event. The Woman's Club of Greenfield was dedicated to bringing programs of high caliber to the area, sharing with the townspeople concerts, plays, and outstanding musical performances.

During World War I the club adopted a British orphan, raised funds to purchase two ambulances, furnished the Mary Potter Lounge at Fort Devens, and was commended for selling many War Bonds.

The club joined the Massachusetts State Federation thru the efforts of Mrs. Arthur Potter, who later became president of MSFWC.

Sunderland Woman's Club

Joined the Massachusetts State Federation in 1898 and the General Federation in 1927.

Founder of the Sunderland Woman's Club was Eloise Tower Fairchild, who met with a small group of women on November 3, 1894, to establish the club. Fifteen charter members made up the club, and they adopted a constitution and decided on the club's purpose: "To consider topics of vital interest, i.e., social, literary and philanthropic, and to promote cordial personal relations among women."

For many years the club took an active part in the social life of the community, and the New Year's Reception and Gentlemen's Night were reported in the newspapers as "brilliant and gorgeous." A talk given on one of these nights in April 1901 was on "The Woman's Club from a Man's Point of View." A Mr. Whitmore was the speaker.

During these early years club members took an active interest in improving the community; making donations of food and money to the Franklin County Hospital; purchasing dishes and other needed items for the chapel meeting place; helping with time and money for the local Girl Scouts; maintaining the first two electric lights on Main Street; and donating books and magazines to the Graves Memorial Library.

The motto chosen in 1918 was "One alone can do little; she can avail, who in the right hour unites her strength with others."

Northfield Fortnightly Club

Admitted to the Massachusetts State Federation in 1928 and the General Federation in 1951.

On September 23, 1904, a few women met at the Dickinson Library, in Northfield for the purpose of forming a literary club. The first meeting took place on October 3 at which time they chose the name "The Fortnightly" and decided on a fifty-cent initiation fee. The topic for the day was "Women who have become famous in New England." Thereafter for several years they chose a theme for each year and one member spoke at each meeting on one aspect of that theme, whether it be famous women, American art, or Japanese history.

At the club's second meeting on October 17th, it was announced that a letter had been received from Mrs. Elisha Alexander, wife of a prominent Northfield resident, commending the women for starting the club and enclosing a check for fifty dollars for the purchase of a desk. She also left a bequest to the town for building a "Ladies Hall," but at that time a new school was needed. Through a special act of legislature, the town was allowed to incorporate the hall into the high school plans. It was not until 1912 that the building was ready and the first club meeting there was held in October.

Throughout the years the members were aware of social and political concerns. In February 1905 the club held a debate on "Resolved: That women ought to have equal rights with men." A vote was taken, and believe it or not, the result was 5 Yes and 11 No!

GROWTH

1918-1942

DURING this time span World War I, the flu epidemic, the Great Depression, and a series of natural disasters challenged the membership. Again our women's clubs demonstrated their ability to cope effectively with a multitude of diverse problems.

Mrs. Herbert J. Gurney, often referred to as the "War President," served from 1916-1919. Clubs throughout the state joined forces in raising money for war relief, increasing food production, and donating medical and surgical supplies. While the war work was outstanding there were other important matters requiring support from the clubwomen. During the flu epidemic dedicated and heroic members turned many club houses into hospitals as they also acted as volunteer nurses. In December 1917 Halifax, Nova Scotia, was partially destroyed when two ships (one loaded with munitions) collided, resulting in a devastating explosion. Again the clubs responded with food, clothing, and other necessities.

When war work concluded Mrs. George Minot Baker (1919-1922) proposed that the Federation shift its emphasis back to peacetime service projects. In her first message she said, "The world is looking to America as the leader of the great moral and spiritual questions of the day. The circle of service is ever widening – the home, the community, the state, the nation, the world, are all dependent upon the life and energy and service of the individual. . . .

> "Take God once more as Counselor
> Work with Him hand in hand;
> Build surely in His grace and power
> The nobler things that shall endure,
> And having done all – Stand"

83

Under the direction of Mrs. Grace Poole Reynolds (1922-1923) the Federation studied and supported legislation related to a new state prison, educational films for schools and colleges, jury service for women, and new immigration measures. In 1922 permanent headquarters for the Federation were established at 585 Boylston Street, Boston.

The Federation also supported the rehabilitation of refugees in the Near East, approved substitution of law for war in settling difficulties, favored our nation's entrance into the World Court, approved the Merit system, and extension of civil service. Members approved a resolution upholding the law which forbade holding games of chance.

No president completes all projects started during her administration and this was true of the Memorial Fellowship established during Mrs. George Minot Baker's presidency. It was completed under the leadership of Mrs. Frederick Glazier Smith (1924-1926). The Music Division was active this biennium with the organization of a Federation Chorale Society, participation in state and national music contests, and publication of a new state song, "Massachusetts, Old Bay State."

Under Mrs. Arthur Devens Potter (1926-1928) the Federation helped organize the Boston Women's Symphony Orchestra. This was the first symphony orchestra in the United States composed entirely of women with a woman conductor. The membership also worked successfully for the preservation of Franconia Notch and inaugurated the Club Institute which was held at the Vendome in Boston.

Mrs. Isabel Packard Westfall, president (1928-1930), was especially identified with the work of the International Relations Committee of the Federation. In recognition of the Tercentenary in Massachusetts, a state forest of 150 acres was presented as a gift to the Commonwealth by the Federation in 1930.

Junior Membership, formerly a special department, became a Federation Committee and a special department called Federation Extension was organized "to bring the joy and friendship of the Federation to the women of the farms and to bring together rural and urban inhabitants."

Mrs. Carl L. Schrader, who served from 1930 to 1932, was called the "Book Lady" because of her many book reviews given before organizations and over the radio. An outstanding program during this administration involved those who could not find employment during the winter of 1930-1931. The serious situation of the unemployed in all walks of life made it imperative that aid be offered. Clothing was collected in Boston for more than 40,000 people and similar work was carried on throughout the Commonwealth. The satisfaction experienced by the clubwomen in helping the unfortunate brought about a unity of purpose and interest.

Three programs made excellent progress during the administration of Mrs. Frank Pierce Bennett, president from 1932 to 1934. The state beautification program created a strong interest in conservation. Town and city commons, highways, church, school, and home grounds were beautified. Dumps were cleared; old, deteriorating buildings were removed.

The State Forest Reservation, 1,000 acres of land in Petersham, was presented to the Commonwealth as a gift to be set aside for the pleasure and recreation of all.

Youth projects, including the establishment of a Greater Boston Information Center for Girls and expansion of the Junior Membership, made significant progress. Mrs. Bennett said of the juniors, "It is a challenge for our clubwomen to encourage and assist them in every way possible and to teach them that success is achieved only by hard work and honest endeavor."

Mrs. Thomas J. Walker (1934-1936) had as her goal: "To modernize the machinery of the Federation so that it might function more efficiently." She appointed Deans of Directors and Deans of Chairmen, naming her first and second vice presidents to fill these capacities automatically. The Junior Department was reorganized to an all-junior membership with a sub-committee of seniors to advise and guide.

The pressing issue during the presidency of Mrs. John H. Kimball (1936-1938) was "Peace." The three objectives of her administration were: "That we cooperate with other individuals and groups doing work similar to that being done by the Federation; that we banish fear and show courage to accept the truth wherever found; that we as clubwomen understand the causes that lead to war, and do something to build for peace." She also encouraged individual clubs to conduct community surveys to better understand the needs and opportunities of their home towns.

As Mrs. Henry W. Hildreth assumed the presidency (1938-1940) she said, "For two years, under the leadership of Mrs. Kimball, we stressed her watchword, 'Peace.' In these days, more than ever, we are interested in peace at home and abroad. To further a continuation of that peace, we have taken as our slogan, 'Good Citizenship,' for without good citizens there can be no peace."

Members and clubs were in full support of this concept and held Good Citizenship Sundays, sponsored community centers for underprivileged youth and in 1939 Congress set aside the third Sunday in May as National Citizenship Day.

Two additional projects undertaken during this biennium included a program called, "Come to New England," a plan to bring visitors to New England which was financed by contributions of a penny per member. The second was to replace trees felled by the 1938 hurricane. This program resulted in replacing trees and also in much roadside beautification.

86

Again during the presidency of Mrs. David A. Westcott (1940-1942) war relief became a focal point for the membership of the Massachusetts State Federation of Women's Clubs.

Prior to the United States entry into World War II clubwomen organized a War Relief Committee. Money was raised and a large mobile feeding unit called a "Rolling Kitchen" was sent to the women of England as an expression of admiration for the bravery with which they were coping with days of stress. Later two more "kitchens" were shipped to England, clothing was sent and many clubwomen opened their homes to receive refugee British children.

Important as it was to support the War Relief Program Mrs. Westcott stressed the need for support of programs at home. Reports submitted by directors and chairmen described work for local charities, hospitals, disabled veterans, and scholarships, while the Junior Clubwomen's project for children with heart ailments had increased.

The following decades of development in our local clubs reflect how they were influenced by the times, the goals of the Federation leaders, and their sense of responsibility.

Southeastern Region

By 1916 clubs were getting into the "swing of things." Among the clubs founded during this era were: the Hingham Woman's Club and the Orleans Woman's Club in 1921; the Braintree Point Woman's Club in 1923; the Sandwich Woman's Club in 1924; the East Freetown Woman's Club in 1925; the Braintree Junior Philergians in 1927; the Rochester Woman's Club and the Somerset Woman's Club in 1928; the Second District Past Presidents' Club in 1929; the First District Presidents' Club in 1931; the Junior Ladies' Library Association of Randolph in 1933; the Third District

Presidents' Club in 1940; and the Mattapoisett Woman's Club in 1941. We discover that the Old Colony Union and the Bourne Women's Club merged in 1921.

The Falmouth Woman's Club members sewed for the War Relief and led successful Red Cross drives, not only for World War I but also for World War II, as did the Philergians. Members of the Edgartown Woman's Club became air raid wardens, spotters, canteen workers; and members of the Abington Woman's Club did much for War Relief including serving as Grey Ladies in camps and hospitals. The clubs ran many money-making projects, the proceeds buying War Bonds and Stamps. The Braintree Point Woman's Club opened a service club and canteen near the railroad depot and servicemen were invited into homes for weekends. Christmas wreaths were made for Camp Edwards. A Red Cross unit was staffed, nurses aid courses and salvage were stressed. Books were collected for servicemen overseas. The Woman's Club of Brockton sold the highest dollar amount of War Bonds for World War II of any club in the Federation. The Cabot Club of Middleboro had an active peace service in 1940 which was a War Veterans Committee. They furnished a room at a local hospital, tended a "Rolling Kitchen" and did Red Cross and relief work. In 1918 the Wareham Monday Club purchased a $500 bond and sent books and knitted articles to the soldiers, and in 1940 performed more war work and supplied a respirator for the Tobey Hospital.

During these formative years, the Falmouth Woman's Club had two of its members elected to the Falmouth School Board, and held health conferences. The Wareham Monday Club set up the first town Christmas tree in 1922, and paid for the tree, trimmings, and lighting for forty years. They added public health to the already existing programs of education, legislation, and home economics; conducted sewing classes for immigrants and provided a hot water tank for the school lunchroom. In 1927 they were successful in continuing street car service for a few more years. The Harwich Woman's Club and The Tuesday Club of Assonet were instrumental in establishing welfare funds and in supplying financial aid to maintain health and dental clinics and scholarships. The Edgartown Woman's Club provided milk for underprivileged children and The Philergians, Ladies' Library Association of Randolph, the Abington, Taunton, New Bedford, Orleans, and Sandwich Woman's Clubs also participated in the clinics and milk funds, and supplied food and clothing for the needy. Mothercraft classes were also held by the above clubs. During these early years, the school nurse was sponsored by many of the clubs in their towns, among them the Taunton Woman's Club; and the

Bas relief plaque symbolizing education presented by the Philergians of Braintree to Braintree High School in 1927.

The Federation Story

Harwich Woman's Club formed the Visiting Nurse Association in their town.

The clubs within the Federation are always working for the beautification of their respective towns – as we can see in the following examples: the Nautilus Club of Provincetown gave a gift of land to their town, planted bulbs, and made markers for paths and trails from town to the sand dunes. The Braintree Point Woman's Club provided equipment for a school playground; members protested an offensive odor emanating from the City Service Oil Company, and were successful in improving conditions there. The Cabot Club of Middleboro planted trees by the railroad depot. The Orleans club also gave playground equipment to their school, placed rubbish cans around town, planted a Christmas tree in Eldredge Park and formed a committee to look into electric lighting for their town. The Philergians presented a sculpture to the high school at its dedication, were also instrumental in securing rubbish collection in the town, worked with the tree warden planting trees throughout the town, and were responsible for erecting the flag pole at the town hall and historical markers at selected sites around the town. The Ladies' Library Association did their part by making sure that houses were numbered for mail delivery, and influencing the town fathers to have the government provide free rural mail delivery in their community. Clean-up days were held throughout the town and a public dump site obtained. Signs were placed at every street and shade trees were donated. The Braintree Junior Philergians collected both cultivated and wild flowers, and distributed them throughout the tenement district.

Many of the clubs formed choral groups within their ranks, such as the Falmouth, Abington, and Wareham clubs, and The Cabot Club of Middleboro not only formed a choral group but sang on the radio and at Federation meetings. In 1930 a Wareham Junior group was formed, only to be disbanded after seven years. During their brief stay in the Federation they sponsored town meeting articles regarding garbage collection and the need for a school nurse. All of the Southeastern Region's clubs volunteered their services for the veterans hospitals and donated generously to scholarships.

The Brewster Woman's Club has yearbooks from the 1920s but no written records prior to 1934. Their yearbooks show that the members wrote papers on topics ranging from "English Poets" and "Corruption in the Government," to "Mothercraft" and emphasis on one's family. A clubhouse was purchased sometime before 1934 which served as a gathering place for many town events as well as the regular club meetings. The

89

clubhouse was rented out to other civic groups and to tourist families in the summer, helping to defray the operating costs. In 1940 Mrs. Herbert Foster, an early member, was selected by GFWC to receive the designation, "Pioneer Clubwoman," and the club also received a citation in connection with this award. Actively involved in politics, the club devoted one meeting each year to discussion of all the articles in the annual town meeting warrant.

The Falmouth Woman's Club encouraged local theaters to present better movies. In 1922 Harwich organized a Girl Scout troop and clubmembers held a successful bazaar to purchase uniforms and equipment for the girls. The Sandwich club sponsored the first youth hostel on Cape Cod, which also was the first hostel to be sponsored by a woman's club. In addition they furnished the teachers' room at the school, urged the New Haven Railroad to install modern improvements including lights and water at the local railroad station; and circulated a petition asking the Massachusetts Medical Society to provide information on birth control to those seeking it. In 1930 Edgartown presented to the public a program, "Pageant of the Shawls," written by a clubmember. It depicted shawls from all over the world, brought back to Edgartown by sea captains. This club also contributed to the Mayhew-Nevin Fund which provided a free hospital bed to a needy person.

In 1935 the Braintree Point Woman's Club's seal was designed by a Braintree high school student. They sponsored the sale of articles made by the blind, supported the Morgan Memorial Fresh Air Camps, and the Norfolk Hospital was aided. In 1939 they were also successful in acquiring a traffic light near the Watson School which greatly improved the safety of the children.

Rochester Woman's Clubhouse was built in 1932 by members and their husbands.

The Simeon Daggett mansion was purchased by the Taunton Woman's Club in 1917 and an auditorium was added in 1923.

The Woman's Club of Brockton was honored to have one of their members, Mrs. H. Gilbert (Grace) Morrison Poole Reynolds, serve as MSFWC president from 1922-1924. During her administration the first permanent headquarters was established in a single room on Boylston Street, Boston. Mrs. Reynolds went on to serve the GFWC, first as corresponding secretary, 1926-1928, then as first vice-president, 1928-1932, and finally as President of the General Federation of Women's Clubs in 1932, an office she held for three years.

During the influenza epidemic of 1918, the Taunton Woman's Club members gave generously of their time and talents to help others. From 1918-1931 the Tuesday Club of Assonet suspended their meetings for a time in order to concentrate on Red Cross and other World War I work. For many years the Rose Hawthorne Lothrop House was enriched by donations of cancer pads and Christmas gifts from the East Freetown and other area clubs. The Woman's Club of Brockton supplied funds to the Brockton Day Nursery for working mothers—these funds were used for rugs, curtains, and food. In 1932, after maintaining a home and office space for the Quincy VNA for twenty-seven years, the Quincy Women's Club gave them a car, office equipment, and $7,000, and turned the organization over to the community. The Rochester Woman's Club was originally an auxiliary of the Men's Country Club, with meetings held twice a month in the men's clubhouse. They continued to grow in number, and moved their meetings to the vestry of the First Congregational Church and organized in 1928 as the Rochester Woman's Club. In 1932 they purchased land and constructed their own clubhouse which they funded by holding chicken pie suppers, clambakes, bazaars, and twice weekly card parties. Through the diligent personal service of the members and their husbands who spent many hours wielding hammers and saws, they saved considerably on the actual construction costs.

The Somerset Woman's Club purchased a former two-room schoolhouse from the town for a token one dollar! The clubmembers remodeled the school to become their clubhouse, upgrading the plumbing and installing a furnace. This clubhouse is still used for meetings and special events. The Orleans Woman's Club was instrumental in forming a local League of Women Voters. They also raised money for the Orleans Athletic Association and Orleans High School, and helped to form a local Girl Scout troop, securing a leader and providing a flag. The Whitman Woman's Club established a student loan fund, and awarded honorary club membership to the two highest ranking girls in the junior class at the high school.

In 1917 the Sippican Woman's Club of Marion acquired the use of quarters at Music Hall. Then in 1922 the club voted to purchase for $7,800 the old house known as Handy's Tavern, built in 1812. With its new heating system, refurnishing, and necessary repairs, the club incurred a debt of $12,000. A portion of the clubhouse was leased for two years

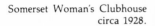

Somerset Woman's Clubhouse
circa 1928.

Built in 1812, the Sippican Woman's Clubhouse on Front Street in Marion was originally known as Handy's Tavern, a meeting place for seamen in the busy port of Sippican. It was later a stagecoach stop.

(1922-1924) at an annual rental of $420 which more than covered the interest, taxes, and insurance. A portion of the house was also used as a "teachery" (boarding place for teachers), another section as a clinic for the Marion Visiting Nurse Association and also as living quarters for the town nurse. Rooms were rented to the nurse and teachers for sums ranging from two to eight dollars a week board. In 1928-1929 club membership grew to 200, making it necessary to abandon use of the clubhouse for meetings and seek larger quarters. The clubhouse was still maintained and rented, however.

Southern Region

In 1918 an epidemic of influenza occurred. The Norwood Women's Club helped set up an emergency hospital and members prepared food for nurses and the state guard who were called to assist. Those with the disease were moved there to prevent it from spreading. In 1922 the members started a doll collection for the children's library and it is now stored in Day House, a historical building which the club helped to restore. Again with children in mind, the club donated $600 for a skating rink and supervised playground programs.

During the years of World War I many clubs preserved food to help the war effort. Clover Club of North Easton reported 2,075 jars canned, 500 jars of jelly, and 250 jars of pickles. Socks, sweaters and helmet liners were knitted.

A Clubhouse Corporation was established by the Framingham Women's Club and a lot was purchased. Later it was sold when a residence was purchased for use as a clubhouse. When the Civic League added an auditorium to its building, the women's club sold the house at a profit and this enabled them to pay rent thereafter to the Civic League. A women's ward and a private room were furnished at the Framingham Hospital as was a room for transients at the Salvation Army and three rooms for the Framingham Girl's Club. Three "daughters" of the club were: Framingham Young Women's Club; the Women's Citizens Club (for women of foreign birth attending Americanization classes whose daughters in turn organized the Danforth Junior Club); and the Framingham Garden Club.

An entrance fee of one dollar and dues of two dollars were charged to Hopkinton Women's Club members in 1920. Tea was served by flickering candles placed on windowsills in the high school where they attended meetings, always wearing their hats and white gloves. After groping their way out, the education committee sponsored an article in the town warrant calling for electricity in the high school. Fourth, seventh, and eighth graders received new one-dollar bills for the best essays on thrift.

In addition to making monetary contributions in 1926 to Mississippi Flood Relief, the Stoughton Women's Club donated to the town unemployment emergency relief fund, the Franconia Notch tree project, and the Foxboro State Hospital. The members also became personally involved with crippled children at the Massachusetts Hospital School in Canton. In 1928 the club served and paid for hot lunches in two schools. In the interest of conservation, the membership which had swelled to 267 by 1940, started one thousand seedlings which when matured were given to the town.

A clubhouse called the "Workshop" was built in 1927 on land donated by the father of two members of the Women's Club of Newton Highlands. They established the Junior Woman's Club and guided it until its demise in 1948.

The Ousamequin Club established and maintained a kindergarten for seven years.

In 1917 when a munitions ship exploded in Halifax, Nova Scotia, wrecking a large part of the city and killing more than sixteen-hundred persons, the Woman's Club of East Bridgewater sent money for relief purposes. A plan to sponsor a public health nurse grew to become the Visiting Nurse Association. They, too, started a school for immigrants.

Raising money for Syrian-American Relief and rolling bandages for Red Cross were the Ashland Women's Club efforts during World War I. After the war a bed was endowed at Children's Hospital. Membership grew to eighty with a waiting list of applicants who hoped to join and take part in serving lunches in the schools. The club was instrumental in starting a PTA in town.

The Community Club of Canton was a far-sighted group that raised money to buy sixty-five acres of land for a playground and town forest. A three day International Bazaar was held in the town hall. A film taken of the town and its residents was the only historical movie made of Canton.

The Walpole Woman's Club started a free kindergarten and established and maintained the Walpole Health Center for twenty years. This included a well baby clinic. A room was furnished for Pond Home.

In 1930 ground was broken for a clubhouse for the Milton Woman's Club. A copper box was placed in the cornerstone containing yearbooks, newspapers containing pictures of the building and officers of the club, ashes from the burnt land mortgage, a letter from the president, and a coin for good luck. In 1941 the building mortgage was burnt. An unusual Christmas tree was decorated with names and addresses promising jobs for the unemployed as this was the start of the Depression. This tree was presented to officials at the town hall along with gifts and clothing.

On December 7, 1941, the Japanese attacked Pearl Harbor in Hawaii. War was declared and women's clubs throughout the region rallied by working for the Red Cross rolling bandages, knitting, and selling war bonds. The Hyde Park Thought Club, New Century of Mansfield, the Junior New Century of Needham, Ashland, Newton Highlands, and Clover clubs were among those which were active in war work.

In 1922 the Newton Centre Woman's Club dedicated their clubhouse and membership was limited to seven hundred. Through the years their programs reinforced their purposes of mutual improvement and service to others. For several years they sponsored an Arts Festival and an Antiques Show. Eventually declining membership and increasing maintenance costs forced the club to sell the clubhouse. The money they

The Milton Woman's Clubhouse, built in 1931, has an auditorium which seats 200 and a parlor for 65 in addition to a kitchen and the usual facilities.

received enabled them to carry on their philanthropic work, to give scholarships and to guarantee the club's financial independence for the future.

Eastern Region

After 1920 the West Concord Club continued its educational programs and raised money for donations to furnish a woman's club room at the hospital. Again in the 1940s, war work involved all members.

Still on file is a reminder of the Golden Rule Bond purchased by the Waltham club in 1931. Money so raised was to be used as wages, twenty-five dollars per man per week "to give worthy, self-respecting citizens an opportunity to earn and pay their own bills rather than become objects of charity." The City Park Commission put the men to work to improve and beautify Prospect Hill Park. That same year club members worked in and donated to the Thrift Store operated by the Waltham Unemployment Committee for those caught in the widespread financial distress of the times. The lessons of the lean years have not been forgotten.

Fifty or more years ago, the Garden Club of the Waltham Woman's

Club was organized with a club motto, "He who has a garden has a future." This club within the woman's club is still active.

In 1932 the Waltham Junior Woman's club, sponsored by the senior club, was organized. Two advisors from the senior club continue to attend its meetings.

In 1922 the Old Folks' Home Fund was established by the Watertown Women's Club and the club assumed responsibility for the dining room furnishings and repairs. In 1925 the clubhouse on the Common was purchased and in addition to being used for meetings of the club it was rented out for parties and even as a home.

In 1926 the scholarship fund was established; 1934, the Garden Club was begun; 1940, the Watertown Woman's Club held an Industrial Fair. Over one hundred industries were exhibited and the slogan "Watertown Serves the World" was heard for miles around.

Bedford Woman's Community Club was organized April, 1920 and entered the Massachusetts State Federation in May, 1920 and the General Federation, 1952.

Knowing that with the end of World War I the women of Bedford would have more time to expand their horizons and serve their community, Florence and Marion Webber drew up a formal purpose for the club, which appears on the title page of every annual year book: ". . . to bring about genuine, well-directed cooperation; to promote a higher, broader culture intellectually, morally, and socially; to sponsor educational scholarships and such other philanthropic projects as our community demands."

Among the contributions to the local and wider community were gifts at Christmas to unfortunate neighbors suffering hard times during the Great Depression; gifts to the Hindman Settlement House, the Rutland Hospital, the State Federation's committee for Friendly Cooperation with Servicemen and their families, and locally, to the Boy Scouts. With music and readings, they entertained the ladies at Worthen House, the forerunner of the Llewsac Lodge, now expanded to Carlton Village. Many events occurred in the following years, in 1936 the Student Loan Fund was established and a successful flower show was held at the home of Florence Webber with 120 entries.

The Belmont Woman's Club came into being as a result of a group of women working together as a Red Cross unit during the turbulent and terrifying days of World War I. The unit met in a store at the corner of Cushing Avenue and Trapelo Road. The workers rolled bandages and sewed garments under the guidance of trained Red Cross instructors. In their desire to continue their associations, working together for a com-

98

The clubhouse of the Belmont Woman's Club, acquired in 1927, was built in 1853 by W. Flagg Homer, uncle of the famed Winslow Homer who painted his well-known "The Croquet Scene" on the front lawn. The fifteen-room building has many elegant features including an oval dining room and a formal parlor of great distinction.

mon cause, the women organized in 1920. The club was admitted to the Massachusetts State Federation of Women's Clubs in 1920, incorporated in 1923, and admitted to the General Federation of Women's Clubs in 1925. They bought the Martha Frost House in 1927 for $25,000. Many fund-raising events were held to redecorate and refurbish the house. Substantial sums of money were solicited from members and friends, and the merchants in the town were very generous with money, supplies, and a central heating system which provided more comfort during the long cold winters to augment the crackling logs used in the many fireplaces. The gaslights were replaced with electricity. In 1947, at its annual meeting, president Mrs. Fred S. MacAlster set a match to the second mortgage of $5,000 which had been paid off in three short months.

In June 1919 the Boston City Federation was hostess to the Massachusetts State Federation at its annual meeting, held at Arlington Street Church. Men and women prominent in public life considered it a privilege to speak at the meetings.

During the thirties programs were held that were pertinent and vital to the needs and conditions in the city of Boston.

During the depression days of 1929 many ways were devised to replenish the treasury of the club, one being the "Home Beautiful Exposition" which brought in $1,300 and this was applied to the mortgage, a new roof, and painting of the clubhouse.

In 1931 a junior club was formed to interest the daughters of members in club movement. It became an important branch of the club, working with enthusiasm and contributing generously to the treasury.

As in the days of World War I, during the crisis of World War II the Red Cross unit carried on its loyal efforts on behalf of suffering humanity at home and overseas.

In 1899 the Mattapannock Woman's Club was organized. All members were "professional" or wives or daughters of professional men. During the 1890-1920 period members were very active in nursing World War I Veterans, and continue to be active in veteran affairs to the present. The club replaced the Lincoln Park iron fence that had been scrapped for the World War II scrap drive. The club also offers two scholarships annually.

Directors' Club in District 6 was founded on December 2, 1931. Its object is the same as the Presidents' Club — to continue friendships formed while serving as directors and to maintain an active interest in Federation work. The club is honored to have had three members serve the State Federation as president, Mrs. F. William Ahearn, Mrs. Edwin M. Troland and Mrs. Raymond N. Peterson.

The club resigned from the General Federation in 1949 when dues were raised by the General Federation, as all members were already members of GFWC through the Massachusetts State Federation of Women's Clubs. Club members gave support to the maintenance and decorating of Headquarters, International Scholarship Fund and restoration of the Clough House, Cathedral in the Pines, (N.H.), "Dimes for Liberty," Garden in the Woods, CARE, Home for Little Wanderers, Memorial Forest, War Relief and scores of other projects.

In 1936 the Past Chairmen's Club was organized echoing the same reasons for organizing as other associated clubs. In 1938 it was presented with an engraved gavel made from the old wood of the original Salem. Court House. It was made for the club and presented by Mr. and Mrs. Dennison Brown of Salem, Massachusetts. In 1940 the club donated money towards the needed $2,000 to send a "Rolling Kitchen" to England by Christmas. In 1941 member Mrs. J. Verrity Smith was appointed by Governor Saltonstall to be assistant director of Labor & Industry. Her duties were to oversee labor conditions of women and minors — to see that these laws were carried out, and rights of women respected. At a 1942 meeting, all women in the club who belonged to the Defense Corps wore their uniforms.

100

Mrs. Chesley A. York resigned from the Chairmen's club. Her MSFWC post took up so much of her time that she could not make the Chairmen's Club meetings, but left with this inspiring thought: "Express the belief that whatever we women want, we can have, if we substitute HOPE for FEAR, and FAITH for DESPAIR. If our hopes are not greater than our fears, we can't be inspiring leaders."

Northeastern Region

The women's clubs, as a whole, have supported all Massachusetts State Federation of Women's Clubs' causes, meeting in stormy weather, snow, threat of hurricanes, under other adverse conditions, but they have made it!

New clubs were organized: Gloucester, 1920; Lynnfield Centre Club, 1925; 8th District Presidents' Club, 1932; 9th District Presidents' Club, 1926; Shawsheen Village Woman's Club (Andover), 1921 and the Lynnfield Woman's Club, 1923. In 1923 Medford Woman's Club joined the General Federation of Women's Club, had built their own clubhouse in 1917, and burnt their mortgage in 1927.

All the clubs during this era performed incredible volunteer duty in war relief work. The Stoneham Club was the backbone of the Red Cross, supervised victory gardens, and gave prizes to school children for the best vegetable garden. They worked hundreds of hours with the Red Cross and British War Relief, served in surrounding veterans' hospitals, collected 900 pounds of clothing for Belgian Relief, peach stones for gas masks, and received an award from the State Federation for selling the largest amount of War Bonds — $4,814. The Wakefield Kosmos Club gave old jewelery and copper plates to the "Melting Pot." Wilmington Woman's Club helped the Red Cross pay for a blind French boy's operation and also sold War Bonds. Woburn Woman's Club did their part by being active in veterans' affairs. The Peabody Woman's Club concentrated entirely on war relief. Nahant held service days, urged everyone to buy thrift stamps, sewed clothes for refugees, and on July 4, 1919, participated in a welcome home parade. They received a medal from the town selectmen for their outstanding wartime service and it is still on display. Amesbury-Elizabeth Whittier Club also supported the war relief program. Littleton made scarves and bandages, gave special aid to the community, sponsored first aid classes and gave complimentary memberships to wives of servicemen stationed at Fort Devens. Groton was instrumental in starting a park in the memory of World War I Veterans. The adoption of babies was also the order of the day: Stoneham, a Greek baby, a Chinese child and Near East orphan support, as did Wilmington, Nahant, and Littleton by supporting a French war orphan.

Reading's federated choral group became an independent club and is well known today as the Reading Choral Group. The Lothrop Club of Beverly has three groups of Hand Bell Ringers which were organized in 1937.

The Woburn Woman's Club began sponsoring a public speaking contest which is still conducted annually. Pepperell sponsored the Girl Scouts in 1936, taking three girls to camp for a week each year. The Lynnfield Woman's Club sponsored a pre-school clinic for babies and also sponsored the Girl Scouts.

Donations were made to the Julia Ward Howe Room at GFWC Headquarters for its maintenance by the Littleton Woman's Club and the Kosmos Club of Wakefield. Peabody Woman's Club purchased a new piano for the Peabody Institute library and realized another dream by sponsoring the children's room at the same library.

In 1928 the 9th District Presidents' Club donated money for the preservation of Franconia Notch. A room at the Winchester Hospital was funded by the Fortnightly Club of Winchester, and Amesbury did her part by raising money for two veterans' families and brightening trays for patients at the local hospital, which they continue to do to the present day.

In 1934 the Winchester Fortnightly received national recognition as the first woman's club to form an antique society and sponsor the Winchester Historical Society. The Reading Woman's Club supported the Parker Tavern and continues to do so. The Woburn Woman's Club started and continues making flower arrangements for the Rumford Historical House and the library.

The Depression of the 1930s caused a drop in membership, dues and income, but clubs such as the Kosmos Club of Wakefield managed to balance their budgets and give the usual amount to worthy causes including the Emergency Relief Fund. Some of the meeting places of the club were changed due to the cost of heating them.

In 1923 Mrs. Homer Bott joined the Lothrop Club of Beverly. Today (1987) she is still an active member. Mrs. Bott received an award (2nd prize) in 1940 from the General Federation of Women's Clubs for her article on the ambulance drive in which she had been so active. The article appeared nationwide in the *New York Herald Tribune*.

Clubs such as the Lothrop Club of Beverly and the Lawrence Woman's Club have done much for the blind in their area. Beverly sponsored the first picnic in 1935 for the blind. Lawrence started a reading circle for the blind in 1925 and conducted the group for fifty years. It would probably be still doing this, but all the clubs are now concentrating on the Talking Information Centers.

Littleton pushed for equal salaries for teachers; campaigned for road signs at the town lines; helped Vermont's flood sufferers; and underlined that "Women should have Mind over Matter – one/third work, one/third recreation, one/third rest." The Shawsheen Village Woman's Club assumed the care and decoration of the Christmas tree in Shawsheen Square. It had been given by William Wood, president of the American Woolen Company, who had established the model village, Shawsheen-Andover, for his mill employees. The Manchester Woman's Club was responsible for getting gas piped into their town. Scholarships have been amply donated and supplied by all the clubs in districts 8, 9, and 10.

In 1919 the Nahant Woman's Club was hostess for the autumn conference of presidents of the Massachusetts State Federation of Women's Clubs at the Nahant Town Hall. In 1922 the Nahant Woman's Club and presumably other clubs throughout the state, were told by Mrs. Nina Del Castillo, the State Federation music chairman, that the Massachusetts State Federation of Women's Clubs "urges clubs and dances to eliminate Jazz – as it is undignified, unmusical, and has a bad influence on the young people. Women musicians should be hired, whenever possible, to play for club dances etc. The Federation is waging a war against the words of popular songs (1922) – Al Jolson songs are always objectionable – it is no use to make a law against such songs, as the one in effect is not enforced – it's vile music. . . ." In the same vein, the 9th District Presidents' Club worked to eliminate movie posters which were both objectionable and misleading.

Typical programs for the Reading Woman's Club and other clubs were "Hum and Strum," Wallace Nutting, and a lecture in 1923 on "The Narcotic Evil."

The 8th, 9th, and 10th District Presidents' Clubs were organized to maintain the friendly relations that the presidents had formed during their terms of office. The 9th District Presidents' Club was the first of its kind in Massachusetts. The clubs have continued their goals which the presidents had maintained during their terms, supporting the Massachusetts State

Federation of Women's Clubs and the General Federation of Women's Clubs in all their projects and contributing magnificently of their time, money, and volunteer work that began with the organization of their clubs and is still going strong.

Central Region

The years from 1918-42 brought many changes to women. The years following the war were at first centered on trying to regain normal life patterns and then changes in life style brought new opportunities for women.

Five new clubs were formed in the District and six joined MSFWC. The Whitinsville Woman's Club, organized in 1921, stemmed from a group called the Study Club, formed in 1896. The Study Club continued as the Whitinsville Library Club and still exists today. In 1931 women wanting to maintain friendships gained in club work decided to form a 13th District Presidents' Club to keep alive the sociability. This club would meet only a few times yearly and not be involved in fundraising.

The clubs' Veterans committees continued hospital visits, knitting afghans etc. and filling ditty bags. In 1922 the clubs in District 13 paid for the upkeep of a memorial to World War I veterans.

In the 1920s, perhaps as town coffers were lowered by war expenses, many clubs undertook new projects in the health field. In 1920 Millbury Woman's Club was instrumental in forming the Millbury District Nursing Society. The same year Harvard assumed financial responsibility for school lunches. Berlin organized classes for girls in sewing and cooking and perhaps to raise flagging spirits, started a masked ball held annually until the Depression. In 1924 the Southborough Woman's Club supported a bed in the Children's Hospital in Boston and raised the necessary funds for ten years. The Gardner Woman's Club established a milk fund for schools and awarded its first scholarship in 1923.

Women's needs for intellectual growth were not neglected. In 1921 Templeton's club had programs on "Women in Politics." In 1922 the Whitinsville Woman's Club heard a lecture by Professor R. H. Goddard of Clark College on "High Altitudes as Investigated by the U. S. Weather Bureau." He is now known as the "father of the space program." Historical areas were not neglected either. In 1923 Lancaster bought the Swedenborgian Chapel, built in 1881, for the huge sum of two-hundred dollars, raised and spent $2,700 to restore it and renamed it Wilder Memorial Building in memory of the founder. Their strong interest in history

Purchased in 1923, the Lancaster Woman's Clubhouse was formerly the New Jerusalem Church which was built in 1881 as a reproduction of a Queen Anne chapel.

encouraged them to take on this responsibility. Also the following year, in a lighter vein, they decided women could wear hats at meetings as long as they did not interfere with other women's views.

Leominster donated hundreds of books to their library and furnished a chapel at the Keystone Nursing Home. Holden set up a library branch at Holden District Hospital. Lunenburg donated funds to improve the burial lots of the town poor. In 1925 the Spencer Monday Club set up beacon lights on their main street. Templeton joined the ranks of many clubs and asked at a town meeting for $2,000 to pay for a district nurse, as well as serving cocoa at noon for three cents a cup to school children. The Fitchburg club asked the school committee to set up classes for foreign-born women.

The Woman's Club of West Boylston came on the scene in 1926 after hearing the 11th District Director talk about woman's club work. In their first year they donated to the Red Cross, the Veterans of Rutland Hospital, and sponsored the lighting of a Christmas tree on the Common; they continued this project until 1937, when they turned it over to the town. They also spoke up on local issues such as the threatened ending of trolley service between Worcester and West Boylston and the possible destruction of maple trees in Oakdale. In 1927 the Shrewbury Woman's Club started loan programs to worthy seniors from the local high school and did so until 1938 when the program was changed to a regular scholarship. The Barre Woman's Club began a prize-speaking contest with monetary awards in 1929 which they continued until 1967. The two hundredth anniversary of Southborough in 1927 saw the woman's club enter the prize-winning float in the town parade. Community marts, public dinners, and mammoth food sales in surrounding towns helped Clinton raise $1,100 for the local hospital.

The thirties brought the Depression. Women's concerns for one another and the community filled many gaps.

The Paxton Woman's Club, organized in 1930, helped to build a town tennis court on the school property and later a school playground. Fundraisers included a carnival to finance the improvement of the Illig property, which had been purchased by the town for recreation purposes, and plays, which were given in the town hall around the twenty-second of February to support local scholarships.

In the same year the Woman's Club of West Boylston formed a Junior Woman's Club for ages fifteen to twenty years involving young women in community service, hospital visits, providing food and clothes for the needy as well as literacy and social functions. This club met until 1944 when it was disbanded. The Lunenburg Woman's Club started delivering Christmas baskets to shut-ins, and continued this until 1953 when a community council took charge, though they still help. The Tatnuck Woman's Club donated tons of coal, clothing and food to less fortunate neighbors through the worst of the depression years.

In the programming of this era health issues were prominent. They presented programs on child labor laws, cancer prevention, helping the retarded child and cooking with aluminum, but at a board meeting of the Clio Club of Ashburnham the discussion of a program on birth control was dismissed with the decision there was "no time and no need." Proving that no task was too big for a woman's club to undertake, Northborough started a campaign to eradicate the common housefly!

Women became more active in town issues, perhaps encouraged by radio broadcasts on WBZ in Boston which were sponsored by MSFWC. These centered on current topics of civic and political interest. The Clio Club even helped to counter unemployment by donating money to the local WPA project — the reconstruction of a children's playground and swimming pool. The Berlin Tuesday Club asked on a town warrant for funds for toilets at the town hall. Lunenburg Woman's Club established a dental clinic and dancing lessons for students. The Spencer Monday Club donated reproductions of fine paintings to the library and schools. They also began donating trees to the town as memorials for members and began to produce plays and musicals involving the community. The Fortnightly Club of Leominster created a job bank to provide jobs for women. Southbridge donated to a milk program for 10 local schools, donating almost 6,000 bottles of milk. Whitinsville Woman's Club started a "clothesline sale" with good used clothes which they continued until welfare programs were introduced in the area.

The Townsend Woman's Club was organized in 1933 as a union of the Townsend Monday Club and the West Townsend Study Club. One interesting note on club expenses of that era — members voted the board the magnificent sum of "seven dollars for a float for the town anniversary parade, two dollars and fifty cents of that sum to be paid to a man to provide and drive the oxen." From 1934 to 1939 this club started buying books for the library as memorials to members, financed the renewing of the scenery at Memorial Hall, had a pageant enacting a typical hospital day demonstrated by the staff of Ayer Community Hospital, and sponsored a Girl Scout troop (which grew to include seven troops).

Many clubs such as Barre, Clinton, Holden, and Townsend donated trees, lights and fixtures for Christmas displays to their towns for many years. In 1936 the Fitchburg Woman's Club gave 130 gift packages to underprivileged children.

In 1933 the Southborough Woman's Club sponsored the Southborough Junior Woman's Club and the Garden Group, active until 1971. They also ran a Well-Child Conference with health examinations for pre-school children from 1935-1943. Members collected jams and jellies for Chelsea Veteran's Hospital as part of their service to veterans. Westborough opened a community thrift shop on Main Street which they ran for eight years. The Tatnuck Woman's Club, organized as a group to support the Tatnuck area of Worcester, continued its concern for local schools and neighborhoods encouraging the development of the Parent-Teachers Association. Hudson planted shrubbery around the primary school buildings. The Webster Woman's Club moved watering troughs, formerly used by horse and buggy taffic, to the front of the town hall and planted them with flowers. They also started a junior woman's club to encourage young girls to become active in the community.

The thirties also saw the start of many flower shows run by clubs such as Hudson, Tatnuck and West Boylston. Musical programs were still prominent. Westborough's drama club spun off and became the Westborough Players in 1936. Club members did not forget their early interest and pride in the history of their land. In 1931 the founder of the Templeton Woman's Club donated $1,000 towards the publication of a history of our Federation by the state. Scholarship funds were maintained and libraries throughout the district were enriched by book and financial donations made by clubs such as Ashburnham, Gardner, and Southborough. Berlin Tuesday Club saw their goal reached in 1930 when they met in the new library as guests of the trustees — a library of 5,000 books. In 1932 the West Boylston club planted a Douglas Fir tree on the town Common to commemorate the two hundredth anniversary of the birth of George Washington.

In 1937 the Templeton Woman's Club was the first in the state to start a memorial to deceased members. Also in 1938 they came to the aid of the town with a loan of $5,000 to cover a budgetary deficit and "save the town the embarrassment of having to borrow from outside sources." (It was returned with interest the following year.) Templeton was one of the clubs fortunate to have some very generous benefactors.

Western Region

Amherst Woman's Club

The visiting nurse project for many years was of prime importance to the club women. The project was started in 1913, and finally in 1922 the untiring efforts of the club's visiting nurse committee was rewarded when the town took over the whole project.

In 1924 the club was contributing $150 for a dental clinic for school children, and the same amount was given toward a nutrition clinic for youngsters who were underweight. Hot lunches for those staying over at noon were financed by the club. A little later a milk fund for school children was established, and like several other club projects, was taken over by the town a few years afterward.

In 1922 a new chapter opened for the Amherst Woman's Club with the acquisition of a beautiful club house, "The Hills Memorial Club House." This building with its two and one-half acres of grounds and a number of pieces of Victorian furniture was willed to the club by Mrs. Alice M. Hills, the widow of L. Dwight Hills, the son of the man who built it in 1863. It was at a special meeting held on May 22, 1923, that the club voted to accept the gifts of Mrs. Hill, together with a $10,000 endowment, "the income to be used for the maintenance of the house and as a memorial to the Hills Family."

Through the years this house has been a marvelous asset to the club and the town, but like all good things it presented constant problems, largely financial. The first rummage sale was held in 1930 in Bolter's store and a similar sale has been repeated annually. Benefit movies have been held and many, many food sales. For many years the annual bridge party has been a highlight of the season providing added income to the house fund. The chief house income is derived from three sources: half of the club membership dues, money taken in from the house and barn rentals, and income from the endowment. The Garden Section, founded in 1924 by Mrs. George B. Churchill, has done wonders in keeping up the house grounds with frequent and arduous work bees, plus the sales of home-grown plants and boxed cards.

For a number of years the sale of articles made by the blind was conducted under the auspices of the club. During the 1932-33 depression year an employment agency was maintained by the club with sixty-five women and twelve men listed, more than half being permanently placed in jobs.

During the next few years the club sponsored the Girl Scouts, and the Civic Section was behind a clean-up campaign which was much appreciated by the town. The Garden Section held an annual tulip show in Sweetster Park and later in Jones Library. These shows were the predecessors of the garden sales on the town green which the section now holds.

It was in 1941 that the club first offered a $50 scholarship to a worthy Amherst girl for further study. The sum was later raised to $100, and now stands at $750.

Chicopee Falls Woman's Club

The year 1923 was a prosperous one enabling the club to support a long list of philanthropic efforts which included Russian Famine Relief, Children's Aid Association, and the Chicopee Visiting Nurse Association. It also saw the establishment of the club's Scholarship Fund which has continued to today. Monies were also contributed for the Julia Ward Howe Room in the GFWC Headquarters Building.

Granby Woman's Club

These were the years of participation and contribution. Club members were active in raising funds for repair of the church, contributing to the

Belgian Relief Fund, and restoring the Longfellow Homestead. In 1920 the club assumed responsibility for serving hot lunches to school children, and sponsored home nursing classes.

On October 16, 1921, the club donated and dedicated a boulder and plaque at the site where the first meetinghouse was built at the corner of West and Amherst streets in 1762. This dedication was in celebration of the 100th anniversary of the present church building of The Church of Christ.

In 1932 the club was given responsibility for the "Aldrich Memorial Cane" donated by Elbert Aldrich, to be passed on to the oldest woman in Granby. The cane is now held by Mrs. Katherine Royston.

During 1937 the club initiated the Well Child Clinics. These were held for several years, the first on May 13, 1937. Of a possible sixty-six children in town, fifty-one were examined. During this time the club also sponsored dental clinics held by the Red Cross.

Southampton Women's Club

In 1923 the club began its affiliation with the State Federation and officially became the Southampton Woman's Club. The thirty-nine charter members chose "For the greatest good" as their motto; the mountain laurel — symbolic of dedication and achievement as their club flower; and green — symbolic of growth and renewal as their club color.

Taking their pledge of growth and renewal to heart, the club members won first place in Western Massachusetts in 1933 and 1935 for extensive roadside beautification projects. In 1937 the scrapbook detailing these projects was featured by *Country Gentlewoman Magazine* and was awarded a blue ribbon.

Southwick Women's Club

Joined Massachusetts State Federation in 1924 and General Federation in 1927.

The Southwick Women's Club was founded in May 1924. The object of the club was and still is "To broaden and strengthen the moral, social and intellectual life of its members; and through them to make itself a power in the community, the basis of membership being earnestness of purpose and love of truth."

Since 1924 the Southwick Women's Club members have dedicated themselves to support the community in any way they could, not only the community of Southwick but an outreach beyond the confines of the community in various capacities.

Ramapogue Women's Club
(Young Women's Club of West Springfield)

Joined the Massachusetts State Federation in 1938 and General Federation 1948.

In the fall of 1937 four small groups of West Springfield women, each group independent of the other, but with a common objective, decided to pool their time and talents so as to more perfectly fulfill that common objective. And so on November 8, 1937, the first meeting of the newly formed "Young Women's Club of West Springfield" was held. The initial membership numbered one hundred.

Club objectives were and are to form a center of moral, intellectual, and social culture; to encourage movements for the betterment of society; and to foster education and public spirit in the community.

In 1938 the Choral, Child Study, Literary, and American Home groups were formed as part of the club. In 1940 President's and Guest's Day was inaugurated, and in 1941 the club sent its first two delegates to Swampscott.

Northfield Fortnightly Club

Members continued to be active and participated in many social and political areas. In 1925 the members formed a chapter of the League of Nations; in 1926 they endorsed the Volstead Act; in 1928 they signed the Kellogg's Peace Pact; and in 1929 they signed a resolution against repeal of the state prohibition law.

During these years, the club has made donations of money or material items to various organizations in support of the community.

Northampton Woman's Club, Inc.

Joined the Massachusetts State Federation 1927 and General Federation 1930.

On June 11, 1926, at the Montague Inn, twenty-five women took the necessary steps to form a woman's club. That afternoon, the Northampton Woman's Club was formed. The nucleus of the club was originally a Delphian Chapter and when it was time to renew the charter, many members expressed a preference for a woman's club. They wanted a club which would have a wider scope, broader contacts, and provide a means by which newcomers to Northampton would find a welcome and a variety of contacts.

There are many departments within the club which enable members to belong to groups having special interests. The first department was the Music Department started in December 1926. This was soon followed by a Civic Department, Department of International Relations, and Garden

Department. Growth took place rapidly and in 1930-31 there were six departments having interesting group meetings along with regular club work.

"Hampton Day" was inaugurated for the first time in 1930-31, comprising clubs of Easthampton, Southampton, Northampton, and including guests from Amherst and Williamsburg. The name of this day was changed in 1938 to "Neighbors Day" and more recently to "Presidents Day."

Depression years found all members along with the public welfare committee active in giving clothing to hundreds of families including more than a thousand children; the formation of a Mother Craft group; taking charge of refugees and providing clothing and food during flood periods; furnishing free milk to hundreds of children. In the late thirties a Junior Club for teenage girls was formed and was active for a number of years.

In the late 1930s and early 1940s voluntary donations were collected for the New England Council, later known as the Pioneer Valley Association. About 1940 a member of the club was responsible for initiation of the broadcasting of Christmas carols from the First Church. This has continued through the years under the sponsorship of the Girl Scout Council.

Tuesday Club of Warren

November 2, 1920, was noted as a "Special Day" in the club calendar, for it was the first national election in which Massachusetts women voted. The "Arts" have always been dear to the hearts of the members. In 1939 they put on two very successful plays entitled, *The Lean Years* and *Command Performance.*

For many years the club contributed generously to the Warren Public Library, and many donations and much effort were given to civic projects. Participation in town celebrations has been a part of the club's commitment.

The Hampden County Women's Club
(Western Massachusetts Women's Club)

During this period, the club grew rapidly until membership reached far beyond the confines of Hampden County. In 1937 the name of the club was changed to "Hampden County Women's Club of Western Massachusetts." At this time the popular informative "Round Tables" were instituted.

In 1941 the long name of the club was changed to "Western Massachusetts Women's Club." At this time the membership represented 27 cities and towns with a membership of over 500 women.

The Wilbraham Women's Club

Emphasis during this period was primarily placed on community service. The projects undertaken during the earlier years were continued and still continue to the present. Each meeting begins with a silver tea, giving the membership time to socialize.

The club bylaws were revised in 1936 and the name was changed from "The Ladies Mission Club" to "The Wilbraham Women's Club."

Athol Woman's Club

In June 1918 a pageant was held at Brookside Park in Orange, Massachusetts, the majority of the cast being from Athol. Proceeds of the pageant would be used for war work, and the total amount of $512.10 realized was divided equally between the local Red Cross and the United War Campaign.

In 1921 with a membership of 250 it was voted to move to the Old Town Hall as a permanent home until a new club house could be built. The Girl's Club was also invited to use the town hall as their meeting place. Many organizations offered furnishings for the town hall, equipment for the kitchen, and with contributions from other sources, the hall's pipe organ was repaired. The club's committee worked tirelessly to raise funds for the anticipated new club house, but sadly this effort was never realized.

During the following years the club continued to offer outstanding programs, some presented by the educational, civics, conservation, legislative and arts and crafts committees. Sizable donations were made to the Society of Prevention of Cruelty to Children, the Longfellow Memorial, Near East Relief, the Hospital International Sunshine Society, and for work among disabled children.

In commemoration of the 40th anniversary of the club, a program which was open to the public was held at Memorial Hall April 8, 1940, with an attendance of about six hundred. It was a gala affair highlighted by Mr. Alton Hall Blackington, noted news photographer, lecturer, and author.

Charlemont Woman's Club

On December 7, 1923, the Charlemont Study Club joined the Federation and became known as the "Charlemont Woman's Club." Their first meeting was held on January 4, 1924, when they adopted their constitution.

During the 1920s the club was responsible for placing articles on the town warrant which would be for the betterment of the community and many of these were passed. Among them were monies for the upkeep of town cemeteries, better school conditions, removal of snow from sidewalks; and a public dump. In 1927 the club sponsored a pre-school clinic which was continued under their sponsorship for many years. In 1928 the club was active in the control of signboards along the Mohawk Trail. (Part of this famous trail is the Main Street of Charlemont.)

In the thirties, a formal dance was held each spring which added much to the social life of the community. During 1937 the club was involved with maintaining and bettering the school cafeteria. During these years the club supported the Girl Scouts and Boy Scouts, a girl to attend Girl's State, the Braille Press, Red Cross, and several state scholarships.

Sunderland Woman's Club

The Thirtieth Anniversary Celebration was held on October 24, 1923, with various speakers presenting a program on the club's history. Having "red fronts" of Sunderland Chain Stores changed to a more conservative color received much publicity through the press and letters from around the state. A newspaper from Hyannis that carried the news stated "To let you known how far that little candle shows its beams." The movement for the abolishment of the red front in a residential district had been endorsed by the Community Service Department of the State Federation.

Other projects and contributions at that time included warm lunches provided for the school children of the town; support for Franklin County Hospital; contributions toward the endowment of the Massachusetts Room in the General Federation Headquarters; and contributions for an acre and a quarter of the State Federation Forest in Sudbury.

Orange Woman's Club

Joined the Massachusetts State Federation in 1922 and General Federation 1929.

The Orange Woman's Club was organized on April 17, 1922, with over two hundred members contributing to the support of various community programs. The early years were devoted to various pursuits (one of which was the parties given for children) and various philanthropic endeavors.

Shelburne Falls Woman's Club

Joined the Massachusetts State Federation July 1925 and General Federation 1953.

The Shelburne Falls Woman's Club was founded in May 1925 and since that time has consistently played an active part in community projects, the primary one being the planting and continued maintenance of the famous "Bridge of Flowers."

Holyoke Women's Club, Inc.

Joined the Massachusetts State Federation in 1924 and General Federation in 1945.

114

The Holyoke Women's Club is the outgrowth of the Women's Municipal League which was initiated in 1915, and whose purpose was "To enlist the cooperation of women in civic problems." The organization recreated itself in 1923 as the Holyoke Women's Club and incorporated in 1924 to hold property.

Under the leadership of the club incorporators the membership reached the awesome number of 1,000, which became the limit of the total membership. There was a waiting list for new memberships for a number of years. Mrs. William G. Dwight was the first president, and the succeeding presidents and membership were and are dedicated to creating a center for moral, intellectual, and social betterment of the citizens of Holyoke and vicinity.

Some of the programs the ladies were involved in are still being carried on today, albeit on a smaller scale: veterans work, child welfare, women's emancipation and recognition as a moving force in the community. In these early years, the Conservation Corps was especially helpful, and were responsible for patient transportation to the Skinner Clinic and local hospitals, while funds were raised for eyeglasses, braces, and other needed items. About three hundred children of all ages were treated to an annual Christmas party with a tree and gifts for all. Veterans were supplied needed items, also recreation tables, books, magazines, etc.

Many noted speakers were presented to expand the horizons of the membership. To quote the words of Mrs. Frank Holyoke, the second club president, 1926-28: "She also reached out for beauty and refinement through art, literature, music and drama." The past members certainly did that, from simple afternoon teas to elaborate garden parties and extravaganzas; revues held at Mountain Park; and a full fledged production of *The Princess* with a cast of 150 club members. Minstrel shows and soirées were an annual occurrence. Many private homes, estates, and gardens were the setting for club entertainment, such as the Skinner Northampton Street Estate and Wisteriahurst.

In 1934 at the May meeting of the Holyoke Women's Club, the first five presidents were asked to give advice to the incoming president. One thing they all agreed on, the fact that with each succeeding administration it was more difficult to obtain expense money, a situation familiar to many Federation members.

The Fourteenth District Presidents' Club

Joined the Massachusetts State Federation in February 1936 and General Federation in 1938.

The 14th District Presidents' Club was organized on November 19, 1935, as an associate club for past and current club presidents within the district. The enthusiasm with which the new club was received soon forced an expansion of its programs, to permit greater service to the active presidents and to extend the privileges of the past presidents.

Because the 14th District Presidents' Club is a working club as well as a social one, programs for the morning sessions covered the following subjects: programs, publicity, parliamentary procedures, money-making projects, junior clubs, scholarships, the American home, and education and better citizenship. The afternoon social sessions have been more diversified, with excellent speakers covering a wide field of subjects.

The Fifteenth District Presidents' Club

Joined the Massachusetts State Federation in 1935 and General Federation 1935.

The Fifteenth District Presidents' Club was organized during 1935. The District consists of eleven clubs which take turns in planning a place for a luncheon, club meeting, and program. Consequently the Presidents' Club luncheons have been varied and the programs most interesting and entertaining.

One of the clubs primary projects has been the collection at each meeting of monies for a scholarship fund to be given to a deserving high school student within the district.

ADJUSTMENT

1942-1960

AS the Golden Anniversary of the Massachusetts State Federation of Women's Clubs approached it became apparent that the lives of women, the direction of humanism, the progress in education, the cultural evolution, government, the entire world had been affected by this organization. Decades of development have been filled with the efforts of Federation members and their leaders to make this world a better place for all. There is still much to be accomplished and women of vision will set more goals, develop more projects, and broaden our horizons.

Mrs. Edith French Anderson, president from 1942 to 1944, led the membership in work on war relief. Clothing, money, and medical supplies were sent to our allies. Many children were "adopted," including 103 from Great Britain, 57 Chinese children, and three blind Chinese babies.

The Federation worked to recruit women for all phases of war work. Their record achievements in the sale of War Bonds and Stamps resulted in naming twenty-six ambulance planes, *Massachusetts State Federation of Women's Clubs*. When reports were finally tabulated the Federation stood third in the list of states, having sold eight million dollars worth of bonds and stamps.

During the biennium other areas of emphasis were consumer concerns and occupational therapy for patients in veterans hospitals. Seed money was set aside as a nucleus for the Memorial Scholarship which would be administered by state past presidents.

When our country faced a nationwide depression and readjustment following World War II, the presidency was assumed by Mrs. Edwin Troland (1944-1946). It was a challenge but once again the Federation demonstrated its strength and resilience. War restrictions resulted in many

The first meeting house at Memorial Forest, shown in the 1980s, was originally a cow shed.

changes. Neither the mid-winter meeting nor the annual meeting were held in 1945. Committee meetings moved from the over-populated, under-staffed YWCA to Federation Headquarters on Newbury Street.

The unity and organization of the Federation resulted in tremendous support of all war services. The final total of War Bonds bought or sold during 1945-1946 was $11 million dollars.

The fledgling Memorial Scholarship became the Memorial Education Fund administered by state past presidents. It would provide fellowships for deserving young women and also memorialize the past state presidents. During this biennium the Memorial Forest in Sudbury was put on the Federation agenda. It would serve as a living memorial to the men and women of World War II who gave their lives for their country.

"The Responsibility of the American Home" was the over-all theme of the administration of Mrs. Harvey E. Greenwood (1946-1948). She said, "Happy homes mean a happy nation and happiness means peace. The result will be a nation of which we shall always be proud and to which the peoples of our lands will look with confidence for guidance."

118

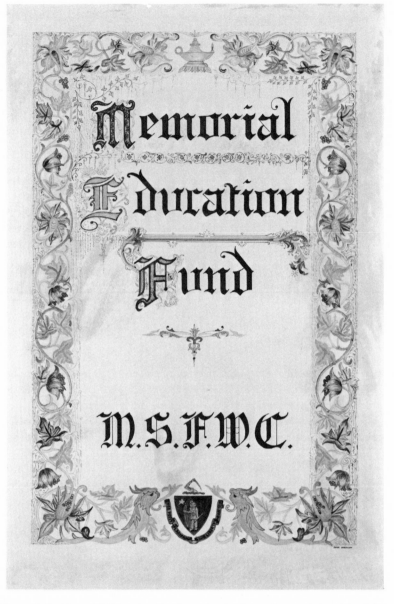

Cover of the Memorial Education Fund scrapbook of contributors designed by John Morrison, each page of which is similarly embellished. Mrs. Herbert F. French proposed establishment of the fund during Mrs. Edwin Troland's administration and it was successfully launched during the administration of Mrs. Henry E. Greenwood.

Federation efforts were also directed toward economic rehabilitation and support of various philanthropic projects throughout the country. Significant progress was made on the Memorial Education Fund and the Memorial Forest. The Cooperative for American Remittances to Europe (CARE) became a leading philanthropy for the Federation.

Mrs. A. Chesley York, president (1948-1950), challenged the membership of the Federation as she took office. She counseled, "May we each be given the vision to seek our path wisely and keep our feet firmly upon it, remembering that good citizenship is not a goal but a journey. Let us travel it together." Travel it they did as member clubs accepted the challenge and educated their members and communities on the responsibilities of citizenship.

The Memorial Forest in Sudbury was dedicated on April 29, 1950. Mrs. York said at the dedication, "This will be a living memorial which shall keep forever green not only the loving memory of those who served in the war, but also the responsibility which is ours to maintain that for which they fought and died. These broad acres will also permit a closer study of soil conservation and preservation so vitally important to our country."

The Evening Division was created as a state committee during the biennium to meet the needs of young women who had reached the state age limit for junior membership but could not attend daytime meetings due to personal and professional responsibilities.

There was strong interest in legislation during the presidency of Mrs. Lewis C. Stevens (1950-1952). An awareness of good citizenship responsibilities was shown as resolutions were passed pertaining to price control, to prevent the sale of alcoholic beverages to minors, to reduce government spending, and to request top priority for school building materials and equipment after the major military needs of the nation had been met.

Clubwomen expressed concern over the shocking increase in the use of narcotics by young people. A long range project was initiated with the consent of the incoming administration, "Crusade for Freedom," with its aim to combat crime, juvenile delinquency, the sale of narcotics, and the spread of communism.

"The Preservation of Our Heritage in a Free World," was the theme of the administration of Mrs. Ralph G. Swain (1952-1954). The objectives were to secure, through community cooperation and better schools, character building and creational opportunities to combat the growing prevalence of crime and delinquency. The goal was strengthening the ideals and freedoms on which the American way of life was founded.

Ninety-five percent of the electorate in Massachusetts went to the polls as a result of the Federation campaign to "Get Out the Vote." ESO (Epsilon Sigma Alpha), a General Federation organization to promote reading of fine books, was established. After twenty-one years, under the supervision of the Federation, the Junior Division achieved status as an affiliate organization and was accepted by the Federation as the Junior Membership, with its own bylaws and officers.

Mrs. Swain sought tax exemption for the Federation and for the Memorial Forest. Tax exemption on the land and on gifts to the forest was granted by the Tax Exemption Office in Washington, D. C. To meet federal standards the Federation charter was changed to establish the Federation as an educational organization instead of an entertainment organization. The Federation was recognized as a civic group engaged in legislative activities beneficial to the general welfare, and this assured tax exemption of gifts made to and by the Federation.

Mrs. David M. Small, president (1954-1956), placed special emphasis on the role of the home in building character and attitudes, promotion of better human relations, and a more responsible attitude toward Civil Defense. Her theme was "Enlightened and Responsible Citizenship." Under her leadership the Federation reached out to many organizations and participated in state and national programs relating to education, communication, health, and legislation. There was increased interest and participation in Veterans' Service as clubwomen donated time and money to this project.

"Community Improvement," was the theme set by Mrs. Kirke L. Alexander (1956-1958). She combined the General Federation of Women's Clubs theme, "Knowledge is Power," saying, "Without knowledge – precise, accurate, realistic knowledge – our dedication to Community Improvement and our every goal would end in frustration."

During her administration the General Federation and Sears Roebuck Foundation launched a two-year competitive contest to build the tradition of community service among clubs to new heights. At the General Federation annual meeting the Veterans' Service of the Massachusetts Federation was cited as the top state organization in the country in service and money given during the previous two years.

"Better Citizens, Better Communities, a Better Country and a Better World," was the theme of the administration of Mrs. Earl R. Weidner, president from 1958 to 1960. She said in her first message to the membership, "Today we are facing many tests in an uncertain world – new calls for service, new duties to perform. But we should in no way minimize the importance of our club life. For by maintaining an orderly, cheerful and cultural existence and by substituting friendship and unselfish service for greed and unrest we may hope to preserve the beauties and values of the life for which the world is struggling." Friendship and culture were reinforced when the Federation established a "Federation Night" at Boston POPS with the first POPS Night being held in May 1959.

121

Resolutions adopted at Federation meetings reflected the attitudes and views of the membership. Resolutions included one to give wholehearted support to the policies and objectives of the President's Council on Youth Fitness; another to protest the proposed discontinuance of women commentators presenting radio homemakers programs; and others to favor bills banning jay walking and promoting highway safety, and to support greater use of educational television programming.

Southeastern Region

With more women finding it necessary to work, it became a sign of the times therefore that many of the clubs now being formed were Evening Division/P. M. clubs. In 1944 the first P. M. club in the country was founded, the P. M. Club of Brockton; in 1947 the Marshfield Woman's Club, Evening Division; in 1949 the Ivy Circle of New Bedford and the Old Colony P. M. Club of South Weymouth; in 1950 the Weymouth P. M. Club; in 1951 the Rockland P. M. Club; and in 1954 the P. M. Club of Hingham which was formerly a junior club. Younger women were taking a livelier interest in their communities as witness the influx of Junior Women's Clubs: in 1948 the Hyannis Junior Woman's Club; in 1950 the Junior Woman's Club of Bourne, the Junior Woman's Club of Taunton, the Wareham Junior Woman's Club, and the Junior Cabot Club of Middleboro; and in 1952 the Harwich Junior Woman's Club was formed. Two general clubs became part of the MSFWC family: the Braintree Women's Club in 1955, and the Dennis Women's Club in 1956.

The clubs such as Brewster, Falmouth, Nautilus, Abington, and the Philergians, continued to work for World War II relief, knitting and rolling bandages, conducting War Bond Drives and so on. In 1944 the Rochester club was responsible for having the town erect an honor roll in the center, for the service people of World War II. In 1945 The Raymond C. Hartley Scholarship was established by Rochester clubmembers in memory of the Rochester boy who was killed in World War II. The Falmouth club purchased War Bonds and adopted a French child. The Nautilus club donated to the European relief organizations. During the war years, the Sandwich club eliminated their annual meeting, gathered games for soldiers' canteens, established a canteen at the Episcopal Church, and sent money to the "Rolling Kitchens" in England. In lieu of a Christmas exchange, they sent money for POW gifts. Through "Save the Children" they adopted a boy from Holland and one from Finland. They collected rubber and metal for salvage, bought War Bonds, and served only crackers and tea at meetings — no sandwiches or sweets. During 1942 the Abington club continued their war relief program; the Braintree Point Woman's Club purchased a movie projector and films and presented them to the veterans of Murphy General Hospital in Waltham. The rehabilitation unit of the Brockton Veterans Hospital was also supported. The Philergians in 1942 supported the Civil Defense Committee and the War Relief Committee, and adopted English and Chinese children. They sent food and clothing to European children. The Ladies' Library Association supplied gifts to ex-servicemen and women at the Norfolk County Tuberculosis Hospital.

The Sandwich club provided the impetus to erect a drinking fountain beside the town hall and landscape the area around it. They also petitioned the post office to establish rural free delivery of mail. The Dennis club contributed to many worthy community projects; and the P. M. Club of Hingham was the driving force in establishing a leash law in their town. The Wareham Monday Club won a Better Community Award in 1949 with a first prize of one hundred dollars which was used to purchase a movie projector and screen for the Youth Center. They opened the thrift shop called "The Screen House", proceeds from which paid for a play seen by one thousand children, for school lunchrooms, bus funds, and a scoreboard for the schools' athletic events. The thrift shop closed in 1949. The Orleans club worked with American Legion Post personnel and other organizations in planning community activities.

A resolution was sent to Orleans, Eastham, and Wellfleet town officials expressing the concern of the Orleans clubwomen over the increasing destruction of the old shade trees, both on private property and along the public highways. In 1960 the Orleans Conservation Department planted flower boxes, shrubs, and climbing roses around the Orleans Information Booth. The club was instrumental in having the parcel of land between the Methodist Church and the Snow Library designated as the

Village Green. Throughout the years, the Gardens and Conservation Department of the Orleans club has maintained gardens throughout the town and contributed to the landscaping at the Snow Library and planted memorial trees at the police station and Village Green. In 1960 Orleans had a spruce tree planted on Village Green in memory of a departed member. The clubmembers notified legislators that the Orleans Woman's Club was in favor of the establishment of a college on Cape Cod. "Trees for Worcester" was a popular project and many clubs took part in this venture. Among them were the Braintree Point Woman's Club, the Weymouth P. M. Club, and the Sandwich Woman's Club which received a state award for their donation.

The Brockton Woman's Club was again honored to have one of their members, Mrs. Ralph (Ada W.) Swain serve as MSFWC president from 1952-1954. During Mrs. Swain's administration the Federation received its charter from Epsilon Sigma Omicron (ESO), a reading sorority sponsored by the General Federation of Women's Clubs. Perhaps this explains the outstanding record of ESO participation achieved by the Brockton clubwomen.

Scholarships in the field of medicine, nursing, or secondary schooling were provided by the following clubs: Braintree Woman's Club, Ladies' Library Association of Randolph, the Nautilus Club, Braintree Point Woman's Club, P. M. Club of Brockton, P. M. Club of Hingham, Marshfield Woman's Club, Rockland P. M. Club, Weymouth P. M. Club, Braintree Junior Philergians, the Mattapoisett, Somerset, and Orleans clubs. The Braintree Woman's Club held field trips on Saturday mornings for 7th and 8th graders to learn about local government. The P. M. Club of Brockton established a bicycle safety program now adopted by the public school system as part of the 4th grade curriculum. In 1960 the Marshfield club petitioned for a public kindergarten and also contributed to educational funds for the school visual aids as well as band instruments, and it provided scholarship aid to a student attending the Vermont Music Camp.

Veterans hospitals and organizations were supported by the Nautilus, Braintree, Mattapoisett, and most of the region's clubs. Braintree Point Woman's Club did their share in supporting the South Shore Hospital Building Fund, as well as the veterans hospitals. The Braintree Women's Club sponsored the first Braintree resident to the Crotched Mountain Foundation, provided six braille watches, a typewriter, and field trips for handicapped children. They held an annual Christmas party for emotionally disturbed and handicapped children and parties for nursing home residents, delivered food baskets for needy families, and provided entertainment for residents at Medfield State Hospital. The Quincy club provided entertainment, outings, and transportation for blind persons; provided gifts and parties for the physically handicapped; as did the P. M. Club of Brockton which spread their service far and wide. The Weymouth P. M. Club gave flood relief to Holland, volunteered hours at South Shore Hospital, donated wheel chairs to the Welfare Department, donated funds to the Well-Baby Clinic and the VNA. The Braintree Junior Philergians supported the New England Home For Little Wanderers, *S. S. Hope,* the USO, and participated in Civil Air Patrol. The Rochester Woman's Club sponsored the Plymouth County Mobile Chest X-Ray Unit, and the Orleans club purchased a hospital bed for the towns of Orleans, Chatham, and Wellfleet, to be kept at the Orleans Fire House. Over the years many contributions have been made to the Chelsea Hospital including wheel chairs. The Orleans clubwomen also did sewing for the Cape Cod Hospital. The Somerset club donated hours of service to the Rose Hawthorne Lothrop Home for cancer patients.

In 1945 the Brewster Woman's Club clubhouse was sold because it had become a financial burden. From 1946 to 1948 the Sandwich club donated money to improve the kitchen and powder room of the Masonic Hall where they met. The Edgartown Woman's Club participated in "Sight Conservation." The Hyannis Junior Woman's Club gave house tours as a fund raiser for nine years with the proceeds going for scholarships, hospice, and other community services. The Falmouth club held a reception for the Mayor of Falmouth, England, and in 1954, they changed their name from the Outlook Club to the Falmouth Woman's Club. In 1954 the Rockland Club introduced the first of many musicals they put on as a fundraising project that united the club and community talent. The Abington club's Little Theater Group was formed in 1956-58 as a club project. In 1958 it was decided by the Old Colony Union Women's Club of Bourne, to honor the outstanding student in the home economics class at the high school by inscribing her name on the silver vase of the Old Colony Union, the vase having been stored in a vault since the Union's classes had been discontinued. The vase was then kept on display at the high school. The Philergians in 1959 donated a stained glass window to the Thayer Academy. The Whitman Club formed the Whitman Garden Club through the woman's club's conservation and gardens committee; sponsored the town's first Girl Scout troop and funded a Memorial Annex at the Whitman American Legion Post. They also gave a set of *Encyclopedia Brittanica* to the high school. The P. M. Club of Brockton

The Abington Woman's Club Choral Group at the Cathedral in the Pines in 1957.

established a sheltered workshop for retarded citizens — BAARC (Brockton Area Association for Retarded Citizens) which is now under the auspices of MAARC (Massachusetts Area Association for Retarded Citizens); and provided a DIAL-A-STORY system to the Public Library. The Weymouth P. M. Club worked to abolish objectionable literature in their community.

The Tuesday Club of Assonet contributed food and clothing to the Foreign Drive. The Cabot Club of Middleboro ran Foreign Students Weekends for a number of years. Annually the Rochester club sponsors an open meeting to discuss the town meeting warrant. The school budget is discussed and candidates for the school comittee and all town officials are present for a Candidates' Night. Members of the Friendly Circle of the Blind were entertained annually by the Taunton Woman's Club. In the spring of 1957 the Wareham Monday Club's clubhouse was destroyed by a heater explosion. Due to their remarkable diligence and hard work, it was rebuilt and dedicated in the fall of the same year!

The Ivy Circle of New Bedford staged fashion shows to benefit Cerebral Palsy; furnished a room at the Soloman E. Mar Hospital for cerebral palsied children; held Halloween parties for children; raised $2,100 in auctions for retarded children; and distributed SOS booklets (Save Our Ship) for the Battleship *Big Mame*. In 1942 the Sippican club "returned home" to its own clubhouse. Two rooms were rented, a portion of the building was used as a store. The club offered the use of several rooms to the Marion branch of the Red Cross for their headquarters. In 1950 "Valentine Varieties" were presented to benefit the March of Dimes; and in 1956 dues were increased from $3.50 to $5.00 and the scholarship fund was doubled from $50.00 to $100.00!

126

Southern Region

During the war years Ashland Women's Club sent a "Rolling Kitchen" to England and arranged parties at Harvey Cushing Hospital which was fast filling with wounded veterans.

Ousamequin Club of Bridgewater established a canteen in the center of the town through which soldiers passed on their way to Camp Edwards on Cape Cod. A building was donated when the canteen flourished and became nationally known. Club members staffed the canteen and provided food as did many in town who were sympathetic to the cause having one or more of their own in service.

Socials for military personnel and USO activities were sponsored by Junior New Century Club of Needham. The Junior Fortnightly Club of Sharon bussed GI's to a school to dance, eat and talk with club members.

Framingham Woman's Club furnished two officers' day rooms at Harvey Cushing Hospital and invited officers' wives to club meetings. They furnished blood donors, served on motor corps and canteen groups, worked as nurses aids, and sold war bonds.

Every club was involved in some aspect of the war effort and due to the stressful nature of the times, many clubwomen found such work a welcome relief from worrying about the constant war news.

In 1940 when President Truman dispatched troops to Korea, the Ousamequin Club sent care packages and the Milton Woman's Club gave $1,000 for fitted bags, a bookmobile, and magazine subscriptions.

Activities undertaken during the fifties by the Junior Fortnightly Club of Sharon included volunteer work at Norwood Hospital with each of its one hundred members required to serve and help by delivering mail and flowers, or doing errands. They also served at the New England Home for Little Wanderers and worked for Project Hope.

A donation to a war memorial building fund was given by the Hopkinton Woman's Club. Some activities of the Evening Division Club of Natick were giving toys for children in Leonard Morse Hospital and conducting baby sitting courses and eye screening for amblyopia. They, like the Ousamequin Club members, gave a piano to the library.

The war years had an effect on clubs because of the added responsibilities women had to assume with so many men gone. This was a time when many married women entered the workplace, a practice which has grown over the years and caused a serious decrease in volunteerism.

Eastern Region

World War I, the depression of the 1930s, and then World War II were serious years in the life of the Waltham club as in the life of the community. Clubwomen joined in every type of war work and contributed time, money, food, and clothing according to the need. The club, as did many of the federated clubs, "adopted" three war orphans, one Chinese, one English, and one French.

In 1941 World War II was declared and responsibility fell upon the Watertown Woman's Club again, with members responding to help the war effort. The sum of $19,000 was credited to the club toward the purchase of an $86,000 bomber ambulance which went into service with the words "Massachusetts State Federation of Women's Clubs" across its nose. The club bought bonds again and completely furnished a sunroom at Camp Devens at a cost of $263 and also sent many afghans. The club supplied many boxes of food and clothing to Russia, which was then our ally. The club also laid a new floor in the Old Folks' Home and bought sterling silver flat pieces for the dining room. The club, as did others in the Federation, "adopted" a French child.

In 1946 the club house was sold because it was inadequate for regular club meetings; in 1951 a Civil Defense Committee was established and many members helped man the Air Raid station and canteens; the club contributed to the Holland Relief Fund and sent materials for the Youth Project in Germany.

In 1959 Mrs. Elinar T. Larson, a member of the Arlington club, was chosen Massachusetts Mother of the Year. In that year the club started honoring the "boy and girl of the month." In order to take an active part in the town's projects, members served on the committee for recycling, the Japanese Youth visit, and the Bicentennial.

In the 1940s the Bedford Women's Community Club activities included an antique show sponsored by the Antique Study Group, lectures on foreign affairs, Home Talent Day, a Country Fair and Auction. In the 1950s one of the members participated in a Seventh District sewing contest. Profits from bazaars, dinner dances, and bridge parties were donated to Emerson Hospital for a crib fracture frame and a wheelchair housed at the police station for the use of a Bedford resident in need.

During World War II days, the Boston City Federation cooperated with every patriotic purpose, working, and praying with courage and faith, that the war clouds would lift and peace would come to all.

During Mrs. Scanlon's administration, the Past Presidents' Scholarship Fund was established. A total of $1,000 was contributed during its first year, and since that time, the fund has grown to well over $5,000, making it possible to give scholarship awards to two outstanding high school students annually.

The Boston City Federation is unique in that it is made up of general club delegates, associate club delegates, and associate members, all supportive of City, State, and General Federation.

During World Wars I and II, in addition to donating to local groups, the Norumbega club members worked by knitting helmets, gloves, mittens, socks, and sweaters for the servicemen. At Christmas time, hospitalized veterans were remembered. In the aftermath of World War II, when the homes of the allies in France and the Netherlands were destroyed, French shawls were knitted for the aged, and crib afghans for the children.

In December 1940 Radio Station WNAC held a quiz and women's clubs were invited to send in four members. The day Norumbega club women went on the air, they scored 100 percent and each member received three dollars for the club treasury.

The Sixth District Presidents' Club was founded on March 22, 1946. Its theme throughout the years is "working together to find the key to achievement and harmony." The club always met at MSFWC Headquarters on Newbury Street until Headquarters moved, and since then the club has met at All Saints' Parish House in Brookline. The club was formed to continue the friendships begun when each member served as a club president. Donations are made annually to a variety of state scholarships, president's projects, CARE, etc.

Northeastern Region

During the war years, the Malden Old and New organized a Red Cross Motor Corps with fifteen members to aid the defense. The Stoneham Woman's Club continued its support of war relief and the Red Cross. In 1943 the Lothrop Club of Beverly adopted a Chinese child through the War Service Committee and an honor roll was compiled by Mrs. J. Vernon Muir in 1944 to honor Beverly young men and women who served in

World War II. In 1942 the women of Pepperell Woman's Club took charge of manning the tower in the town hall all night to watch for planes. The final climb was up a steep ladder, fortunately there were a few brave enough to scale it. During World War II, Mrs. George Scoville, chairman of the ambulance drive, raised $1,250 and through the Red Cross an ambulance was purchased and sent to Beverly, England. Mrs. Cole, chairman of War Bonds and Stamps, worked tirelessly and sold $28,846 worth of bonds and stamps. In 1942 Nahant collected money for Russian Relief. During 1943-1944 the club donated Christmas trees, decorations, and candy to soldiers stationed at Nahant and the Coast Guard Station. Curtains were made for Fort Richman, and knitted helmets were sent to England. Club teas were discontinued, members felt the money was better spent on war supplies. In 1949 a Christmas box was sent to an aged woman in England while books were donated to school children in Norway.

In 1942 Littleton sent money to help support the fatherless children in France and provided support to children's hospitals. In 1950 Nahant Woman's Club sent sheets and flannel blankets to Germany, CARE packages to Korea, and money to the Holland Relief Fund. In 1942 the 9th District Presidents' Club sent contributions to Iceland to purchase musical instruments (the writer wonders why).

Mrs. Chesley A. York of the Medford Women's Club was elected president of the Massachusetts State Federation of Women's Clubs from 1948-1950 and Mrs. Natalie B. Weidner, of the Malden Old and New, served as state president from 1958-1960.

The Stoneham Woman's Club organized a fresh air picnic for mothers and children of underprivileged families in Boston. Starting in 1950 Wilmington Woman's Club established a summer play program and home and nursing courses at the high school. The members also landscaped the Regional Health Center and bought the children's chairs for the library.

In 1959 the Salem Woman's Club disbanded and the Lothrop Club of Beverly took over the sponsorship for their Blind Circle. The Evening Division of the Lynn Woman's Club was organized in 1950. It was formerly a part of the Lynn Woman's Club which was disbanded in 1983. They made tray decorations for the hospital and children, and still do. The proceeds from one of their auctions bought uniforms for three "Gray Ladies," volunteer workers for the Red Cross. In 1958 members gave a party for twenty-five seven to eight year old under-privileged children. The following year they began the current programs to aid the retarded.

Parker Tavern is supported by the Reading Woman's Club American Heritage committee as a club project. Built in 1694, it is listed in the National Register. (Sketch courtesy of the *Daily Chronicle*.)

In 1945 Kosmos Club of Wakefield sponsored a concert to sell bonds in the Victory Loan Drive and in 1948 raised money for their room at the Hartshorn House in Wakefield.

The Reading Woman's Club Juniors were organized in 1950. Initially it was a small group of twenty-five to thirty members who met in their homes. They managed to put in nearly a thousand volunteer hours of community service each year and made generous financial contributions. In October 1957 the Reading Woman's Club had a clubroom of their own at the Community Center and Mrs. Robert Barclay received second prize for her story on the Parker Tavern restoration. In 1957 the Medford Women's Club organized their annual lawn party, the monies raised from this event supported the Scholastic Fund. In 1958 a bowling group was organized and continues to the present. A Medford Women's Club Juniors Club was started at this time, unfortunately it was disbanded two years later due to lack of interest.

When the John Greenleaf Whittier Bridge was dedicated in 1954, the Amesbury-Elizabeth Whittier Club took an active part in its dedication, wearing appropriate colonial costumes. During this period the Peabody Woman's Club continued their aid to historical societies and provided camperships and scholarships. The Manchester Woman's Club began the Christmas Community Gathering, supplying hot chocolate to singers and providing the Christmas lighting for the town. They also made it a practice of ringing the bells on July 4th. The Shawsheen-Village Woman's Club supplied ditty bags to veterans and maintained the level of their scholarships.

Throughout the years of 1941-1960, all the clubs of districts 8, 9, and 10 continued their support of scholarships for high school seniors as well as the Massachusetts State Federation of Women's Clubs scholarships, and worked diligently for veterans relief.

Central Region

Between 1942 and 1962 five new clubs were founded. The 1940s were the war years and clubs such as Barre, Clinton, Holden, Southborough, Paxton, and Webster were again very active in selling bonds, manning defense centers and warning systems, working at canteens, driving mobile blackout units, serving as air raid wardens, working on Red Cross relief funds, and ration committees. The 11th District clubs voted to furnish a room for convalescents at Fort Devens Hospital. Cushing, Burbank, Bedford, and Rutland veterans' hospitals saw hours of volunteer work and countless donations by the 11th and 13th districts.

Proud to say, there was not a club that did not participate in some way. In 1942 the Leicester Woman's Club, in addition to salvaging fats, tires, metals, and silk stockings, organized a community project called "the Buddies Club," involving representatives from local groups and all churches. Various fundraisers conducted by this group enabled it to send 142 boxes to servicemen at Christmas. Southbridge adopted an English war orphan and even sold 200 chairs (bought in 1914) to purchase War Bonds. Every club participated in selling War Bonds but three clubs were outstanding. The Woman's Club of West Boylston sold $34,665 worth of bonds. Both the Fitchburg Woman's Club with sales of $35,656.25 and the Shrewsbury Woman's Club with sales of $51,949.50 were recognized by government agencies.

Anxiety about war in 1943 led to the organizing of a group of young women in Sterling who wanted to serve, too. Serve they did—immediately becoming involved with veterans at local hospitals.

Many clubs such as the Barre Woman's Club, the Templeton Woman's

Club, Clio Club of Ashburnham, the Fitchburg Woman's Club, the Hudson Woman's Club, and the Shrewsbury Woman's Club adopted war orphans. The Clio Club furnished three "Rolling Kitchens" for England and started a newsletter for the 275 Ashburnham servicemen and women every month. This newsletter was sent again during the Korean and Vietnam wars. Gardner Woman's Club drove a mobile blackout unit and manned the defense center warning unit. Lancaster also worked at the airplane spotting center observation post. The Hudson Woman's Club also furnished "Rolling Kitchens" for England and their war relief committee sponsored a group of young women known as the MacArthur Club to do volunteer work at Camp Devens as well as attend dances there which were chaperoned by club members. Local servicewomen were made honorary members of the Hudson club. The Woman's Club of West Boylston, along with many in the district, contributed to a sun room at Fort Devens Hospital. Guest speakers were given defense stamp corsages. Many clubs such as Lancaster stopped serving tea at meetings. Each month Shrewsbury sent knit articles to the War Relief Headquarters in Boston, Christmas gifts to Camp Devens, and invited soldiers to members' homes for Christmas. In 1944 the Fortnightly Club of Leominster held an all day fair for war relief and charities and for four years after gave gifts to veterans at Fort Devens. The Townsend Woman's Club worked as USO hostesses in Ayer and donated surgical dressings.

Community efforts were also continued during these years. In 1945 Fitchburg donated $1,150 as a memorial gift to the YMCA for a ladies' lounge. Lunenburg started a project of buying a portable resuscitator for the town. Hudson had charge of the anti-tuberculosis seals campaign and sponsored chest x-ray clinics for high school students until 1947, when it was taken over by the South Middlesex Health Association. The Gardner Woman's Club helped establish the District Nursing Association.

The Sterling Woman's Club gave the school a sterilizer for its dental office, donated books to the library, and ran puppet shows, record hops, craft classes, and Halloween parties for town youngsters for many years.

In 1942 the Northborough Woman's Club began donating books to the library as memorials, doing so until 1960. The Townsend Woman's Club worked with the town to provide a permanent skating rink in 1947. The following year the Paxton Woman's Club, concerned about violence in films, reviewed and selected movies for children to be shown in the town hall. The Tatnuck Woman's Club fully furnished the dining room of the Sterling Health Camp (now called Camp Putnam), a summer camp for

132

under-privileged children. This was a ten year project and Camp Putnam is still the main concern of this club.

In 1944 Millbury Woman's Club took a big step and purchased a clubhouse, using it until 1980 when maintenance became too burdensome. In 1945-46 Westborough started kindergarten classes that ran until 1976 when the school system took over. The Eleventh District formed a Presidents' Club in 1946 to continue the friendship found in club work.

The 1950s brought numerous changes to women's clubs. With many women joining the work force, changes were made to accommodate them in meeting days and times. With the return of the servicemen hospital visits were increased. Ditty bags were filled and delivered, Christmas parties given, and carols sung by the many choral groups. Countless knitted goods were worked on through the years. Armed forces sent overseas for the Korean police action made for renewed effort. Clubs continued to run mobile blood units and visit nursing homes. The Uxbridge Woman's Club, founded in 1950, immediately formed a veterans' committee and started visiting hospitals.

At the same time, clubs kept up their efforts at home. They became more vocal on legislative issues and town concerns. In 1950 the Hudson Woman's Club protested to selectmen about prohibiting billboards being put up in the town square and the dumping of rubbish in the Assabet River. In 1953 they held a state conference for the American Home Committee of the State Federation. The Chaffin Woman's Club, founded in 1951 with 137 members, focused on scholarships. The Harvard Woman's Club supported a dental clinic for school children. Gardner Woman's Club donated funds to build a new wing on the hospital in 1953. They also decided against a clubhouse and instead transferred the building fund to the scholarship fund. They sponsored bloodmobiles, were active in passing state legislation, and supported local beautification projects. Green stamps became an important part of fundraising. Many clubs joined the General Federation to profit from their knowledge and programs. The clubs seemed filled with energy — the Westminster club, founded in 1953 — started a chorus, focused on veterans' work, and sponsored an anniversary ball for the town's 200th birthday. In 1958 they sponsored the public health nurse, now funded by the town.

The Holden Woman's Club was very active in youth activities, winning the MSFWC Build Freedom with Youth contest. In addition, much time and effort was directed to the local hospital.

In 1953 the Southborough Woman's Club began an extensive volunteer

133

program at Westborough State Hospital, giving birthday parties, book reviews, musical programs, and occupational therapy to the patients. This was a continued effort until 1970.

In 1956 the Whitinsville Woman's Club held an outstanding fashion show, realizing a profit of $1,500 for its scholarship fund.

Libraries still benefitted from donations. Westminster and Winchendon donated books, Berlin Tuesday Club gave new book shelves and magazine racks. Between 1958 and 1961 the Shrewsbury Woman's Club held community fairs, earning a total of $9,082 which they deposited in a savings bank until 1975. The total amount of $27,000 was then turned over to the trustees of the Shrewsbury Public Library towards the purchase of a bookmobile. West Boylston Woman's Club raised funds for a van for transportation for the elderly. In 1956 the Clio Club spearheaded a drive for funds for a visiting nurse association. Winchendon helped maintain a community building that has an olympic-sized swimming pool. The Worcester Woman's Club continued its efforts through the fifties and sixties — at one time reaching a membership of one thousand members plus a waiting list. Countless projects such as Lincoln Square Senior Citizens Club, Faith Inc., a home for women alcoholics, support for YWCA programs, and camp scholarships for underprivileged children were carried out.

In 1953 a local disaster caused by a tornado in the Central Region (Worcester area) banded clubs together as they offered support in donations of clothing, food supplies, and funds. Worcester Woman's Club sold 2,123 sets of placemats at one dollar each to benefit the fund for tree replacements in the area. The Northborough Woman's Club received a citation from the town for aid given the storm victims.

Historical interest was still maintained. In 1955 Ashburnham restored the town's oldest document, their charter, for the club's 50th anniversary, and went on in 1958 to lead in the establishment of the Ashburnham Historical Society.

Western Region

Agawam Women's Club

The first "Friendship Tea" for Senior Citizens was started in the fall of 1940 and has continued yearly to the present day. Currently the club holds two teas a year, one in the fall and the other in the spring.

In 1947 the Club Collect was written by Mrs. H. Preston Worden and is printed annually in the front of the club's yearbook.

During the war years of World War II the women worked diligently to help the servicemen at Westover Field. They furnished a Day Room there and also held parties for the personnel right up through the 1950s.

In 1957 when membership of the club was well over two hundred, and there was a long waiting list especially of young women, it was decided to form the Junior Division, a group which is very active today.

Amherst Women's Club

The austerities of World War II days were keenly felt, and every effort was made to share in the problems of those grim times. A flag was promptly purchased and properly displayed, money was given to Camp Devens, Christmas boxes for soldiers were packed, courses in home nursing were initiated, a Red Cross blood bank was sponsored by the club, magazines were taken to the State Hospital in Northampton, and innumerable cookies made for the Leeds Veterans Hospital. Also throughout these days there was extensive and well-organized entertaining for soldiers in the club house, with senior and junior hostesses. Nearly six hundred service men were in the club house between April and August of 1946.

Chicopee Falls Woman's Club

The main effort of the club during these years was support of the Massachusetts State Federation projects and continuing the club's local scholarship funds.

Granby Woman's Club

In 1950 the club sponsored the formation of the Evening Division of The Granby Woman's Club, known as the P. M. Club. The young mothers and working women of the town are members of this group and they have been very active in Federation projects.

Under Civil Defense, in 1952 the first Ground Observer Corp Post in Granby was activated with the Granby Woman's Club assuming the responsibility of manning the post for twelve continuous hours weekly. In another branch of the civil defense project, one of the members, Mrs. Margaret Dickinson, was appointed chief warden. Mrs. Dickinson and her wardens were very active during some of the hurricanes which hit the area. Club members were also active in the Red Cross Canteen Service during this time. An Armed Services Committee was established for remembering the local boys who volunteered or were drafted for military service.

In 1950 the club published a book on *The Old Homes of Granby*. For many years, the club, together with the Granby Grange, helped defray the expense for the care and upkeep of the lovely town Common.

Southampton Woman's Club

During the forties the club increased its volunteerism with an emphasis on veterans' service and the war effort. A baby sitting service was formed to aid the club women in their work and the club was credited with $3,375 worth of bond sales toward the purchase of an ambulance plane. The records of the forties tell of such projects as the underwriting of dental work for needy children, the purchase of food and clothing for the poor, and books and craft items for shut-ins.

The club grew in membership during the fifties and began to meet at the church hall. Its efforts in community projects, especially those of town beautification, continued to be of prime importance.

Southwick Women's Club

During World War II the club women supported the Holyoke Soldiers Hospital. They rolled bandages, made afghans, lap robes, quilts, and volunteered their services to do menial jobs to alleviate the understaffed nurses. After the end of the war, the women supported the Leeds Veterans Hospital. Every year baskets of apples or peaches were delivered to the hospital. Donations of money were sent for veterans' Christmas gifts and also for veterans to buy gifts for their family members.

Donations towards scholarships for Southwick High School students as well as donations for Federated sponsored scholarships and local programs have always been supported by the club members. The beautification programs have kept out oversized and unsightly billboards from cluttering up the town's roadsides. The women organized and conducted town roadside cleanups. The house numbering project, sponsored by the club, saved the town thousands of dollars that it would have cost to have a professional company do the same job.

Ramapogue Women's Club

In 1943 the name of the club was changed from the Young Women's Club of West Springfield to the Ramapogue Women's Club. The name Ramapogue was selected for its significance and legendary appeal. Ramapogue is an Indian word meaning branching water and also a meadow under a hill. It was the Indian name for West Springfield.

During 1947 a scholarship fund was originated to be awarded to a deserving West Springfield High School student. During earlier years, awards of money were given to young women at the school to encourage them to enter the field of nursing. The club also made donations to the West Springfield YMCA and to the Neighborhood House, known as the West Springfield Boy's and Girl's Club.

The club in 1950 sponsored formation of the Ramapogue Junior Women's Club. This was proven to be very beneficial as many junior members have moved up to the women's club to become active members and leaders.

In 1957 the club reached an all-time high in membership with 235 members. New groups added to the club were the Women's Golfing and Bowling League, and Drama Group. In addition to the scholarship given each year to a graduating West Springfield High School student, the club began giving scholastic aid scholarships to residents of West Springfield attending college and needing further financial assistance to continue their studies.

Northfield Fortnightly Club

The war years found the club busy with donations of money and services to the Leeds Veterans Hospital and internationally, contributions to the War Relief Fund, blankets for the elderly in Germany in 1951, woolen clothing for Japan in 1951, and aid to the Holland flood victims in 1953.

The club has also helped with the children's immunization clinics, the Red Cross Blood Mobile, and providing aides in the library and the school. In February 1950 the club sponsored adult education classes under the direction of the superintendent of schools. Classes in typing, decorative arts, dressmaking, rug hooking, and chair caning, were carried on for several years.

Northampton Woman's Club, Inc.

The work of the club during the war years was largely in support of the demands of the war. Bonds and stamps were sold at monthly club meetings, members sewed and knit for the soldiers, and afghans were made for the Veterans' Hospital. In 1942 the American Home Department initiated a campaign for salvaging waste fats which enabled the department to contribute to many worthy causes such as the Springfield Naval Convalescent Hospital, the "Phone Home" Fund, needy families of navy men, subscriptions of Boston papers to the Veterans' Hospital, and veterans' Christmas bags. The fat salvage money also purchased files for Forbes Library to preserve the records of veterans, and for all honor boards in the county.

In the following years, among the many causes receiving donations, the American Home Department has given a prize to a girl in the graduating class at Smith's School and nurses loans have been made to many worthy students at the Cooley Dickinson Hospital.

Tuesday Club of Warren

During World War II Marcia Shepard was very active in promoting the sale of War Bonds, and in response to a Federation request, members also contributed to a quarter of a million dollar fund to establish furlough houses in France for American soldiers.

Wilbraham Women's Club

During the war years the club contributed to and served the American Red Cross, European Aid, the sale of War Bonds, adoption of war orphans under "Save the Children Federation," Korean Relief, and it also gave aid to a Finnish refugee.

The Wilbraham Women's Club Choral Group formed as a study group in 1945, later became a performing group that continues to sing for area hospitals, nursing homes, women's and civic organizations.

Athol Woman's Club

Due to the added war work during 1942, meetings for Red Cross sewing, and surgical dressings were arranged. Funds were raised to purchase a comfortable chair for the soldiers at Fort Devens. In 1945-46 the club made donations to the Athol School Band, scholarships were increased an additional fifty dollars, and a great deal of sewing was done for the Red Cross. During the fifties the community service committee sponsored the March of Dimes with outstanding results. Members offered their services for the March of Dimes, and at the Bloodmobile and Heart Drive. The charities supported included the Salvation Army, Halloween celebration for children, Veterans, Red Cross, Penny Art Fund, Camp Fire Girls, and the local YMCA.

Lake Pleasant Women's Club

Joined the Massachusetts State Federation 1942 and General Federation 1943.

The Lake Pleasant Women's Club was organized in 1941. Although it is a small club, its members are active in village affairs. Their efforts are devoted primarily to the maintenance of the "Rutter Memorial Bridge"; helping to send children to camp; funding all Lake Pleasant children's parties; and it was instrumental in sponsoring the library for the children of the village.

All original records/notes on the history of the Lake Pleasant Women's Club were destroyed by fire.

Charlemont Woman's Club

In 1943 it was voted to meet once a month instead of twice a month, this practice continues to the present time. During this period a Reading Club was sponsored with meetings held at a time other than that of the regular club meeting. The club sponsored first aid classes and was very active in the selling of War Stamps and War Bonds.

The club reached its largest membership during 1948-1949, having ninety-two members. From the start a roll call had been taken at each meeting. This custom was dropped about 1950, but was reinstated in 1955 and mentioned in the February 1956 "TOPICS" as a unique and commendable part of the Charlemont Woman's Club.

The Reading Club which was formed in 1943 became an independent club in the fifties.

The Woman's Club of Greenfield

The club adopted a Korean orphan in 1956 and continued to support him until he finished his education. The club continued with its scholarship program to local youths and support of community projects.

Sunderland Woman's Club

One of the outstanding events of this period was the Golden Anniversary Celebration of the club held in 1944, a highlight in the history of the Sunderland Woman's Club.

Orange Woman's Club

A Garden Club was formed in the 1950s and the members helped beautify the park and river bank. The Bloodmobile became a yearly endeavor in 1960 and is still being supported. In 1960, Florence Alexander of the Orange Woman's Club was elected president of the Massachusetts State Federation.

Shelburne Falls Woman's Club

During the 1950s the club completely renovated the "Bridge of Flowers" and planted trees along the main streets of Shelburne and Buckland.

Agawam Junior Women's Club

Joined the Massachusetts State Federation 1958 and General Federation 1958.

The Agawam Junior Women's Club was organized in April 1957. The first years were extremely fulfilling. The very first act performed for the town was the reactivation of the "story hours" at the Agawam Center

The Bridge of Flowers, award-winning community service project of the Shelburne Falls Woman's Club in 1929 and again in 1978. Formerly a 390-foot railway bridge, it was converted to serve as an aqueduct in 1929 and later that year was transformed into the famous Bridge of Flowers which has since brought millions of visitors from all over the world.

Library. Two years later, in 1959, the club had raised enough money to present one graduating senior high school student a science award. Later, American history and language awards were added.

The Agawam Juniors showed they cared in many ways in the early years of the club. Yearly camperships to the YMCA were given to needy children of the town. In 1960 the Juniors took over the always rewarding task of "Clearinghouse." This project grew every year until by 1977 the juniors delivered seventy-five baskets of food and goodwill to grateful families in Agawam.

MATURITY

1960-1988

DRASTIC CHANGES in lifestyles, a permissive society, drugs and alcohol, more affluent and aging club memberships challenged the leadership of the Massachusetts State Federation of Women's Clubs during the decades of the 60s, 70s, and 80s. Our state presidents and local clubs met these challenges with programs designed to fulfill the goals and purpose of the organization.

"Building Firm Foundations for the Future", was the theme under the presidency of Mrs. Charles E. Shepard, 1960-1962. This was the second time a state president was elected from the 14th District. Mrs. Shepard believed community improvement was a club responsibility and that it could be achieved through the organized efforts of women. Local clubs fulfilled her belief by their 100 percent participation in the Community Improvement Program. The second volume of *Progress and Achievement* was published during her administration. Other areas of Federation concern were public higher education, highway safety, conservation of natural resources, and the support of legislation to oppose legalized gambling.

Mrs. Thomas L. Porter, president, 1962-1963, had as her theme "Horizons Unlimited". Within four months of her election Mrs. Porter became ill and her first vice president, Mrs. Frederick J. Wood, assumed the responsibilities of the presidency. Club women gave generous support to educational television and their contributions to Channel 2 in 1962 were matched by the Ford Foundation. An outstanding project initiated during this administration was the restoration of the Clough-Langdon House and its garden area which adjoined the Old North Church. Interest in the Community Improvement Program (CIP) was stimulated when the Federation hosted the Community Improvement Seminar held in Boston by the northeast region of the General Federation of Women's Clubs.

Blind children pat a deer on the "Touch and See" nature trail at the Hale Reservation, a Westwood Woman's Club Junior Membership project.

"Our Heritage — to Dream, to Dare, to Do" was the theme and the challenge made by Mrs. Frederick J. Wood, who served as president, 1963-1965. The two day Fine Arts Festival held in Worcester was outstanding and set a cultural standard for local clubs. Restoration on the Clough-Langdon House next to the Old North Church continued. Highway safety was the main thrust of the legislative program and the Truth in Lending legislation supported ' he Federation became a model for national legislation. Work continued for club volunteers in hospitals, youth work, helping the blind, reading to the elderly, and increased support of the scholarship program.

Programs that would "Cherish the Past — Challenge the Future", were reinforced under the leadership of Mrs. Americo Chaves, president, 1965-1967. Self education in current legislation was accomplished through a series of "Days at the State House". The main thrust of the legislative program was a bill to regulate installment sales. More than 300 women passed the Driver Improvement Course as part of the highway safety program sponsored by the Federation. Conferences were held in the fields of art, conservation, safety, public health, community service, and publicity. Federated members traveled to the United Nations and to Washington, D. C. Clubs demonstrated their support of the Clough-Langdon House restoration with generous contributions.

143

Common goals for senior club women, the Evening Division and Junior Membership were established under the leadership of Mrs. Clarence F. Clark, president, 1967-1969. Her theme, "Today's Best Is Tomorrow's Beginning". Hosting the General Federation of Women's Clubs convention in Boston was a major event during Mrs. Clark's presidency. Workshops held throughout the state featured conservation, education, scholarships, fine arts, public health, community improvement, and community affairs. Three legislative workshops were held and members made two visits to the J. F. Kennedy Federal Building at Government Center. Improvements were made at the Memorial Forest on the clubhouse and caretaker's cottage.

The shoreline of Massachusetts provided a campaign slogan during the presidency of Mrs. Raymond N. Peterson (1969-1971). "Save Our Shores" addressed the threatened extinction of the shores and waterways of historic Dorchester Bay and the islands in Boston Harbor. Her theme "Rise Up and Build" reinforced the goal for the biennium. Club members' interest was stimulated with workshops featuring conservation, consumer affairs, justice, and rehabilitation. The Federation sponsored a trip to Majorca and two Club Institutes were held in Worcester. Support continued for the Clough-Langdon House and improvements at the Memorial Forest where a trail was cut near the old windmill and to the second bridge.

"Freedom and Responsibility", was the theme under which Mrs. Marshall W. Ross assumed the presidency for 1971-1972. She established the Presidents' Fund for maintenance of the Memorial Forest in Sudbury and to support an educational program on prison reform and criminal justice. The response was excellent. To keep clubwomen informed on all Federation programs, lines of communication were improved with round tables for members, the Federation Packet and statewide workshops. The *Blueprint for Action,* a plan to reorganize and revitalize the Federation, was implemented. Strong support was given to the Memorial Forest and to programs for crime prevention and rehabilitation.

Unifying the three segments of the Federation was a major goal for Mrs. Paul E. Congdon, president from 1972-1974. She believed the General Clubs, Junior Membership, and Evening Division should work together toward common goals. The "Touch and See Trail" was developed at

From the Past to the Future

Cathedral of the Pines, Rindge, New Hampshire. At left is the Memorial Bell Tower, above is the bell which is a memorial to American women who served in World War II, and below is a view of the Monadnocks from the Cathedral grounds.

At top left is Clough House in Boston, restoration of which has been a continuing project of the Federation. The Old North Church is at the right. Above, interior restoration begins, and at left is a typical restored room. The newly-restored garden between the Old North Church and Clough House is shown below.

146

Laughing Brook. Uniting with the Juniors, women worked together on education, legislation, and fund raising for the mentally retarded. "Special Help for Special People". Federation members opposed legislation to legalize marijuana, they operated HOT LINES, and helped with youth centers in their efforts to cope with the growing problem of drugs in our society.

"Improve the Quality of Life," said Mrs. Eugene G. Faucher, when she assumed the presidency for 1974-1976. Her four-thrust program included education, legislation, developing opportunities for women, and celebrating the bicentennial of our country. "Federation Focus," a legislative bulletin, was published to inform the membership of issues at the State House. Members gave strong support to the Equal Rights Amendment and were delighted with its passage in Massachusetts. The restoration at the Clough House was completed. Chapter 766 became an integral part of public education as it provided education for all, not only the bright students but for everyone no matter their ability or disability. The "Help for Children" program was a special interest for many clubs.

Clubwomen's concern for their fellowmen was revealed in the theme selected by Mrs. John W. Holland, Jr., president, 1976-1978, as she challenged the membership with, "Concern, Courage, Commitment – A Better World for All." Nutritional workshops were held statewide. "Hands Up," was a popular crime reduction program. At Tabor Academy the Federation held "A Day of Learning," for the membership. World renowned scientists led discussions that emphasized conservation and the bounty of the sea at the "Conference by the Sea" held for members at Woods Hole. Horizons were extended for members and their friends when they traveled to Holland, to the United Nations, the World Trade Center, and the Metropolitan Opera in New York City. Children, a constant focus of the Federation, were addressed by the program "Prevention of Cruelty to Children."

"Invest in the Future," challenged Mrs. Edward C. Warner, president, 1978-1980. Recognizing the importance of leadership in such a program,

Logo of Priority One, WNEV-TV award to the Federation for crime awareness and reduction.

A Community-Wide
Alliance to Halt Crime

The Federation Story

The Federation's present headquarters building in Memorial Forest, Sudbury shown above was dedicated in August 1987. At right construction begins in 1986 and below, President Nancy Beatty checks the foundation.

148

General Federation of Women's Clubs International headquarters at 1734 N Street N. W.,
Washington, D. C.

a Leadership Seminar was held at Wheaton College and participants created a Leadership Membership Packet for the Federation. The establishment of Great Decisions discussion groups was encouraged on the local level. Boundaries were extended as members raised monies to build a school in Huacho, Peru. The Boston Public Library volunteered to publish the ESO reading list. Safety, a continuing concern for Federation members, was addressed with the installation of highway reflective markers throughout the state under the urging of the Federation. The concept of leadership under Federation standards included woman as person and a leader; club as leader in the community; MSFWC as leader financially; and leadership in the world through peace and understanding of other cultures.

Mrs. Garry R. Keessen, president, 1980-1982, asked Federation members to "Reach Out" to learn, to teach, to serve, and to enjoy. Regional conferences were held stressing home life and the subject matter dealt with adolescent suicide, leadership-membership, and parliamentary law. Many special programs were held to emphasize that "Families are Forever." At the Old North Church a vesper service was held together with a Colonial Tea at the Clough House. Reaching out to the future, the Headquarters

The Federation Story

A day at the State House in 1982, typical of annual Federation days at Beacon Hill, Boston.

149

Building project was started. In developing a program for the print handi-capped, the Federation supported the Talking Information Center finan-cially and with volunteer readers. In the area of health members were urged to participate in the early detection of colon-rectal cancer testing.

Volunteerism was stressed as clubwomen worked to achieve the goal, "for the common good," under the leadership of Mrs. F. William Ahearn, president, 1982-1984. Members gained insight into leadership during a two-day seminar. Guides at the Clough House distributed the new brochure, "Historic Clough House," to visitors from around the world. Clubs demonstrated their continued support financially and individually for the Talking Information Center. Efforts by the Federation were recognized when Channel 7 Priority One gave them the "Good Neighbor Award" for their program on crime awareness and crime reduction. Regional con-ferences addressed the public relations/communication program and members learned to use the manual, "Tell the Federation Story."

"Our nation needs informed, caring, daring leaders...let us work together to that end," said Mrs. Theodore Billias as she assumed the presidency for 1984-1986. Her theme "with malice toward none" was reflected in many Federation programs. The Talking Information Center

The Talking Information Center (TIC) microwave relay system tower at Liberty Plaza in Marshfield . . . the culmination of three presidential administration's efforts from 1980 to 1986. Above, operating a special TIC receiver for programming to the print handicapped.

was supported generously by the membership. During the fall, conferences were held in all the regions with presentations on family economics, public affairs, community improvement, membership, public relations, and veterans' service. The Family Economics Booklet was published and members attended "A Day at the State House" to meet with their legislators and inform them about our concerns. The abundance of history was enjoyed by members and friends who had traveled to Greece, a source of culture, the arts, and leadership styles.

Culminating the dreams and commitment of several administrations, the new Headquarters building was dedicated in August 1987; a major event during the presidency of Mrs. Royce E. Beatty, president, 1986-1988. Her theme "Sharing is Caring" has been reflected in many Federation programs. Conservation, an emphasis for the administration focused on the goal, "Conservation, the Future Depends on You and Me." Clubwomen helped make the "Garden in the Glade" at the Forest a thing of beauty as they began planting bulbs with an initial planting of 2,500 bulbs. Hazardous waste, beautification, and clean water were addressed by clubs

𝔅𝔦𝔠𝔢𝔫𝔱𝔢𝔫𝔫𝔦𝔞𝔩 𝔄𝔫𝔫𝔦𝔳𝔢𝔯𝔰𝔞𝔯𝔶 𝔅𝔞𝔩𝔩

The Harwich Woman's Club
The Harwich Junior Woman's Club
and The Evening Division

cordially invites you to attend a

Colonial Cotillion

Friday the twenty first of November
Nineteen hundred and seventy five
at eight-thirty o'clock

Harwich Port
Wychmere Harbor Club

Colonial dress optional

Dancing the minuet at midnight at the Harwich Bicentennial Anniversary Ball.

throughout the state. Members shared and cared as they contributed club histories to the newest Federation history, *From the Past to the Future*, published in 1988.

152   Stability has been given to the Federation with the establishment of our Headquarters at the Memorial Forest. Decreasing membership in some of the local clubs has certainly been a sign of the times as more and more women joined the work force. However, the commitment to Federation goals has been reflected in our strong leadership, in the support of community improvement programs, the escalating scholarship awards, and the enthusiastic participation in cultural events. The Federation is building on the past to meet the needs of the future.

Southeastern Region

More new clubs were formed in this era: in 1963 the Dennis Junior Women's Club; 1965 the Nauset Junior Woman's Club of Orleans; 1969 the Harwich Woman's Club, Evening Division; 1970 the Sandwich Junior Women's Club; 1971 the Dartmouth Enrichment League, an Evening Division club; and the Weymouth Club which was formed in 1976 from the merger of the Old Colony Club (1897) and the Monday Club of Weymouth (1896).

Winning design for Federation cup plate sold to help fund Headquarters building construction.

All of the clubs in the Southeastern Region continue to provide scholarships for worthy students, give many volunteer hours to the veterans hospitals and nursing homes, provide Meals-on-Wheels, and support their local libraries with book donations and other services. More and more of the clubs are concentrating on assisting the senior citizens' centers, such as the Sandwich club supplying cooking utensils, dishes, bridge tables and chairs, for Shawme Heights. The Harwich club supports the "Albro House" and performs many services for the local shut-ins. The Whitman club established a park at Harvard Court, and the P. M. Club of Hingham provides transportation for the Golden Agers to and from their meetings.

Mrs. Marshall W. (Eleanor) Ross, a member of the Mattapoisett Woman's Club, served as president of the MSFWC from 1971-1972. This one year term enabled the Massachusetts Federation to synchronize its administrations with those of the General Federation. Mrs. Ross established the Presidents' Fund, the money collected was divided between the maintenance of the Memorial Forest in Sudbury and an educational program on prison reform and criminal justice.

Mrs. John W. Holland, Jr. (Ann), a member of the Falmouth Woman's Club, served as president of the MSFWC from 1976-1978. She went on to serve two consecutive terms as the GFWC chairman of conservation from 1978 to 1982; was elected to the office of GFWC treasurer, 1982-1984; GFWC recording secretary, 1984-1986, and served as the second vice president of the GFWC from 1986-1988.

The members of both the Mattapoisett and Falmouth clubs are justifiably proud of the accomplishments of Eleanor Ross and Ann Holland.

There are many imaginative methods of fund raising, and at times it seems that the Massachusetts clubwomen have tried them all! There are balls, fashion shows, auctions, plays and musical productions, house and garden tours, "chicken pie" and other type suppers, antique shows, flea markets, candy sales, craft fairs, bake sales, card parties, sales of calendars, and board games, to name a sampling. Cookbooks have also been popular projects through the years, and some of the clubs which have used this method of funding some of their charitable contributions and scholarships are The Tuesday Club of Assonet, the Mattapoisett, Sandwich, and Marshfield clubs. Despite all of the fund raising, sometimes clubs have to make difficult choices when the subject of spending comes up. As each club strives to do as much as possible to better their communities and the wider world around them with necessarily limited financial resources, some of the old customs have to come to an end. One small example of this

154

Jericho House, site of the Dennis Women's Club board meetings, was built in 1801 and given
to the town by authoress Elizabeth Reynaud.

is when the Old Colony Union Women's Club of Bourne was forced to place their cherished old silver vase in the custody of the Bourne Archives, because the insurance on the vase had risen to become a burden. They preferred to channel their money toward the future rather than toward the past. An example of much greater scope is the number of clubs which have found through the years that they were no longer able to maintain their clubhouses.

In 1970 the Brewster club members traveled "en masse" making a "Pilgrimage to Plymouth," marking the 350th anniversary of the landing of the Pilgrims. In 1973 the Sandwich club members convinced the town to save the Deacon Eldred House (now the Thornton Burgess Museum), for which the club members did all of the interior restoration. They also print their own newsletter "The Sandpiper," as do the Mattapoisett, Sippican, and many other clubs throughout the region. These newsletters are very effective tools in strengthening and unifying the clubs. Sandwich is also among those clubs which sponsor house tours and flower garden shows as fund raisers. The Harwich Woman's Club, Evening Division, hosted a town-wide reception for a local teacher who had taught three generations of some local families. The Abington club promoted a safety first and better street lighting program in 1966-68, and in 1976-78 was among the many clubs which supported the Crime Watch Program featuring "McGruff."

Volunteers from the Braintree Point Woman's Club assisted "Brain Injured Children" weekly. For their CIP project, the Braintree Woman's Club installed a rope ski tow at East Junior High School, and provided ski instruction for the children. They presented a glass display case and a school directory to the high school for the media center, donated Talking Information Center (TIC) receivers and saw completion of five years work furnishing a room in the maternity wing of the South Shore Hospital. The Dennis club's many services include Meals-on-Wheels, Vision, the Rescue Squad, Shriners Burn Institute, Hospice, and the Cape Cod Homemakers program. The Dennis Juniors also have an extensive well-rounded program of activities and service. The Edgartown club provided clothing and gifts for needy children through their contributions to the "Red Stocking Fund."

The Philergians prepared, published, and presented a book of the town history, and distributed copies to the schoolchildren. Scholarships and other charitable support by the Quincy club is assured because of the income from a trust fund established from the proceeds of the sale of their clubhouse in 1985. Although their clubhouse had served them well for over twenty-five years, its disposition will perhaps serve them even better in this way. This has been the decision many clubs were forced to make which have been unable to maintain their clubhouses due to escalating costs.

Almost every club in the region participated in the TIC (Talking Information Center) project through donations and/or purchasing and donating receivers. This project, which aided the print handicapped, was a very popular State Federation project that extended through three administrations. Among those purchasing receivers were the Rochester, Taunton, Ivy Circle of New Bedford, and Weymouth clubs. The Weymouth club also conducted walk-a-thons for the Ethiopian famine. The Whitman club took part in the Toll House renovation and still maintains window boxes at the post office. The P. M. Club of Brockton supports "Womansplace," a shelter for battered women and children; "Camp Jabberwocky," a cerebral palsy camp on Martha's Vineyard; and clubmembers transport the blind. The P. M. Club of Hingham provides a baby sitting clinic at the library. The Marshfield club distributed a poison control kit to school children, participated in the "Wally Worm" nature trail project; in 1971 took over full responsibility of the Bloodmobile; and in 1974 supplied Tot Finder stickers for aid in identification of childrens' bedrooms in the event of fire. The Rockland P. M. Club conducts a "Christmas in July" at Camp

156

Hillside, home of the Quincy Women's Club, overlooks Quincy Center and the harbor. It is said to be a copy of Abbotsford, home of Sir Walter Scott.

Jabberwocky which is a high point for the cerebral palsied children staying there. Club members saw to it that the Heimlich Maneuver was demonstrated in every school in town, and began a two-year project in 1983 to fingerprint all town children. Another State Federation project that was very popular was our research which helped bring about the installation of reflecting markers on Massachusetts highways.

The Braintree Junior Philergians have supported the South Shore Center for brain damaged children and Pilgrim Center (a halfway house for troubled teen-aged boys); organized Braintree FISH (temporary emergency service for local residents) and assisted the Lupus Foundation projects. They donated bolts of cloth and blankets to a Braintree missionary working in South Africa — spreading their good works around the world. The Hanover Juniors provided "stop-arms" for local school buses. The Tuesday Club of Assonet took second place in the Shell Oil Company contest, planted flowers, shrubs and trees on community sites, promoted land conservation, and worked diligently to help prevent a potentially hazardous plant from being built in the watershed forest area of their community.

The Cabot Club sponsored a Girl Scout troop for handicapped youngsters at Lakeville Hospital. The Rochester club maintains two ancient watering troughs in town areas, filling them with annuals in the spring and Christmas greens in the winter. Every student at Rochester Memorial School was presented with a seedling in the spring of 1985, in support of conservation. The Taunton club planted trees in local parks and at public buildings, and has been actively involved in the hazardous waste problem, both in terms of educating the public and in conducting "pick-up" days. The Sippican club has also worked conscientiously on this problem. The Wareham Monday Club has held six Trade Fairs at Town Hall to promote their town. They gave funds for the renovation and the furnishings for the "Publik Room" at the old Fearing House. Libraries are faithfully supported by many clubs, including the Nautilus, Brewster, Marshfield, P. M. of Hingham, Harwich and Wareham clubs.

Even though they have suffered a decrease in membership and a lack of community response to so-called "social affairs," the Ivy Circle of New Bedford manages to maintain its high percentage of participation in charitable campaigns. In addition, an annual party for the blind continues to be held and a local nursing home was provided with a TIC receiver. They also support all MSFWC projects. In December 1979 the New Bedford Woman's Club's clubhouse building, the Standish House, was sold to the YMCA. The club retains the privilege of holding meetings there. The Standish House is officially entered in the National Register of Historical Buildings, and continues to be a focal point for community activities such as concerts, and other events.

The Harwich Junior Woman's Club in 1973 began a local AFS Chapter for international student exchange; in 1974 started the Harwich Youth Center which is still functioning and is an annual recipient of funds raised at their charity ball. To mark the bicentennial, in 1976 the club members planted thirteen cherry trees at Harwich High School; they helped revitalize a small town park by installing a surrounding fence; purchased a "Jaws of Life" life pack for the town; and in 1980, as the culmination of a two year CIP project, purchased an ice boat for the fire department. They saw that all local school children were fingerprinted and in 1985 began a child registry program. These industrious young women are truly an asset to their community.

In 1962 the Orleans club formed a "Watch-Dog" committee in an endeavor to keep the architecture of new buildings in the Cape Cod Tradition, and to stimulate the interest of business and individual property owners in maintaining the appearance of their respective properties. They sent a resolution to the town officials requesting denial of variances of building codes, and signs that did not adhere to town regulations; and secured an agreement with the planners of the Stop & Shop Market regarding the general character of the building, sign, and planting space in the parking lot. The year 1968-69 was important for the Orleans club with three members being singled out: Mrs. Kallock's work at the Job Corps in Wellfleet was featured in *McCall's* magazine; Amy Jarvis was honored by *Yankee* magazine with a story about her first experience as a country school teacher; and Alice Lowe's book *Nauset On Cape Cod*, a history of Eastham, was published. Orleans took house numbering as a CIP project in 1970, and yellow ribbons were widely distributed in 1980 to be displayed as a reminder for all to think about and pray for the Americans held hostage in Iran.

The following community projects have been supported admirably by the P. M. Club of Hingham: New England Home for Little Wanderers, and the South Shore Association for Retarded Children. They supplied toilet articles for incarcerated women at various correctional institutions. They also initiated a children's eye screening program in their town. The Sippican club supported town and State Federation projects to the utmost. Holding dental clinics and bringing hot soup and cocoa into the schools for the children, maintaining a lifeguard and a boat at Wharf Island, providing a slide for children at Silver Shell Beach, safety vests for newsboys, movies, gifts, and parties for the local veterans at the Kendrick House, were only a few of their community projects. The Dartmouth Enrichment League members are actively serving on community boards such as the New Bedford Preservation Society; and Massachusetts Governor Michael Dukakis appointed club member Edith Andrews as a Commissioner on Indian Affairs, a position she has held for twelve years.

The General, Evening Division, and Junior Membership clubs of the Southeastern Region, like their counterparts throughout the state, have given a wealth of service to their communities through the years. They have initiated new programs and supported existing organizations, local hospitals, libraries, schools, the veterans, youth and the aged. They have given both monetarily and personally with their time, energy and loving concern. They will long stand as shining examples of what women can accomplish when they band together to reach out to others — opening their caring hearts and sharing their many talents in service. In future years they will draw on their past accomplishments as they continue to be a vigorous force in their neighborhoods, their state, and in the world community.

Southern Region

As the nation became more involved in the Vietnam War, the Junior Fortnightly Club of Sharon sent packages to soldiers and children there. Although membership fell to twenty-five these dedicated women adopted patients at Wrentham State Hospital, worked to combat drugs, fingerprinted over twelve-hundred children, contributed to Hospice, and adopted a local family at Christmas, giving the children toys, clothes, a tree, filled stockings, and a fifty dollar certificate for shoes.

Books in memory of deceased members were given to the library by the East Bridgewater Woman's Club. An autoclave was donated to the Visiting Nurse Association and maple trees were furnished to the town.

Dresses for the Salvation Army dolls are sewed by the Ashland Women's Club members who also make tray favors for nursing homes.

All clubs in the Southern Region give scholarships to the schools, many from permanent funds established for that purpose.

The Milton P. M. Club was formed to accommodate women who worked and were unable to attend Milton Woman's Club (which met in the afternoon), or the Junior Woman's Club which has an age limit of twenty-eight. They all share the same clubhouse which has beautiful murals of old Milton in the entrance hall. There are many active committees to raise money to maintain the clubhouse and contribute to their many civic and charitable obligations.

When the Brockton Fuller Art Center opened, Ousamequin Club of Bridgewater gave a $3,000 painting by Conger Metcalf. This club underwrote the cost of transporting three hundred fourth graders to Brockton to enjoy Sarah Caldwell's production of Mozart. A thirteen-volume set of the *Oxford English Dictionary* was given to the library as the club's seventy-fifth anniversary gift. Supplements are given annually as memorials and club members formed a "Friends of the Library" organization.

As the need for senior housing increased the Foxboro Woman's Club was instrumental in placing an article on the warrant to create the Foxboro Housing Authority and the club president served on that board. Boyden Library was the recipient of $1,500 from the club to buy chairs for the conference room. *Reader's Digest* large print books are subscribed to annually for the library.

Former mental patients live in Alpha House furnished by Kalmia Club of North Attleboro whose members also assist serving lunch at the Senior Center.

160

Southborough club members admire afghans knitted for veterans, a continuing project of every Federation club.

Westwood Woman's Club provided an amblyopia clinic in the elementary school.

Veteran service committees of all clubs worked for veterans' hospitals, giving Christmas parties and gifts, cookouts in summer, teas for veterans and their visiting families, besides making afghans. One member of the Stoughton Woman's Club received a certificate for 5,631 hours of volunteer service.

In addition to becoming foster parents to an adolescent girl in Central America, the New Century Club of Needham provided a family in their town with a tree, food, and gifts at Christmas. The Natick Woman's Club also provides help to needy families at holiday time.

A Vietnam Memorial was erected on the town common by the Hopkinton Woman's Club paying tribute to those who lost their lives in that unpopular war. The club also built an access ramp for the library and sponsored fingerprinting the children.

Bellingham Junior Woman's Club gave mimeo and video equipment to the schools.

Scholarship aid has been a priority of all clubs. Dedham Junior Woman's which started in 1976 with six members conducted many fundraisers to provide two scholarships: one to a high school graduate, and a second to a woman who is returning to school to finish her education before entering the work force.

In addition to providing $2,000 in scholarships annually, the Evening Division of Natick which had seventy-two charter members has donated over $38,000 to Leonard Morse Hospital since 1950.

The fourth, fifth, and twelfth districts Presidents' Clubs bring together many talented women who share offices of the Federation, thus fulfilling its main objective to encourage friendship, unity and an exchange of ideas.

Eastern Region

Up until 1965, Christmas parties were held by the Watertown Woman's Club for fifty needy children. In the 1960s the wearing of hats, fur stoles and white gloves, all dear to the hearts of the clubwomen, ended and clothing became more casual and informal.

During the 1984-1985 season members reported 10,000 hours of volunteer work and $1,600 worth of knitted items were donated to veterans' hospitals.

It should be noted that the tall, stately pin-oak tree, which stands at the rear of the Watertown Free Library, was planted by the Watertown Woman's Club on April 29, 1938, to commemorate the 150th anniversary of the United States Constitution. A large boulder, which sits at the base of the tree, holds a commemorative plaque which was permanently set in place in 1985. The Watertown Woman's Club sold Statue of Liberty bonds.

Several times in the 1960s the Bedford Woman's Community Club entered the Shell Oil Scholarship Contest and twice won five hundred dollars. The club's educational efforts also won three hundred dollars. For several successive years the fund raiser was an Evening in Scandinavia, in India, in Japan etc., with an authentic dinner and an entertainment appropriate for the particular country.

Members have made every effort to abide by the founders' purposes, and with hard work and original ideas, have stimulated the growth of membership and good works for the community. In cooperation with the Town of Bedford, the club organized the Great Road Beautification Project and the Bedford Citizens for Environmental Quality. With cultural aims in mind, the big social event and fund raiser for the past seven years has been An Evening At Pops, when small city symphony orchestras and the Greater Boston Youth Symphony Orchestra have brought delightful entertainment to Bedford.

162

The Bedford Club maintains a booth on Bedford Day and helps to construct a float for the parade. The clubmembers of the community service committee of the Bedford club serve coffee and home-made cookies, and crackers and cheese at the Veterans' Administration Hospital in Bedford on a series of Sunday afternoons. Annually the members send gifts at the holiday season, and make afghans for the veterans.

On April 11, 1980, the 60th anniversary jubilee luncheon of the Belmont Woman's Club was celebrated at the clubhouse. President Mrs. John J. Puma accepted many citations for the club congratulating the women on their fine work. A certificate of commendation was awarded to the Belmont Woman's Club for its active participation in the General Federation of Women's Club Free Enterprise Program, in addition to a certificate from CARE.

In December of 1982 the clubhouse opened its doors to the public for the first time. From December 1 to December 4 the Christmas Show House Tour of the Belmont Woman's Club was presented. The historic mansion was elegantly and festively decorated in a Christmas holiday theme by florists, antique dealers, interior decorators, and members of the Belmont Garden Club. Funds raised by these tours are applied to the restoration of the clubhouse and philanthropic endeavors including scholarships to Belmont High School.

On January 21, 1984 the Belmont Woman's Club cooperated with the police in its town by fingerprinting over 500 children and was presented a Certificate of Appreciation from the Belmont Police department.

It is interesting to note also that the Belmont Woman's Club clubhouse is recorded in the National Register of Historic Buildings and the Massachusetts Historical District Commission. The club continues to contribute to all projects proposed by the State Federation and extra philanthropies.

The New England Women's Club contributed to the Pan American Scholarship begun in 1944 and given that year to a girl from Argentina, and also to the International Scholarship available since 1950. Currently the New England Women's Club is dedicated to finding homes for the homeless.

The Women's Italian Club of Boston has two $1,000 scholarships for the Christopher Columbus Catholic High School. During World War II money was raised for an ambulance and presented to the War Department. The members worked at the YMCA and K. of C. buildings, making beds, and running canteens into the wee hours of the morning. The club also ran dances for the veterans and saw that there was plenty of entertainment for them; they sold war bonds; folded thousands and thousands of bandages; and the club received a citation from the War Department. Annual donations are made to the Massachusetts General Hospital covering the maintenance of a bed, the Italian Home for Children, Boys' Town of Italy, Home for Little Wanderers, Rosie's Place, and all the Massachusetts State Federation projects.

On the observance of the Past Chairmen's Club's 50th celebration in June 1987, Aina McMann, president, remarked "this is not the time to rest and look backward, rather the 50th anniversary should be only a step on the continuing ladder of our club's growth. Now we must look forward to the challenge of the next fifty years. We hope each member will cherish and use this opportunity for further creative service to her family, her club, her community, and her nation."

Northeastern Region

The clubs have continued to meet their obligations as laid down by their founders — many have added to their volunteer work, supplying time and money where needed. Values have changed, new needs have arisen and some projects are no longer necessary.

Nahant Woman's Club raised funds to purchase a "Jaws of Life" tool for the town. As a result they received awards from the Massachusetts State Federation of Women's Clubs and the General Federation of Women's Clubs and money from these awards was used to purchase supplies for the town police ambulance. They also raised funds to purchase a survival suit for the police force and in 1968 sent eighty pounds of clothing to South Vietnam children.

In 1984 the Nahant Woman's Club was honored to have Penny Billias elected president of the Massachusetts State Federation of Women's Clubs for the years 1984-1986. The Lynn Woman's Club was dissolved in September 1983 and Rockport continued to give to the scholarship funds and local projects as did the Revere Women's Club. The Danvers Women's Association celebrated its 100th birthday in 1982. Since 1970 the Evening Division of the Lynn Woman's Club has continued its work with the retarded, donating a pool table and cookingware to a home for retarded adults, and a food freezer and chain link fence to a home for retarded teenagers. They hold spaghetti suppers and auctions for these worthwhile projects. The Groton Woman's Club developed and completed the "Avenue of Flags" for the town.

The Pepperell Club donated $1,000 to the Nashoba Hospital to help furnish a room. Many boys came back from the wars to the Nashoba Hospital and should you visit that institution, make sure to note the tablet on the door proclaiming the gift of these women. Christmas 1980 marked the fifty-seventh anniversary of carol singing by the Winchester Fortnightly Club on the Winchester Green around an evergreen that the club had presented to the town. In 1986 a large bronze plaque for the Winchester Hospital consultation room was given by the Fortnightly Club at a cost of $3,000. In 1980 the Lothrop Club of Beverly was awarded the Community Improvement Program (CIP) scroll from the General Federation of Women's Clubs, and they were proud that one of their members, Beverly Carlman, had been selected State Chairman of the Bicentennial for the nation's 200th birthday. In 1977 Anna White, member of the Lothrop Club of Beverly, was awarded second prize by the General Federation of Women's Clubs for her winning slogan — "America to the Future through the Past". In 1981 the Lothrop Club of Beverly beautified the new Vietnam Park and also installed two drinking fountains. In 1986 they held a luncheon to raise money to continue the upkeep of Vietnam Park. Seven hundred and fifty Beverly veterans served in Vietnam, nine of whom never returned.

As with other clubs the Lynnfield Woman's Club sold home smoke detectors at the fire station. It supports SADD (Students Against Driving Drunk), and veterans with parties, laprobes, and bibs at the Bedford Veterans Hospital. The Lynnfield Woman's Club also gave a television set to the West Roxbury Veterans' Hospital and money for a senior citizen van, as did the Kosmos Club of Wakefield. Since 1966 monthly parties and annual picnics were organized for a Lynn convalescent home which has expanded from 40 to 109 residents. The same home was presented a receiver from the Talking Information Center. The Stoneham Woman's Club works with veterans at the Bedford and Chelsea veterans' hospitals, as well as in local nursing homes. Members have also participated in the Crime Watch program as did the Reading Woman's Club.

A "new" club was organized in October 1984 by merging the Melrose Woman's Club and the Melrose Highlands Woman's Club. Within the two years the new club has been in operation, it has donated five hundred dollars to the Memorial Forest, three hundred dollars to the Talking Infomation Center, and has awarded eight scholarships, plus overseeing the well-being of approximately twenty-six residents in a local nursing

164

home. The Kosmos Club raised money at a luncheon for a child in Chile, while Esther Osborne was honored for having performed a thousand hours of volunteer work. The members held a paper drive in 1986 which broke all records, receiving $531 as their share. The Woburn Woman's Club was honored at the Massachusetts State Federation of Women's Clubs May annual meeting, receiving a CIP award from Sears for their restoration of the Count Rumford (historical) House Gardens. They also provide permanent plantings around the Choate Hospital. One of the most popular club projects is making hand puppets for the pediatric department of the Choate Memorial Hospital. These puppets have proved a very useful tool for the nurses when administering medication to their young patients and when a child leaves the hospital, he or she receives a puppet.

The Reading Woman's Club entered into the excitement of creating the Massachusetts State Federation of Women's Clubs' Room at the Clough House in Boston. In 1962 the Old North Church corporation purchased the adjoining Clough House from the White Fund. It is one of the two remaining houses in Boston, dating from the early eighteenth century. During the past twenty years or more, money has been raised to restore the house, including $20,000 donated by the Massachusetts State Federation of Women's Clubs. The gardens in the rear of the house, originally a rubbish pile, have been transferred into a place of beauty with terraced gardens by the MSFWC Conservation and Gardens Committee under the direction of Louise Templeton, former president of the Reading Woman's Club. The north chamber of the Clough House, under the supervision of the MSFWC Council, has been furnished with furniture, china, and artifacts of the Clough period. Georgia Grebenstein, past president of the Reading Woman's Club, along with her husband and other volunteers, cleaned out the chimneys and scraped the woodwork to restore the north chamber. Audrey Houghton of the Stoneham Woman's Club donated an oil painting and the curtains were handmade by another member. In 1975 Kay Faucher and Ann Holland opened up the house to the public as the start of the Bicentennial festivities. The Clough House is now open every Wednesday throughout the summer with the clubmembers acting as hostesses.

In 1975 Mabel Coolidge, wife of the former lieutenant governor, was honored as a fifty-year member of the Reading Woman's Club. She also starred in a movie made by her grandchildren, *An Old-Fashioned Woman*, prints of which are kept at the public library for anyone to see. The Reading Woman's Club initiated the annual strawberry festival during the 1970s. It was begun by Marian Tyminski, then president of the club, who was assisted by Georgia Grebenstein and Florence E. Magrane. It has become an annual occurrence, with the help of Florence E. Magrane, who arranged with the Parker Tavern to have the festival held on its grounds with the ladies dressed in Colonial costumes. Tours are conducted by Miriam Barclay throughout the tavern. The year 1987 saw the Reading Woman's Club donating towards the purchase of a thirty-foot American beech tree to replace the Common's last elm, which fell victim to old age and disease. The Reading Woman's Club also donated money for Christmas lights which enliven the Common during the holidays. The club, under the direction of Thelma Blanchard, past president, and Phyllis Evensen, present president, participated in serving a collation to the Readingites celebrating the 200th birthday of the Constitution in September 1987.

The Reading Woman's Club was saddened by the death of Lucille Templeton this past year, but her memory will live on in the memory of her donation made to further the cause of women in clubwork.

The 8th District Presidents' Club recognized twenty-three members in 1986 as twenty-five year members. Betty Lasselle of the Stoneham Woman's Club penned the following verse in their honor and it applies to all of the clubwomen in the Federation be it one year or fifty years: "More than twenty-five years of membership, We're mighty proud of you! We're grateful for your loyalty and this brings our love to you."

Central Region

From the 1960s until the present day the club picture has been ever-changing. Differences in the life styles of women was a strong force in the formation of junior clubs. Young mothers with small families were restricted to evening hours for their private activities. Clubs gave them an opportunity to "get out of the house" while still contributing to the community and expanding their interests. In most cases evening meetings were a necessity. The following clubs not only were founded but joined MSFWC and GFWC within a year: Marlborough, 1964; Apple Valley, 1973; Northborough, 1975; Auburn, 1985; and Tri-Community Junior, 1986.

The 1960s again brought loss and sadness to our nation, with the onset of the Vietnam War. It seemed that veterans' committees were never left with idle hands. Volunteer hours in hospitals were increased. Record players, radios, TVs, coffee pots, books, and magazines were donated. In 1962 the Leicester Woman's Club was re-organized and immediately was involved in sending books and packages to Vietnam servicemen.

Countless community projects were undertaken in the early 1960s. Lancaster Current Topics Club checked and registered all bikes with the police department. They also continued to provide hours of service to the Clinton Hospital. Chaffins Woman's Club ran the first baby sitting safety training course ever offered in Holden. In 1961 Uxbridge Woman's Club assumed responsibility for beautifying the town Common, planting flowers around the war memorial, and adding park benches — a project continued until today by the conservation committee. In 1963 Lunenburg started a yearly project of planting flowers at the library each spring. Southbridge also planted hundreds of bulbs, as well as helping the state department identify poor roads in the area, and raffling off a quilt each year for their scholarship fund. In 1961 the Clinton Women's Club donated towards a new x-ray machine for the hospital.

Many clubs continued historical endeavors. Uxbridge furnished a room at the historic John Cornet Farnum House. During the 1960s the Holden Woman's Club helped support the Jenny Hendrick's House run by the Holden Historical Commission. In 1963 Millbury won first prize for their float in the Sesquicentennial parade, later won second prize in an Oxford parade and finally sold their float, depicting an old style open trolley car, for one hundred and fifty dollars. Marlborough Juniors cleaned up and beautified Holts Grove — a local historic site.

A strong point in clubs were the civic activities entered in CIP (Community Improvement Projects) contests by such clubs as the Berlin Tuesday Club's donation to the town hall of a new side entrance with railing, and card tables, and the Clio Club's building and equipping a playground in South Ashburnham. The club went on to win future awards totalling $2,800 for the project and in true "Woman's Club Spirit" donated the cash awards back to the project. The Current Topics Club of Lancaster held a community fair, raising $1,028 to use for improving and beautifying the town forest, a prize-winning project. They also held dance classes for students which were a tremendous success. These classes were continued for many years.

The Fitchburg Woman's Club took part in the town's Bicentennial pageant in 1964 and undertook a CIP project to recognize with awards the retarded students in schools. In 1967 they received special congratulations from Senator Edward Kennedy for this program. The Townsend Woman's Club supplied Christmas gift boxes to the local welfare office and bought bike stands for the Townsend Youth Library.

As a CIP project in 1962, the Sterling Woman's Club, with the support of the townspeople, rejuvenated the town Common with a new lawn and shrubs, repaired and painted the fence, and installed two new tennis courts for town use. In 1965 they started teaching babysitting courses.

The Oxford Woman's Club ran glass recycling drives, supplied drivers for cancer patients, and had a very active veterans' department. In 1963 the Westborough club saw another spin-off from their musical endeavors in the formation of the 100th Town Chorus.

In 1964 the newly formed Marlborough juniors supported the need for a mental health clinic and helped to renovate the building, donated to a concert piano for the library, and headed the campaign to buy a car for a kidney dialysis patient to travel to Boston for treatment. In 1965 Leominster hosted the fall meeting of MSFWC for the first time with eight hundred members in attendance.

In 1966 the Woman's Club of West Boylston worked at Holden and Oakdale nursing homes running bingo games, presenting club shows, and taking books from the library biweekly. Winchendon ran blood pressure clinics as well as paper and bottle drives. In 1967 a new chapel at the Keystone Nursing Home was furnished by members of the Fortnightly Club of Leominster. The Upton Woman's Club started a country fair in the late 1960s as their main fund raiser and are still making it an annual event.

The early 1970s saw many cookbooks being published as fund raisers, and perhaps to help offset the resulting gain in weight, many clubs such as West Boylston held "Slim 'n Trim" classes!

In 1971 the CIP committee of the Lancaster Current Topics Club sponsored a community-wide cancer detection clinic with ten area doctors participating. The same year they fed one hundred volunteers who worked in a "clean up Lancaster" campaign and participated in a green stamps project to send children to Operation Blind Camp. The Current Topics Club members earned funds by catering and had an excellent reputation for their meals. In the 1970s the Hudson Woman's Club was very active in the local girl's club and along with another organization sponsored a "girl of the month" program. In addition, equipment and funds were donated to help support the Girl's Club. In 1970 the Clinton Women's Club marked Christmas by donating gifts to the Paul Dever State School in Taunton. They also supported the Clinton Citizens' Council Recreation Project that year.

Slow learners in Spencer grade schools were assisted by "The Right to Read Program" begun by the local club in 1970.

In 1972 the first of very popular Octoberfests run by the Sterling Woman's Club was held to raise scholarship funds. This was continued with great success until 1984 when it was taken over by a local foundation set up by one of the founders.

The Upton Woman's Club donated trees to be planted around the town library. In 1972 the Fortnightly Club of Leominster donated several scholarships for needy children to Lincoln Woods Natural History and Ecology Day Camp.

In 1973 a group of young women wanting mutual support and involvement in the community organized the Apple Valley Young Women's Club in Hudson. Fashion shows, auctions, and bake sales helped to finance their many community projects such as "Breakfast with Santa" for the youngsters, holiday baskets for the needy, and support for the local senior centre, as well as many MSFWC and GFWC programs. In 1972-74 the Templeton Woman's Club sponsored a program called "Better Biking Day" in conjunction with the Baldwinville Woman's Club, the police department, and local businesses. Bicycles were engraved for identification purposes and a film shown on bicycle safety. A trip to the Freedom Trail in Boston for children in Templeton schools was planned for the next two years, again with the support of the Baldwinville club and local schools.

After much deliberation the Worcester Woman's Club sold their clubhouse in 1975. Shortly afterwards they donated a valuable twenty-volume set of the works of Henry David Thoreau to Clark University for their rare book collection. The first volume is an original manuscript in Thoreau's own handwriting.

In 1973-74 Westborough started plantings on the rotary area which were completed in 1975. That same year Northborough Juniors were started by a girl who belonged to another junior club and their first speaker was from the Red Cross. They ran a blood drive in 1976, and have been visiting nursing homes, supporting the library, and donating to needy families. They continue their educational aspects as well and have donated reference books to the Zeh School Library.

The Bicentennial year was marked by each club in some significant manner. Following are just a few of the projects:

Westborough donated to the Council on Aging for their first minibus; Hudson gave funds to the restoration of a neglected town park, and presented a flag and stand to the library.

Leicester presented the town an heirloom quilt designed by the woman's club, depicting buildings past and present; Shrewsbury donated to the historical society for the restoration of Old #5 Red Brick Schoolhouse, and bought draperies and play equipment for the children's room in the library.

Clinton planted a tulip tree in Central Park and had a Bicentennial plate made with an etching of the first town hall which they sold as a fund raiser.

Townsend planted a flowering crab tree on the town common.

Many clubs such as Barre, Hudson, Lunenburg, Northborough, Spencer, and Sterling performed historical pageants, plays, and tea parties, often jointly with local historical societies and using authentic costumes. The artistic talents of clubwomen in towns were displayed on beautiful floats in town parades.

Perhaps the proudest club of all at this time was the Lancaster Current Topics Club. What better year than 1976 to have their clubhouse placed on the National Register of Historic Places! This accomplishment took years of dedication, research and fund raising. Planting trees and flowers as well as painting and repairing this beautiful building is a lifelong project for the club.

The late 1970s and 1980s led to many cutbacks in federal government funded welfare and community projects. It was left to individuals to fill the gaps and again women stepped to the fore. We focused once more on helping one another.

In 1976 the Barre Woman's Club started printing a Community Calendar with information about local organizations, birthdays, and anniversaries — a service still continued. Beginning in 1975-76 a very active member of the Clinton Women's Club began running bus trips as a fund raiser. The substantial amounts raised led to CIP projects such as a donation of two record players, a screen and projector, Sesame Street records, and other equipment to the Bigelow Free Public Library. They now show movies to the public on Thursday evenings. The Fitchburg Woman's Club continued their work with the Burbank Hospital and manned the Salvation Army Kettles at Christmas as well as providing knitted goods for distribution to the needy. From 1973 until 1983 the Southborough Woman's Club ran a lead screening clinic and in 1976 staffed the flu shot clinics which they still maintain. Since 1979 Crotched Mountain Center for Crippled Children in New Hampshire has benefitted from the handmade Christmas tree ornaments and colorful lap robes donated by the club.

The Sterling Woman's Club continues till today an Interfaith Thanksgiving service begun in 1975 and introduced a health clinic with free monthly blood pressure checks. Two years later a cardiac pulmonary resuscitative heart saver program started and the club was awarded two Resusi-Ann mannequins by Channel 5 WCVB and the Massachusetts Heart Association for instructional use. In 1978 the woman's club joined with other local organizations to blaze "the Butterick School Nature Trail."

The Westborough Woman's Club donated a stereo to their library and gave funds toward purchase of an Explorer Post 85 van. The Westminster Woman's Club aided the community in the purchase of Jaws of Life equipment and introduced young women students to community service by inviting them to become junior complimentary club members and help with the annual fashion show — their main fund raiser for scholarships.

Harvard ran three Powder Puff Clinics for local women and participated in the Nashoba Hospital Building Fund. They contributed five hundred dollars to landscaping around the library and donated a granite drinking fountain placed on the common.

Programming returned to the early days as history repeats itself. The cost of professional programs led to local speakers, health and community groups, and our own members.

In the line of self-help programs many clubs sponsored Crime Watch programs and ran rape clinics and object identification marking programs. The Gardner Woman's Club worked on crime prevention projects featuring "McGruff" and continues to donate to the police department's safety patrol fund. Running Bloodmobiles and visiting nursing homes are their primary concerns. The Clio Club of Ashburnham in 1986-87 raised funds for the restoration of the Dolly Whitney Adams School to house the town library. The members continue to sponsor Bloodmobiles, candidate nights, and beautification of three traffic triangles in town. CPR (cardiac pulmonary resuscitative) classes were conducted by many clubs in their communities.

Many clubs such as Shrewsbury, Westminster, Harvard, Holden, and Hudson, donated to the purchase of Jaws of Life and CPR equipment including video equipment for classes, resuscitation equipment, and airbags and other equipment for volunteer fire and ambulance groups. In 1980 the Hudson Woman's Club supported the Hudson Beautification Committee's plans to landscape the town hall grounds. The following two years the Hudson Girls' Club benefitted from the ongoing support of the club with the donation of an Audubon Society learning program, records, and other equipment, plus monetary donations for their clubhouse. Crime prevention was also focused on during the eighties. Support for a bandshell to be erected in Wood Park (Hudson's Bicentennial Project) continues to be given, and many members are active in conservation, working to clean up the Assabet River which flows through the park and Hudson.

In 1981 Westborough installed fire hydrant spotters on their community roads to help fire fighters. The oldest club, Worcester, celebrated its 100th anniversary in 1980 with a special program. The Auburn Woman's Club donated a closed-circuit radio to their public library.

In 1980, as the Clinton Women's Club CIP project, a generous donation started a drive to purchase a new curtain for the stage in the town hall auditorium. The following year, money raised by bus trips paid for a curtain at the back of the stage as well. In 1986 the CIP Project was the reupholstering of two antique round seats owned by the Clinton Historical Society.

Since 1982 the Holden Woman's Club has held an annual antique show and craft fair as a fund raiser for scholarships. In 1985-86 the club made a generous donation to the White Oaks Conservation Commission for repairs to a dam in Holden.

The Southborough Woman's Club redecorated the front hall and powder room of the local Community House in 1981 and continues a practice begun that year of donating staples to the Salvation Army every November.

The Spencer Monday Club has a CIP project this year (1987) of distributing house numbers for the town and continues to focus on veterans' services.

In 1981 the Sterling Woman's Club celebrated the town's two hundredth birthday by contributing to a colonial-type bandstand in the new Memorial Park.

The Upton Woman's Club continued its community service through the eighties with a CIP project in 1985 of planting a flowering pear tree, celebrating the one hundredth anniversary of the town hall. The town of Upton had its 250th anniversary in 1985 and the club sponsored a float in the parade. In addition, many club members were involved in publishing a history called *Upton's Heritage.* The club is donating planters and shrubs to beautify the area around the town library building as its project this year.

Millbury Woman's Club participated in the renovation of the library donating $11,500 to furnish the children's section. Westminster, from 1982 to 1984, undertook sponsoring a community bulletin board and from 1984 to 1986 helped finance the first computer for public use in the library, and is now working on buying a set of software for it.

Leicester Woman's Club is currently raising funds to provide a hearing ear dog for a resident of the town and completing plans for a recognition dinner for FISH volunteers.

The Fortnightly Club of Leominster sponsored a historical twenty-two page coloring book called *My Leominster,* written by one of its members.

Lunenburg continues to support the Ritter Memorial Library, football boosters, and Music Aiders formed to encourage young people in the music field.

The Federation Story

In 1984 and 1985 the Templeton Woman's Club applied for and received an Arts Council grant to conduct poetry and creative writing contests in the Narragansett Regional District. Continuing their support of the upgrading of recreational areas, the Paxton Woman's Club in 1986 served 140 hot meals at the construction site of the new Richard Leather-designed playground, and are donating benches for the theater area.

173

Winchendon continues to visit five veterans' hospitals and three local nursing homes. In 1986 the Current Topics Club in Lancaster continued its never-ending work on their clubhouse by applying for grants to insulate and install storm windows.

West Boylston raised funds for a permanent concession stand for public use at town athletic fields. In 1985 the Auburn Woman's Club started a beautification project in Auburn.

Scholarship programs continue strong with many clubs, such as Clio Club of Ashburnham, Whitinsville, and Westborough, sending students to attend Hugh O'Brian Foundation programs. Students in our state have received thousands of dollars in scholarships. The clubwomen in the central region became much more active in legislation — calling legislators, writing countless letters in support of safety on the highways, better roads, highway markers, clean air and water, preservation of wetlands, and support for victims of crime. Many women have positions in town and state government. Thousands of volunteer hours are logged by clubwomen in town and school libraries, hospital auxiliaries, blood donor clinics, crime prevention campaigns, such as Channel 7 (WNEV) Boston's "Priority One," election days, and cancer screening clinics. There is active participation at Federation meetings and service on various committees. Such state programs as "Day at the State House" and Home Life Department conferences are well attended.

In addition to local concerns, through the years support was always given to the Federation focal points — the restoration of Clough House in Boston, the bell tower at Cathedral of the Pines in New Hampshire, the Memorial Forest in Sudbury, as well as rallying to support the state presidents' programs such as the Talking Information Center. The central region clubwomen, in addition to demonstrating intelligence, compassion, dedication, persistence, and farsightedness, have one more quality — that of salesmanship! Countless buttons, cookbooks, crafts, stuffed toy symbols such as McGruff, the crime prevention dog, and cup plates have been sold to help us reach our goals. Tickets to antique and craft fairs, fashion shows, plays and musicals, card parties, and auctions are constantly passing through their hands.

Their greatest source of leadership and inspiration has always been the women who serve as the State Federation presidents. The Central Region is proud of the fact that seven state presidents have been chosen from its clubs: Miss Georgie A. Bacon, 1908-11, Worcester Woman's Club; Mrs. Thomas J. Walker, 1934-36, Whitinsville Woman's Club; Mrs. Harvey E. Greenwood, 1946-48, Clinton Women's Club; Mrs. Lewis C. Stevens, 1950-52, Worcester Woman's Club; Mrs. Thomas L. Porter, 1962-63, Worcester Woman's Club; Mrs. Garry R. Keessen, 1980-82, Whitinsville Woman's Club; and Mrs. Royce E. Beatty, 1986-88, Upton Woman's Club.

Members from the Central Region who served the General Federation of Women's Clubs in leadership roles included Miss Georgie A. Bacon, Mrs. Garry R. Keessen, and Mrs. Royce E. Beatty.

Though there has been a membership loss because of the return of women to the work force, clubs continue to be formed — Auburn Junior Woman's Club in 1985 and the newest club in the region, the Tri-Community Junior Woman's Club of Southbridge, founded in 1986.

Priority changes and new problems arise to be addressed. The suicides among young people in Leominster has encouraged that club to work actively, developing suicide awareness programs, a sad example but nonetheless encouraging that we are identifying the problems of a new generation and seeking ways to solve them.

August 30, 1987, was a red letter day in the history of MSFWC with the dedication of our new headquarters building in the Memorial Forest in Sudbury. The beautifully-designed cup plates sold to promote this undertaking now grace the homes of members and friends far and wide. Each club in the Central Region, either by donation or personal effort, shared in this huge undertaking, but the Southborough Woman's Club with the first five hundred dollar donation in 1984, and the Clinton Women's Club with a $1,000 donation, must be recognized. Now that MSFWC has its "home", the long-sought recognition as a viable volunteer organization will be obtained. As a part of this organization, hopefully the accomplishments of the Central Region in the past will be equalled or surpassed in the future.

Western Region

Agawam Women's Club

The "Friendship Tea" for senior citizens which was started in the fall of 1940 has continued yearly till the present. The club now has two "Teas" yearly, one in the spring and one in the fall.

Though the club has grown smaller in number it continues to work diligently for the town. The club has always taken an interest in the young people, which is demonstrated by the Annual Scholarship Food Sale which raises funds not only for club projects, but also to award a scholarship to a deserving high school senior. Club members have a deep interest in the drug problems facing our youth, and not too many years ago the club furnished a Counseling Center and two members served on the board of directors.

A great deal of history has been written since Minerva Davis, a charter member, purchased the Captain Charles Leonard House and told the club they could call it "home". The club has met there ever since and continues to carry out the traditions started many years ago.

Amherst Women's Club

For many year club members entertained patients of the Northampton State Hospital at regular teas. This practice was discontinued when the hospital no longer functioned.

In 1971 the members decided to reject an offer to buy the Club House, tear it down, and build a modern building which would contain a suite of rooms for club use. Following this decision, the club embarked on an extensive program of renovation and refurbishment of the Club House, a labor of both love and frustration that continues to this day. At present the house is rented almost every weekend as the beautiful site of weddings, receptions, and parties, in addition to seminars and meetings that occur during the week.

In 1975 the club held the first annual arts and craft show and sale. This event has grown and developed until it outgrew the Club House and is now held each fall in the Amherst Regional Junior High School and has become a major fund-raising event.

Members of the Amherst Women's Club continue to adhere to the original ideals set forth by the founders. The club is proud of its contributions to the community as club members support with their time and gifts the Amherst Boys and Girls Club, the Senior Surrey, Cooley Dickinson Hospital, the Chorale of Amherst Regional High School and other local projects. Each year "ditty bags" are filled for the Veterans Hospital as well as contributions of one or more afghans.

Granby Woman's Club

In 1964 the club joined with the Granby PM Club to raise money each year for a scholarship to be given a high school graduate. During

1970 the club helped beautify the former Durant property. This property was presented to the town by Elbert Aldrich, and the club had a boulder moved onto the lawn with a plaque inscribed to the memory of Elbert Aldrich. Also in 1975, the club established the Brown-Ellison Memorial Park as a bicentennial project and still takes responsibility for the upkeep of the park.

The club has sponsored Girl Scout and Brownie troops; given camperships; sponsored the girls' basketball team of the Granby Athletic Association; and a children's ballet at the school. The home and community service committee distributes Christmas plants or remembrances to the shut-ins in the community at Christmas time, and they keep the historical monuments clean and plants growing.

Southampton Woman's Club

In 1964 the club was honored to win the State CIP award for its efforts in dramatizing and effecting the improvement of unsanitary sewage disposal at the center of town near the park. This health hazard was corrected and the park further improved by planting the Woman's Club Memorial Grove. In recent years, the club has sponsored candidate nights; has awarded scholarship grants to high school seniors; has held flu and diagnostic clinics for the elderly and a town-wide informational health fair; has aided in staffing and improvement of the Clark-Chapman Historical House; has worked with the Park Commission and other service clubs to plan and equip a playground at the town park, and has completed a large project of numbering the streets in town. Club members worked to compile an informational booklet to be given to new residents in town.

Presently many members work outside their homes in business, health, education, and public service fields. The founders of the original "Home Economics Club" would be pleased to know that the women of Southampton are still working to fulfill the motto "For the Greatest Good."

Southwick Women's Club

Perhaps one of the most gratifying projects of the club has been the Bloodmobile. During World War II the American Red Cross started the blood bank and the women's club ran the canteen that went with it. At that time the American Red Cross came to Southwick but once a year, collecting approximately eighty-eight pints of blood. In 1980 the Southwick Women's Club began sponsoring five Bloodmobiles a year, now collecting between 400-488 pints of blood a year. Club members are volunteers among the nurses, clerical workers, canteen attendants, with behind the scene workers making telephone calls, posters, and doing other publicity to promote this worthy cause.

Probably the most talked about service presented by the club is its service to the senior citizens. The members bake and donate cakes for their birthday parties and other important functions. The main affair though is the Senior Citizens Christmas Party. The Southwick Congregational Church donates the use of their facilities for this occasion. The women provide food galore for a pot-luck luncheon, and there is entertainment and gifts for the enjoyment of 100 to 150 senior citizen guests.

The Adult Education Program in Southwick was created by a group of women in the club but was later assumed by the public school system. The Safety Programs devised by the club's safety committee brought awards from the Sears Foundation as well as the Liberty Mutual Insurance Company Foundation. There were bike registrations and Safety Clinics, and in the last few years the club sponsored the Crime Watch Program and the finger-printing program in conjunction with the local police department and Woodland School.

There are many needs, and the Southwick Women's Club is doing their best to take care of as many as they can and pass the torch of human services on to others. Part of their job is to create awareness to the needs of others. In this way the women of the Southwick Women's Club are doing their part.

Northfield Fortnightly Club

In 1969 the first Scholarship Fund was established. In 1975 the club helped the Historical Society document the Main Street houses, and in 1981 an exhibit of art by the local elementary school children was held.

In 1984 a chicken pie supper was served in October as a fund raiser. It proved so successful that it has been made an annual event and provides an opportunity for participation in some form by all members.

The Fortnightly Club has met its aim to stimulate intellectual improvement, civic interest, and social service.

Tuesday Club of Warren

The club has a long history of women serving the Federation in various capacities, most notably Mrs. Charles E. Shepard who served as president of the Massachusetts State Federation in 1960-62. She not only served the Federation with enthusiasm and dignity, but has helped many a Tuesday Club president with advice and guidance when called upon.

Several years ago the name of the club was changed from Tuesday Club of Warren to Tuesday Club, since many members were from West Brookfield and Brimfield.

178 ## Western Massachusetts Women's Club

For many years the club had its traditional Spring Card Party, which was its only fund raising event of the year. In 1981 this was changed to a Fashion Show and Wine Tasting and has proven very successful.

The Western Massachusetts Women's Club is unique in the respect that its members come from so many different communities, the club does not attempt to carry out any projects of the Federation in any particular community. Rather, it supports the programs and projects of the Federation and donates to its various departments and scholarships.

The Western Massachusetts Women's Club has had four presidents of the Massachusetts State Federation: Mrs. Charles Shepard of Warren, Mrs. Clarence F. Clark of Sunderland, Mrs. Paul E. Congdon of Springfield, and Mrs. Edward C. Warner of Sunderland.

Wilbraham Women's Club

Following a survey by the club in 1965, Housing for the Elderly became a reality. The Council on Aging was formed and a second survey resulted in Home Care Services, a hot lunch program, a Health Clinic and Senior Citizen transportation. Later the club implemented the "Vial of Life" program. A preschool vision and hearing screening program was organized in 1971, now in its sixteenth year, tests about 300 children annually. CPR programs, a Bloodmobile, and swimming instruction are also conducted each year. Our encouragement and financial assistance have been extended to the Children's Museum, the Atheneum Society, Wilbraham Counseling Center, the Wilbraham Public Library, and other community needs as they arose.

Much emphasis has been placed in recent years upon the Scholarship Endowment Fund. Craft fairs, fashion shows, home tours, bake sales, bridge parties, and a cook book have contributed greatly to this effort. The most financially rewarding projects have been participation in the Wilbraham United Players' Gilbert and Sullivan productions. A source of great pride has been the Wilbraham Telephone Directory, published by the club every other year.

The Wilbraham Women's Club honors the past, enjoys the present, and builds for the future.

Athol Woman's Club

The sixties were mainly devoted to community service projects. The March of Dimes club volunteers collected $1,236, and in 1966 the club members gave a total of 965 hours to community service.

Charlemont Woman's Club

In the early sixties the club was active in supporting the formation of an ambulance service for the town. The year 1975 found the club taking over the town Christmas tree; working with several other organizations who supplied oranges, candy, Cracker Jack, etc. and then packaging all items for presentation to children of all ages to the sixth grade. This continues to be a club project.

The club was active in 1980 in initiating a drive to expand the area of toll free telephone calls. Today townspeople are now able to call toll free throughout the Franklin County area.

At the present time club projects consist of: the Charlemont Town Christmas Tree, maintaining a flower bed at the "Hail to the Sunrise" statue on the Mohawk Trail, giving a scholarship of at least one hundred dollars to a local student, and holding a candidates' night for local elected town officials.

Though the club has dropped to a membership of less than thirty members, it is still active and working to meet the purpose of the club: "To promote the intellectual and social life of its members and to contribute to the welfare of the community."

The Woman's Club of Greenfield

The club is one of the most active groups in the area, its members volunteered over 2,000 hours in support of community projects in 1985 and can always be depended on for donating knitted and crocheted afghans, lap robes, hats, mittens, and therapy balls for the veterans, both men and women, in the Holyoke Soldiers' Home and Leeds.

In 1985 the club donated Temple Woods, "the 56 acres of land", to the Town of Greenfield to be kept in its natural state for the benefit of the townspeople.

The Sunderland Woman's Club

The Sunderland Woman's Club through the years has furnished leadership for the State Federation, and in 1967-69 Mrs. Clarence Clark (Frances), was elected president of the MSFWC. Her theme, "Today's Best is Tomorrow's Beginning", was a challenge to the Federation to move forward to new goals and to higher levels of achievement. Perhaps this was best demonstrated on the local level when in April 1967 the Frances M. Clark Award was announced in Sunderland to honor her at the beginning of her administration and to establish a scholarship to be given each year at commencement to a high school senior going to college. Over the years this award has helped more than twenty-five young people during their first year at college.

A Sunderland Woman's Club book of "Favorite Recipes" published during her term of office showed the high regard the members had for her as expressed on the dedication page — "with pride in her past service, with faith in her future accomplishments, with gratitude for her loyalty, and with affection from all."

Achievements on the state level under her leaderhip made an impact on the local level in many ways. Attendance at meetings increased, new members were added, and broader goals were set. A few of the highlights within the Federation had a way of spilling over into the work of the local club. There was the 75th Anniversary Celebration of MSFWC — the Diamond Jubilee, the New England Conference held at the Yankee Drummer Inn, and those five days in Boston when MSFWC was host to the General Federation annual meeting in June. In addition, the lease of a "right of way" through Memorial Forest in Sudbury to the Tennesee Gas Company was made possible through her leadership — a real benefit to the Federation. Then the fire at New Ocean House, meeting place of MSFWC for years, made it necessary to change the place of the annual meeting within three days with the same program! Frances proved equal to the leadership task here again.

In 1978 the Sunderland Woman's Club furnished another president to the MSFWC, Mrs. Edward C. Warner (Mary). Her theme — "Invest in the Future" was demonstrated early in her administration when she presented the first ten souvenir shares for the Endowment Fund for the State Federation to the Sunderland Woman's Club.

The stand-up bulletin board placed on the grounds of the Graves Memorial Library in Sunderland was a constant reminder of Mary's interest in education and her confidence in young people, as well as the close tie between the club and the library through the years. One important achievement under her leadership was the building of two elementary schools in Huacho, Peru, through CARE, Inc. It was a thrill to see this project become a reality for a group of youngsters in another part of the world and to know that the club members in Sunderland really cared enough to support this project.

Under the leadership of Mrs. Warren Bennett, club president in 1978-80,

Souvenir stock certificate was used for enrollment in president's project during Mary Warren's administration, 1978-1980.

the club started sponsorship of the "Great Decisions" discussion group, and since then it has offered the community the opportunity to participate each February and March.

In reviewing some of the activities of the Sunderland Woman's Club since its inception, the members are grateful for the fine leadership represented, and for the spirit of cooperation and goodwill among members that have made all accomplishments possible.

Agawam Junior Women's Club

In the 1960s there was no Agawam Senior Center or transportation van. Much of the responsibility for giving service to senior citizens was accomplished by the juniors. They supplied needed transportation as well as companionship, especially at holiday times. Children of members sent cards, sang Christmas carols, entertained at local nursing homes, and sometimes just spent time with many of Agawam's senior citizens. Because of the time, the caring and the thoughtfulness, the Agawam Council for Aging awarded the Golden Deeds Award in 1965 and 1966 to the Agawam Junior Women's Club.

The American History and Language Awards given to two high school seniors were changed to two scholarships awarded to two deserving seniors, largely due to the success of the Juniors' Annual Fall Dance and Fashion Show.

During the Vietnam years, the juniors pitched in to let the hometown boys know they were remembered. Through the years 1965-1974, the juniors put together boxes of books, pens, razor blades, soap, writing paper, and, of course, baked goods which were sent to Vietnam hospitals as well as to thirteen Agawam men serving in Vietnam. This service was done twice each year, Christmas and Easter.

The girls embarked upon the second ten years of club membership by donating much time and effort helping to redecorate the State School at Belchertown. Because of these efforts, the juniors were awarded a Certificate of Merit in 1969 from the school.

Continuing their efforts during Vietnam, the juniors began a town letter-writing campaign to Hanoi to help in the release of the 1,500 American POWs held there. Over a thousand letters were mailed in 1970. Next, they erected a billboard in Feeding Hills Center to promote the awareness of the plight of our prisoners of war. In 1974 the Agawam juniors again were there with a contribution towards the Vietnam Orphan Airlift.

During the past ten years the juniors have turned much of their time and efforts toward local concerns. This began with sponsoring a local candidates' night in 1977. This was closely followed in 1978 by the first Arts and Crafts Festival, held yearly ever since, on the Capt. Charles Leonard House grounds. It is from this annual effort that funds for the scholarships they award are now derived. During this same year, funds were donated to the town to supply all crossing guards with signs, and the juniors received the Olympics Bronze Medal for their contribution in clearing the town of trash, metal, and other debris.

About this same time the Agawam juniors also began the annual Safety Bus Tours, using a local police officer and the "Safety Bug" to introduce new bus-riding students to school transportation safety. Safety film strips were also donated to Agawam schools by the juniors. In recognition of their efforts in "Safety-Awareness," Liberty Mutual awarded the Agawam juniors their Safety Award in both 1978 and 1979.

The juniors were quick to respond with their time and love when volunteers were needed to help with patterning exercises for a local boy recovering from a drowning accident. Many of these same girls continued their support in 1980 thru 1982.

Understandably concerned about the increasing numbers of missing children, the Agawam juniors and the local police department organized a fingerprinting clinic in 1982-83 for all town children. This was such a success that the juniors are planning to conduct a second clinic in 1987 or 1988.

In 1984 the "HAPPE" handicapped puppets were first introduced into the elementary schools by the Agawam juniors. These puppets are still being used to teach children about the different aspects of their handicapped peers.

The juniors' 1986-1988 club project was "Teen Suicide." They held their annual Valentine Dance in February 1987, with all profits going toward this very timely problem. They were also considering other projects as well as becoming involved with the Task Force on Teen Suicide being directed by the Springfield Area Center for Human Development.

Whenever there is a worthy project, or a problem that needs attention, you can be sure the Agawam Junior Women's Club will be there, trying to accomplish something!

Meadows Junior Woman's Club, Inc.

Joined Massachusetts State Federation in 1972 and General Federation 1972.

The Meadows Junior Woman's Club was founded in September 1972 by Judy Lederer and sixteen other members.

Since its inception the club has been active in community affairs. From 1972-1973, thirteen hundred poison plant sheets were distributed to all the elementary grades, kindergarten to grade 4; a pre-school eye clinic was held with 140 children tested; a Punch and Judy Puppet Show was held at the East Longmeadow Library and Longmeadow Elementary School with a total of 330 adults and children attending; a benefit softball game was held with proceeds going to the Hampden County Association for Retarded Children; and a candy sale was held to benefit the Kidney Foundation.

In 1974 the club sponsored a baby-sitting course which was attended by over seventy boys and girls at four one-hour sessions. During this time the club's education committee did extensive work to form a local association of children with learning disabilities, and in the years that followed money was raised for LUPUS and information concerning this disease was put in newspapers and the Longmeadow Library; a CPR course was organized by the public affairs committee; children's activity books were finished and distributed to area hospitals; and Thanksgiving baskets were made and distributed to the needy.

In recent years a toy, book, and clothing drive was held for the

Children's Study Home; clothes were collected for Loretto House (a home for battered women) and the local Loaves and Fishes; and books were donated to the East Longmeadow Nursing Home to fill their bookcarts which the club had previously donated.

These are just some of the major works that the Meadows Junior Woman's Club has accomplished in the past fourteen years. This history does not include those numerous details that every clubwoman, past and present, has to attend to in order to achieve a successful year and a successful club.

Wilbraham Junior Woman's Club

Joined the Massachusetts State Federation in 1977 and General Federation 1977.

The Wilbraham Junior Woman's Club was started in 1977 by Helene Trombley, a former member of the Agawam Junior Women's Club. The club serves the Wilbraham community by conducting an annual "Baby-sitting Clinic" for junior high school students; sponsors the town Easter Egg Hunt each year; and awards an annual scholarship to a deserving local high school senior in June.

In 1980 The Wilbraham Junior Woman's Club placed second as a state winner in the Massachusetts Federation Community Improvement Program for their "Mr. Yuk" project. This was a twenty minute original animated safety skit which stressed "Mr. Yuk," the poison warning symbol used by poison centers in the National Poison Center Network. The skit warned against the dangerous products found around the home and was presented to over 3,000 school children in Western Massachusetts. In 1985 the club, in cooperation with the Public Access Cable Television Station of Longmeadow, videotaped the skit and now VCR tapes are available to all schools through their local libraries.

Holyoke Women's Club, Inc.

Today, the Holyoke Women's Club holds its meetings at the Holyoke War Memorial Building, except for Christmas dinners and American Home Day. These are necessarily not as elaborate as in past years, but still enjoyable and always to be anticipated with joy.

Many services performed by this club have become unnecessary to continue because of existing social reforms and programs. The women do not have to keep a list of acceptable bakeries and grocery stores, and make periodic checks to maintain names of cleanly operated establishments. Children now have many champions that do past tasks; milk is now

distributed in schools; hot lunches are served, etc. The poor will always
be with us, but today there are agencies and resources. Nevertheless,
members still help wherever or whenever they are called upon to do so.

The Holyoke Women's Club members have in the recent past been involved in many community projects: crime prevention, veterans' welfare,
library work, etc. The members have always been loyal and ready to serve,
and the years ahead will be marked by the same cooperation, although
the members are fewer in numbers. They are not faint of heart.

NO GREATER or more drastic
changes in lifestyle have occurred
since the Federation was orga-
nized in 1893 than during the last quarter century. As today's teen-agers
would say, "It's awesome!" Not only was the women's work force increasing
but we were also facing the "graying of America." These factors certainly
affected the Massachusetts State Federation of Women's Clubs. Another
subtle influence was the attitude nationwide towards the Vietnam War
which aroused negative feelings of patriotism for many citizens.

Reflecting the "graying of America," club memberships became older.
Many imaginative programs were devised and supported to meet the needs
of senior citizens, such as senior housing, the Vial of Life, and Meals-on-
Wheels.

Members were concerned with the growing number of missing
children and sponsored fingerprinting. Other concerns included the drug
scene and many clubs initiated programs to combat this menace. Retarded
and brain-damaged children were another priority. Some clubs urged the
use of safety vests for newsboys while others established Crime Watches
in their home towns and shelters to protect battered women. Scholarships
were another priority for all clubs and reaching out beyond our borders,
the Federated women built two elementary schools in Peru.

The Bloodmobile, Jaws of Life, flu clinics, an ambulance service —
all these showed our support of good health in many communities.

Indicating its continued respect for history, the Federation helped
with the restoration of the Clough House. In addition the Fearing House

and Standish House were restored by local clubwomen, as well as the Thornton Burgess Museum.

To complete the Federation record the following section presents brief vital statistics about each member club, and the final part lists for ready reference a chronology of important events during the Federation's first century of service.

Thus we have walked through the pages of history of the Massachusetts State Federation of Women's Clubs for ninety-five years. Beginning with the visionary goals of the Federation members in 1893, we have been inspired by the difference our Federation has made on our lives, on our Commonwealth, our country, and even on our world. Reaching out from coast to coast and across the oceans we have helped make this world a better place. Time and again we have received the gauntlet, we have accepted it and won. There is still much to do but we have the past to guide us into the future of an even better world.

MEMBER CLUBS

Town	Club	Founded	State Federated
Abington	Abington Women's Club	1898	1900
Acton	Acton Junior Woman's Club	1972	1972
Acton	West Acton Woman's Club	1896	1899
Agawam	The Agawam Junior Women's Club	1958	1958
Agawam	The Agawam Women's Club	1926	1926
Allston	Brighthelmstone Club	1896	1897
Amesbury	Elizabeth H. Whittier Club	1896	1897
Amherst	Amherst Community Women's Club (Jr.)	1970	1970
Amherst	Amherst Junior Woman's Club	1970	1970
Amherst	Amherst Woman's Club	1893	1895
Andover	The Shawsheen Village Woman's Club	1921	1922
Andover	Tuesday Club	1904	1905
Arlington	Arlington Heights Study Club	1907	1913
Arlington	Arlington Woman's Club	1895	1896
Arlington	Kensington Park Study Club	1911	1921
Ashburnham	Clio Woman's Club of Ashburnham	1905	1909
Ashland	Ashland Woman's Club	1890	1899
Assonet	The Tuesday Club of Assonet, Massachusetts, Inc.	1893	1937
Athol	Athol Junior Woman's Club	1973	1973
Athol	Athol Woman's Club, Inc.	1900	1911
Attleboro	Attleboro Round Table	1895	1896
Attleboro	Etaerio	1894	1902
Attleboro	Junior Woman's Club of Attleboro	1957	1957
Attleboro	New Century Club	1897	1905
Attleboro	North Purchase Club	1900	1901
Attleboro	Pierian Club	1896	1899

Town	Club	Founded	State Federated
Auburn	Auburn Junior Woman's Club	1985	1985
Auburn	Auburn Woman's Club	1924	1926
Auburndale	Auburndale Woman's Club, Inc.	1914	1914
Ayer	Ayer Woman's Club	1898	1899
Baldwinville	Baldwinville Woman's Club	1899	1899
Barnstable	Barnstable Woman's Club, Inc.	1922	1922
Barre	Barre Woman's Club	1916	1921
Bedford	Bedford Woman's Community Club	1920	1920
Bellingham	Bellingham Junior Woman's Club, Inc.	1972	1973
Belmont	Belmont Woman's Club	1920	1920
Berlin	Berlin Tuesday Club	1898	1898
Beverly	Lothrop Club of Beverly	1895	1896
Billerica	Billerica Young Woman's Club	1973	1973
Billerica	Nineteen Hundred Club of Billerica	1900	1904
Blackstone	Blackstone Alpha Club	1896	1896
Boston	Agnes Carr Writers' Club	1941	1942
Boston	Beta Sigma Phi, Boston Area Council	1931	1967
Boston	Boston City Federation of Organizations, Inc.	1912	1912
Boston	Boston Eastern Star Women's Club	1923	1923
Boston	Boston Parliamentary Law Club	1912	1913
Boston	Boston Teachers' Club, Inc.	1898	1950
Boston	Canadian Women's Club	1907	1920
Boston	The Chatterbox Club	1919	1954
Boston	The Continued Interest Club of Boston	1944	1945
Boston	Council Club	1958	1958
Boston	Daughters of Canada	1944	1953
Boston	Daughters of Vermont	1894	1896
Boston	The Directors' Club	1931	1932

Town	Club	Founded	State Federated
Boston	Evening Division Past Presidents' Club	1964	1964
Boston	Goodwill Auxiliary to Morgan Memorial	1905	1924
Boston	Greek Ladies Philoptohos Society – Philoptohos Society of the Greek Orthodox Cathedral of N.E.	1912	1954
Boston	Harvard Woman's Club of Boston, Inc.	1913	1915
Boston	Junior League of the Women's Italian Club	1920	
Boston	Junior Past Presidents' Club	1969	1969
Boston	Ladies' Physiological Institute	1848	1899
Boston	League of Women for Community Service, Inc.	1918	1920
Boston	Massachusetts International Relations Club	1946	1946
Boston	Massachusetts-Maine Daughters	1918	1918
Boston	Massachusetts State Committee of the American Mother's Committee, Inc.	1954	1968
Boston	Music Lovers' Club of Boston	1911	1953
Boston	National Association of Railway Business Women	1953	1965
Boston	National Council of Jewish Women, Inc. (Greater Boston Section)	1896	1905
Boston	The New England Hotel Women's Relief Association, Inc.	1927	1929
Boston	New England Women's Club	1868	1893
Boston	Old Glory Club	1924	1966
Boston	Past Chairmen's Club	1936	1937
Boston	Past Junior Officers Club	1982	1982
Boston	The Presidents' Club of Massachusetts	1916	1916

Town	Club	Founded	State Federated
Boston	The Professional Women's Club, Inc.	1907	1907
Boston	Resthaven Junior Club	1937	1952
Boston	Sepia Hi-Fi Club of Boston	1955	1958
Boston	The Women's Italian Club of Boston	1916	1917
Boston	Women's Organization, Boston Association Retail Druggists	1906	1907
Boston	The Women's Service Club of Boston, Inc.	1919	1959
Boston	1st District Presidents' Club	1931	1935
Boston	2nd District Past Presidents' Club	1929	1939
Boston	3rd District Presidents' Club	1940	1946
Boston	4th District Presidents' Club	1965	1965
Boston	5th District Presidents' Club	1931	1932
Boston	6th District Presidents' Club	1946	1946
Boston	7th District Presidents' Club	1932	1932
Boston	8th District Presidents' Club	1932	1932
Boston	9th District Presidents' Club	1926	1926
Boston	10th District Presidents' Club	1939	1939
Boston	11th District Presidents' Club	1946	1967
Boston	12th District Past Presidents' Club	1940	1941
Boston	13th District Presidents' Club	1931	1932
Boston	14th District Presidents' Club	1935	1935
Boston	15th District Presidents' Club	1935	1935
Bourne	Bourne Junior Women's Club	1950	1950
Bourne	Old Colony Union Women's Club of Bourne	1911	1914
Braintree	Braintree Junior Philergians	1927	1927
Braintree	Braintree Point Woman's Club	1921	1924
Braintree	Braintree Women's Club	1955	1955
Braintree	The Philergians	1899	1901
Brewster	Brewster Woman's Club	1911	1913
Bridgewater	Bridgewater P. M. Club (Evening Division of Ousamequin Club)	1947	1951

Town	Club	Founded	State Federated
Bridgewater	Ousamequin Club	1898	1899
Brockton	Junior Women's Club of Brockton	1934	1934
Brockton	P. M. Club of Brockton	1944	1951
Brockton	Woman's Club of Brockton	1898	1899
Brookline	Brookline Woman's Club, Inc.	1917	1917
Burlington	Burlington Junior Woman's Club	1970	1970
Cambridge	Cambridge Women's Club	1892	1892
Cambridge	The Cantabrigia Club	1892	1893
Canton	The Community Club of Canton	1912	1913
Carver	Sassamanesh Junior Women's Club	1976	1976
Charlemont	Charlemont Woman's Club	1898	1924
Charlestown	Norumbega Woman's Club	1893	1895
Chatham	Chatham Junior Woman's Club	1977	1977
Chatham	Chatham Woman's Club, Inc.	1915	1915
Chelmsford	Chelmsford Junior Woman's Club	1975	1975
Chelsea	Chelsea Woman's Club	1893	1895
Chicopee Falls	Chicopee Falls Woman's Club	1894	1897
Chilmark	Woman's Community Club of Chilmark	1927	1932
Clinton	Clinton Women's Club	1896	1897
Cohasset	Cohasset Women's Club	1927	1927
Concord	The Concord, Massachusetts Woman's Club	1895	1896
Concord	West Concord Woman's Club	1902	1911
Danvers	Danvers Women's Association	1882	1893
Dartmouth	Dartmouth Enrichment League (EDM)	1971	1972
Dartmouth	Dartmouth Woman's Club	1948	1954
Dedham	Dedham Junior Woman's Club, Inc.	1979	1979
Dedham	Dedham Women's Club	1893	1895

Town	Club	Founded	State Federated
Deerfield	Deerfield Woman's Club	1925	1925
Dennis	Dennis Women's Club	1956	1956
Dennis	GFWC Dennis Junior Women's Club	1963	1963
Dennis and Yarmouth	Dennis-Yarmouth Junior Woman's Club	1963	1963
Dorchester	Athena Club	1897	1897
Dorchester	Dorchester Woman's Club	1892	1893
Dorchester	Ladies Unity Club, Inc.	1892	1893
East Boston	Woman's Club of the East Boston School Center	1913	1920
East Boston	Sachem Young Woman's Club of East Bridgewater	1961	1961
East Bridgewater	Woman's Club of East Bridgewater	1913	1914
East Freetown	East Freetown Woman's Club	1925	1928
East Longmeadow	Meadows Junior Woman's Club, Inc.	1972	1972
Easthampton	Woman's Club of Easthampton	1917	1920
Easton	Outlook Club of Easton, Inc.	1888	1902
Edgartown	Edgartown Woman's Club	1898	1924
Everett	The Friday Club of Everett	1891	1894
Falmouth	Falmouth Junior Woman's Club (Junior Outlook Club of Falmouth)	1950	1950
Falmouth	Falmouth Woman's Club (Outlook Club)	1904	1915
Feeding Hills	Feeding Hills Community Women's Club	1926	1948
Fitchburg	Fitchburg Woman's Club	1894	1895
Foxboro	Foxboro Woman's Club	1901	1912
Framingham	Framingham Junior Woman's Club (Framingham Young Woman's Club)	1957	1957
Framingham	Framingham Women's Club	1889	1894

194

Member Clubs

Town	Club	Founded	State Federated
Framingham	Lake Shore Women's Club	1954	1955
Franklin	Alden Club	1892	1893
Gardner	Gardner Woman's Club	1909	1909
Gloucester	Gloucester Woman's Club	1920	1921
Grafton	Grafton Woman's Club	1911	1915
Granby	Granby P. M. Club	1950	1950
Granby	Granby Woman's Club	1908	1909
Great Barrington	Thursday Morning Club	1892	1893
Greenfield	Poet's Seat Junior Woman's Club	1973	1973
Greenfield	The Woman's Club of Greenfield	1911	1912
Greenfield	Young Women's Club of Greenfield	1969	1969
Greenwood	Greenwood Junior Woman's Club	1938	
Greenwood	Greenwood Woman's Club	1934	1934
Groton	Groton Woman's Club	1913	1913
Groton	Mountain Lakes Woman's Club	1936	1938
Hanover	Hanover Woman's Club Juniors	1970	1970
Harvard	Harvard Woman's Club	1913	1913
Harwich	Harwich Junior Woman's Club, Inc.	1952	1952
Harwich	The Harwich Woman's Club	1921	1927
Harwich	Harwich Women's Club, Evening Division	1969	1970
Haverhill	Haverhill Woman's Club	1904	1905
Hingham	Hingham Junior Woman's Club	1954	1954
Hingham	Hingham Woman's Club	1921	1921
Hingham	P. M. Club of Hingham	1954	1955
Hingham	Riverview Woman's Club of Hingham	1954	1954
Hingham	Timely Topics Club	1923	1923
Holden	Chaffins Woman's Club	1951	1951

Town	Club	Founded	State Federated
Holden	Holden Woman's Club	1915	1915
Holliston	Holliston Woman's Club	1956	1956
Holyoke	Holyoke Women's Club, Inc.	1923	1924
Hopedale	Hopedale Community House Woman's Club	1924	1928
Hopkinton	Hopkinton Woman's Club	1920	1926
Hudson	Apple Valley Young Women's Club (Jr.)	1973	1973
Hudson	Hudson Woman's Club	1898	1899
Hull	Hull Woman's Club	1919	1919
Hyannis	Fine Arts League	1970	1970
Hyannis	Hyannis Junior Woman's Club	1948	1949
Hyannis	The Hyannis Woman's Club	1900	1901
Hyde Park	The Hyde Park Current Events Club	1894	1895
Hyde Park	Hyde Park Thought Club	1881	1893
Ipswich	Ipswich Woman's Club	1898	1900
Jamaica Plain	Jamaica Plain Tuesday Club, Inc.	1896	1897
Jamaica Plain	Women's Association of the Massachusetts Osteopathic Hospital	1927	1940
Lake Pleasant	The Lake Pleasant Woman's Club	1941	1942
Lancaster	Lancaster Current Topics Club, Inc.	1897	1898
Lawrence	Greater Lawrence Italian Women's Club	1933	1948
Lawrence	Lawrence Woman's Club	1892	1893
Lawrence	Tuesday Sorosis of Lawrence	1899	1904
Leicester	Leicester Woman's Club	1962	1962
Leominster	Fortnightly Club of Leominster	1897	1914
Littleton	Littleton Woman's Club	1897	1899
Longmeadow	Junior Women's Club of Longmeadow	1985	1985

Member Clubs

Town	Club	Founded	State Federated
Lowell	Middlesex Woman's Club	1894	1895
Ludlow	Ludlow Woman's Club	1908	1909
Lunenburg	Lunenburg Woman's Club	1913	1923
Lynn	Atalanta Club of Lynn	1903	1904
Lynn	Evening Club of Lynn, Inc.	1953	1953
Lynn	Outlook Club	1896	1897
Lynn	Woman's Club of Lynn, Inc.	1936	1936
Lynnfield	The Centre Club	1925	1926
Lynnfield	Lynnfield Woman's Club	1923	1938
Magnolia	Women's Community Club of Magnolia	1947	1948
Malden	Junior Old and New of Malden	1931	1931
Malden	Linden Woman's Club (Linden Mothers' Club)	1924	1931
Malden	Maplewood New Century Club	1900	1901
Malden	Old and New of Malden	1878	1895
Malden	Suburban Club	1965	1965
Manchester	Manchester Woman's Club	1908	1908
Mansfield	New Century Club	1900	1907
Mansfield	P. M. Division, New Century Club	1956	1956
Marblehead	Harbor Women's Club	1963	1963
Marblehead	Hobbs Community Club	1931	1934
Marblehead	Marblehead Women's Club	1913	1915
Marion	Sippican Woman's Club	1904	1906
Marlborough	Marlborough Junior Woman's Club	1964	1965
Marlborough	Marlborough Woman's Club	1906	1906
Marshfield	Marshfield Woman's Club	1927	1928
Marshfield	Marshfield Woman's Club, Evening Division, Inc.	1947	1951
Mattapoisett	Mattapoisett Woman's Club	1941	1941
Maynard	Maynard Woman's Club	1904	1905
Maynard	Maynard Young Woman's Club	1973	1974
Medfield	Hannah Adams Woman's Club of Medfield	1894	1894

Town	Club	Founded	State Federated
Medford	Medford Women's Club	1892	1894
Medford	The Mothers' Club of Medford Hillside	1905	1929
Medway	Medway Woman's Club	1911	1911
Melrose	Melrose Highlands Woman's Club	1898	1901
Melrose	Melrose Woman's Club	1882	1895
Melrose	Women's Club of Melrose, Inc.	1984	1984
Merrimac	Merrimac Woman's Club	1914	1915
Methuen	Methuen Women's Club	1927	1928
Methuen	Woman's Civic Club of Methuen	1949	1950
Middleborough	The Cabot Club	1897	1900
Middleborough	Junior Cabot Club	1950	1950
Middleton	Middleton Women's Club	1928	1931
Milford	Milford Junior Woman's Club, Inc.	1974	1974
Milford	Quinshipaug Woman's Club	1897	1899
Millbury	Millbury Woman's Club, Inc.	1894	1897
Millis	Oak Tree League of Millis	1975	1975
Milton	Milton Junior Woman's Club, Inc.	1933	1933
Milton	Milton P. M. Club (Milton Woman's Club, Evening Division)	1950	1950
Milton	Milton Woman's Club	1898	1900
Monson	Monson Woman's Club	1899	1922
Montague	Montague Junior Woman's Club	1965	1965
Nahant	Nahant Woman's Club	1895	1896
Natick	The Evening Division Club of Natick	1950	1950
Natick	Natick Woman's Club	1895	1896
Needham	The Junior New Century Club	1935	1935
Needham	The New Century Club of Needham, Massachusetts	1909	1909

198

Town	Club	Founded	State Federated
New Bedford	Ivy Circle of New Bedford (EDM)	1949	1949
New Bedford	The New Bedford Juniors	1967	1967
New Bedford	New Bedford Woman's Club, Inc.	1897	1981
Newburyport	Newburyport Woman's Club	1896	1896
Newton	Newton Community Club	1919	1919
Newton	Newton Community Club, Inc. Evening Division	1952	1952
Newton	Newton Federation of Women's Clubs	1895	1901
Newton	Nonantum Women's Club	1970	1970
Newton Centre	Newton Centre Woman's Club, Inc.	1887	1896
Newton Centre	The Oak Hill Park Woman's Club	1949	1950
Newton Highlands	Woman's Club of Newton Highlands	1917	1917
Newton Upper Falls	Newton Upper Falls Woman's Club	1919	1920
Newtonville	Newtonville Woman's Club, Inc.	1884	1892
Norfolk	Norfolk Neighborly Club	1912	1914
North Adams	Fortnightly Club	1892	1900
North Andover	North Andover Woman's Club	1935	1935
North Attleboro	Fidamie Club	1955	1955
North Attleboro	The Kalmia	1895	1897
North Easton	The Clover Club of Easton	1891	1904
North Grafton	North Grafton Junior Woman's Club	1935	
North Grafton	North Grafton Woman's Club	1911	1915
North Leominster	Whalom Woman's Club	1921	1924
North Quincy	Atlantic Women's Club	1918	1920

Town	Club	Founded	State Federated
North Reading	The Upland Club	1911	1912
North Reading	West Village Women's Club	1912	1915
Northampton	The Northampton Woman's Club, Inc.	1926	1927
Northborough	Northborough Junior Woman's Club, Inc.	1975	1975
Northborough	Northborough Woman's Club	1894	1897
Northfield	The Fortnightly	1904	1928
Norwood	Norwood Woman's Club	1900	1900
Norwood	Young Women's Evening Division of the Norwood Woman's Club	1960	1960
Oak Bluffs	Triad Club	1908	1926
Onset	Onset Woman's Club, Inc.	1923	1923
Orange	Orange Woman's Club	1922	1922
Orange	Pioneer Junior Woman's Club	1971	1971
Orleans	Nauset Junior Woman's Club (Orleans Junior Woman's Club)	1965	1965
Orleans	Orleans Woman's Club	1921	1923
Oxford	Oxford Woman's Club	1950	1951
Palmer	The Palmer Woman's Club	1902	1903
Paxton	Paxton Woman's Club	1930	1931
Peabody	The Peabody Woman's Club	1895	1897
Pembroke	Hanson-Pembroke Women's Club	1957	1977
Pepperell	The Pepperell Woman's Club	1906	1907
Plymouth	Plymouth Woman's Club	1912	1987
Provincetown	Nautilus Club	1907	1908
Quincy	Montclair Women's Club	1949	1954
Quincy	Peninsula Women's Club	1951	1951
Quincy	P. M. Club of Quincy	1982	1982
Quincy	P. M. Division of Quincy Women's Club	1945	1945

Town	Club	Founded	State Federated
Quincy	Quincy Federation of Women's Organizations	1914	1915
Quincy	Quincy Women's Club	1905	1906
Quincy	Quincy Women's Club Juniors	1929	1936
Quincy	Squantum Women's Club	1912	1914
Randolph	Junior Ladies' Library Association	1933	1933
Randolph	Ladies' Library Association	1855	1895
Reading	Reading Junior Woman's Club	1954	1954
Reading	Reading Woman's Club	1893	1895
Revere	Revere Junior Woman's Club	1931	1931
Revere	Revere Women's Club, Inc.	1894	1897
Rochester	Rochester Woman's Club, Inc.	1928	1934
Rockland	Rockland P. M. Club	1951	1951
Rockland	Rockland Woman's Club	1906	1906
Rockport	Rockport Woman's Club	1914	1915
Roslindale	P. M. Club of Roslindale	1936	1936
Roslindale	Roslindale Woman's Club	1911	1911
Roslindale	Roslindale Young Woman's Club	1936	1936
Salem	The Thought and Work Club of Salem, Inc.	1891	1893
Sandwich	Sandwich Junior Woman's Club	1970	1970
Sandwich	Sandwich Woman's Club	1924	1924
Saugus	Cliftondale Woman's Club	1911	1920
Saugus	M. M. Club	1915	1930
Saugus	Riverside Club of Saugus	1898	1899
Saugus	Saugus Woman's Club	1911	1920
Scituate	The P. M. Club of Scituate	1949	1959
Scituate	Scituate Woman's Club	1904	1906
Sharon	The Fortnightly Club of Sharon, Inc.	1897	1898
Sharon	Junior Fortnightly Club of Sharon	1935	1935

202

Town	Club	Founded	State Federated
Shelburne Falls	Mohawk Junior Woman's Club	1970	1970
Shelburne Falls	Shelburne Falls Woman's Club	1925	1925
Shirley	The Altrurian Club, Inc.	1893	1901
Shrewsbury	Shrewsbury Woman's Club	1904	1907
Somerset	Somerset Woman's Club, Inc.	1928	1928
Somerset	Somerset Woman's Club, Inc., P. M. Division	1950	1950
Somerville	Forthian Club	1899	1899
Somerville	Heptorean and Somerville Woman's Club	1894	1895
Somerville	Old Powder House Club	1905	1905
South Ashburnham	Bay State Woman's Club	1914	1925
South Boston	The Mattapannock Woman's Club	1899	1899
South Deerfield	South Deerfield Women's Club	1897	1906
South Easton	The Browning Club	1895	1915
South Hadley	South Hadley Woman's Club	1898	1901
South Hadley Falls	South Hadley Falls Woman's Club	1898	1901
South Hadley Falls	The Club of Sohaywo	1957	1957
South Weymouth	Old Colony Club	1897	1897
South Weymouth	Old Colony Junior Women's Club of South Weymouth	1961	1961
South Weymouth	Old Colony P. M. Club	1949	1950
South Yarmouth	South Yarmouth Woman's Club	1915	1924
Southampton	Southampton Woman's Club	1917	1923
Southborough	Southborough Woman's Club	1903	1904
Southbridge	Southbridge Woman's Club	1914	1914
Southbridge	Tri-Community Junior Woman's Club	1986	1986
Southwick	Southwick Women's Club	1924	1924
Spencer	Spencer Monday Club	1892	1895
Springfield	Early Morning Club	1899	1916

Member Clubs

Town	Club	Founded	State Federated
Springfield	East Springfield Women's Club	1924	1930
Springfield	Italian Women's Club of Springfield	1921	1926
Springfield	Valley Women's Club	1960	1960
Springfield	Western Massachusetts Women's Club	1912	1914
Sterling	Sterling Woman's Club	1943	1944
Stoneham	Stoneham Woman's Club	1899	1899
Stoughton	Fieldbook Young Women's Club of Stoughton	1960	1960
Stoughton	Stoughton Woman's Club	1926	1926
Stoughton	Stoughton Woman's Club Juniors	1940	1940
Stow	Stow Woman's Association	1913	1921
Sudbury	Sudbury Woman's Club	1910	1911
Sudbury	The Natural Resources Club	1948	1950
Sunderland	Sunderland Woman's Club	1894	1898
Swampscott	Swampscott Fortnightly Club	1914	1917
Swampscott	Swampscott Woman's Club	1888	1893
Taunton	Evening Division of the Taunton Woman's Club	1960	1960
Taunton	Junior Woman's Club of Taunton	1950	1951
Taunton	Taunton Woman's Club	1910	1910
Templeton	Templeton Woman's Club, Inc.	1899	1935
Tewksbury	Tewksbury Junior Woman's Club	1975	1975
Townsend	The Townsend Woman's Club	1933	1933
Turners Falls	Turners Falls Young Woman's Club	1965	1965
Turners Falls	Women's Club of Turners Falls	1911	1912
Upton	Upton Woman's Club	1900	1906
Uxbridge	Uxbridge Woman's Club	1950	1950
Waban	Waban Woman's Club	1896	1899

Town	Club	Founded	State Federated
Wakefield	The Kosmos Club	1895	1896
Wakefield	Wakefield Junior Woman's Club (Greenwood Junior Woman's Club)	1938	1938
Walpole	The Junior Woman's Club of Walpole	1963	
Walpole	Walpole Woman's Club	1895	1895
Waltham	Waltham Mothers' Club	1895	1915
Waltham	Waltham Woman's Club	1893	1896
Waltham	Watch City Woman's Club (Waltham Junior Woman's Club)	1932	1932
Ware	Social Science Club	1885	1913
Wareham	Wareham Junior Monday Club	1950	
Wareham	Wareham Monday Club	1889	1912
Warren	Tuesday Club	1888	1898
Watertown	The Watertown Woman's Club	1894	1894
Wayland	Wayland Woman's Club	1902	1963
Webster	Webster Woman's Club	1916	1916
Wellesley Hills	Wellesley Hills Junior Woman's Club	1947	1947
Wellesley Hills	Wellesley Hills Woman's Club	1890	1894
West Acton	West Acton Woman's Club, Inc.	1896	1899
West Boylston	Woman's Club of West Boylston	1926	1927
West Newbury	The Lamplighters	1964	1964
West Newbury	West Newbury Woman's Club, Inc.	1914	1916
West Newton	The Community Service Club of West Newton	1920	1938
West Newton	West Newton Woman's Club	1962	1962
West Newton	West Newton Women's Educational Club	1880	1893
West Roxbury	Newell Woman's Club	1927	1927
West Roxbury	West Roxbury Woman's Club	1911	1911

Town	Club	Founded	State Federated
West Springfield	The Ramapogue Junior Women's Club	1950	1950
West Springfield	Ramapogue Women's Club	1937	1938
West Springfield	West Springfield Junior Women's Club	1941	
West Springfield	West Springfield Woman's Club	1909	1921
Westborough	Westborough Woman's Club	1916	1917
Westfield	Hampton Ponds Women's Club	1953	1957
Westfield	Westfield Woman's Club	1914	1915
Westford	The Tadmuck Women's Club, Inc.	1905	1913
Westford	Westford Junior Woman's Club	1976	1976
Westminster	Westminster Woman's Club	1953	1953
Westwood	Westwood Woman's Club	1946	1947
Westwood	Westwood Young Woman's Club	1959	1959
Weymouth	Weymouth P. M. Club	1950	1951
Weymouth	Weymouth Women's Club	1976	1976
Weymouth	The Monday Club of Weymouth	1896	1897
Whitinsville	Whitinsville Woman's Club	1921	1921
Whitman	Whitman Woman's Club	1907	1907
Wilbraham	Wilbraham Junior Woman's Club	1977	1977
Wilbraham	Wilbraham Women's Club	1905	1910
Williamsburg	Williamsburg Women's Club	1923	1924
Wilmington	Wilmington Women's Club	1901	1902
Winchendon	The Winchendon Woman's Club	1898	1898
Winchester	The Fortnightly	1881	1896
Winchester	Winchester Woman's Club, Juniors (Winchester Young Woman's Club)	1974	1974
Winthrop	Popular Authors Literary Club	1896	1898

From the Past to the Future

Town	Club	Founded	State Federated
Winthrop	The Zenith Woman's Club of Winthrop	1922	1926
Winthrop	Winthrop Woman's Club	1897	1898
Woburn	Woburn Woman's Club	1883	1893
Wollaston	Wollaston Woman's Club	1913	1913
Wollaston	Wollaston Woman's Club, Juniors	1933	1933
Woods Hole	Woman's Club of Woods Hole	1914	1917
Worcester	Fireside Club	1896	1914
Worcester	Tatnuck Woman's Club	1912	1914
Worcester	Worcester Woman's Club	1880	1896
Wrentham	The Holly Club	1898	1913

IV

CHRONOLOGY

1847	The Ladies' Physiological Institute of Boston established.
1867	New England Women's Club organized.
1880	Ladies' Association of the First Parish Church of Brighton chartered by Commonwealth of Massachusetts.
1890	General Federation of Women's Clubs organized.
1892	Cambridge Women's Club and Newtonville Woman's Club, Inc. joined State Federation.
1893	Massachusetts State Federation of Women's Clubs founded.
1893-1898	Julia Ward Howe (Mrs. Samuel G.), Federation president.
1893	Following clubs joined Federation: Alden Club, The Cantabrigia Club, Danvers Women's Association, Dorchester Woman's Club, Hyde Park Thought Club, Ladies Unity Club, Inc., Lawrence Woman's Club, New England Women's Club, Swampscott Woman's Club, The Thought and Work Club of Salem, Inc., Thursday Morning Club, West Newton Women's Educational Club, Woburn Woman's Club.
1894	Federation joined General Federation of Women's Clubs. Following clubs joined Federation: Framingham Women's Club, the Friday Club of Everett, Hannah Adams Woman's Club of Medfield, Medford Women's Club, the Watertown Woman's Club, Wellesley Hills Woman's Club.
1895	Following clubs joined Federation: Amherst Woman's Club, Chelsea Woman's Club, Dedham Women's Club, Fitchburg Woman's Club, Heptorean and Somerville Woman's Club, Ladies' Library Association, Melrose Woman's Club, Middlesex Women's Club, Old and New of Malden, Norumbega Woman's Club, Reading Woman's Club, Spencer Monday Club, The Hyde Park Current Events Club, Walpole Woman's Club.
1896	Following clubs joined the Federation: Arlington Woman's Club, Attleboro Round Table, Blackstone Alpha club, Daughters of Vermont, Lothrop Club of Beverly, Nahant Woman's Club, Natick Woman's Club, Newburyport Woman's Club, Newton Centre Woman's Club, Inc., The

Concord, Massachusetts Woman's Club, The Fortnightly, the Kosmos Club, Waltham Woman's Club, Worcester Woman's Club.

210

1897   Following clubs joined the Federation: Athena Club, Bright-helmstone Club, Chicopee Falls Woman's Club, Clinton Women's Club, Elizabeth H. Whittier Club, Jamaica Plain Tuesday Club, Inc., Millbury Woman's Club, Inc., Northborough Woman's Club, Old Colony Club, Outlook Club, Revere Women's Club, Inc., The Kalmia, The Monday Club of Weymouth, The Peabody Woman's Club.

1898-1901   Miss Olive M. E. Rowe Federation president.
Following clubs joined Federation: Berlin Tuesday Club, Lancaster Current Topics Club, Inc., Popular Authors Literary Club, Sunderland Woman's Club, The Fortnightly Club of Sharon, Inc., The Winchendon Woman's Club, Tuesday Club, Winthrop Woman's Club.

1899   First Federation manual published.
Following clubs joined Federation: Ashland Women's Club, Ayer Woman's Club, Baldwinville Woman's Club, Forthian Club, Hudson Woman's Club, Ladies' Physiological Institute, Littleton Woman's Club, Ousamequin Club, Pierian Club, Quinshipaug Woman's Club, Riverside Club of Saugus, Stoneham Woman's Club, The Mattapannock Woman's Club, Waban Woman's Club, West Acton Woman's Club, Inc., Woman's Club of Brockton.

1900   Following clubs joined Federation: Abington Woman's Club, Fortnightly Club, Ipswich Woman's Club, Milton Woman's Club, Norwood Woman's Club, The Cabot Club.

1901-1904   Mrs. William G. Ward Federation president.

1901   Following clubs joined Federation: Maplewood New Century Club, Melrose Highlands Woman's Club, Newton Federation of Women's Clubs, North Purchase Club, South Hadley Falls Woman's Club, South Hadley Woman's Club, The Altrurian Club, Inc., The Hyannis Woman's Club, The Philergians.

1902   Following clubs joined Federation: Etaerio, Outlook Club of Easton, Inc., Wilmington Women's Club.

1903   *The Federation Bulletin* first published.
Following club joined Federation: The Palmer Woman's Club.

1904-1907   Miss Helen A. Whittier Federation president.

1904   Following clubs joined Federation: Atalanta Club of Lynn,

Nineteen Hundred Club of Billerica, Southborough Woman's Club, The Clover Club of Easton, Tuesday Sorosis of Lawrence.

1905 Following clubs joined Federation: Haverhill Woman's Club, Maynard Woman's Club, National Council of Jewish Women, Inc. (Greater Boston Section), New Century Club, Old Powder House Club, Tuesday Club.

1906 San Francisco earthquake and fire; Federation as well as individual clubs donated money and clothing.

1906 Following clubs joined Federation: Marlborough Woman's Club, Quincy Women's Club, Rockland Woman's Club, Scituate Woman's Club, Sippican Woman's Club, South Deerfield Women's Club, Upton Woman's Club.

1907-1908 Mrs. William G. Ward Federation president.

1907 Following clubs joined Federation: New Century Club, Shrewsbury Woman's Club, The Pepperell Woman's Club, The Professional Women's Club, Inc., Whitman Woman's Club, Women's Organization, Boston Association Retail Druggists.

1908-1911 Miss Georgie A. Bacon Federation president.

1908 Membership contributed food, clothing, and money to victims of the great Chelsea (Mass.) fire.

1908 Following clubs joined Federation: Manchester Woman's Club, Nautilus Club.

1909 Following clubs joined Federation: Clio Woman's Club of Ashburnham, Gardner Woman's Club, Granby Woman's Club, Ludlow Woman's Club, The New Century Club of Needham, Massachusetts.

1910 Following clubs joined Federation: Taunton Woman's Club, Wilbraham Women's Club.

1911-1913 Mrs. Henry C. Mulligan Federation president.

1911 Federation endowment fund established with goal of $10,000.

1911 Following clubs joined Federation: Athol Woman's Club, Inc., Medway Woman's Club, Roslindale Woman's Club, Sudbury Woman's Club, West Concord Woman's Club, West Roxbury Woman's Club.

1912 Following clubs joined Federation: Boston City Federation of Organizations, Inc., Foxboro Woman's Club, The Upland Club, The Woman's Club of Greenfield, Wareham Monday Club, Women's Club of Turners Falls.

1913-1916	Mrs. George W. Perkins Federation President.
1913	Following clubs joined Federation: Arlington Heights Study Club, Boston Parliamentary Law Club, Brewster Woman's Club, Groton Woman's Club, Harvard Woman's Club, Social Science Club, The Community Club of Canton, The Holly Club, The Tadmuck Women's Club, Inc., Wollaston Woman's Club.
1914	Following clubs joined Federation: Auburndale Woman's Club, Inc., Fireside Club, Fortnightly Club of Leominster, Norfolk Neighborly Club, Old Colony Union Women's Club of Bourne, Southbridge Woman's Club, Squantum Women's Club, Tatnuck Woman's Club, Western Massachusetts Women's Club, Woman's Club of East Bridgewater.
1915	Resolution on woman's suffrage approved by vote of 203 to 99.
1915	Following clubs joined Federation: Chatham Woman's Club, Inc., Falmouth Woman's Club (Outlook Club), Grafton Woman's Club, Harvard Woman's Club of Boston, Inc., Holden Woman's Club, Marblehead Women's Club, Merrimac Woman's Club, North Grafton Woman's Club, Quincy Federation of Women's Organizations, Rockport Woman's Club, The Browning Club, Waltham Mothers' Club, West Village Women's Club, Westfield Woman's Club.
1916-1919	Mrs. Herbert J. Gurney Federation president.
1916	First annual meeting held at New Ocean House, Swampscott.
1916	Following clubs joined Federation: Early Morning Club, The Presidents' Club of Massachusetts, Webster Woman's Club, West Newbury Woman's Club, Inc.
1917	Federation membership sent aid to Halifax, Nova Scotia to aid victims of explosion.
1917-1918	World War I. Federation second among members of General Federation in raising funds for soldiers' recreation overseas.
1917	Following clubs joined Federation: Brookline Woman's Club, Inc., Swampscott Fortnightly Club, The Women's Italian Club of Boston, Westborough Woman's Club, Woman's Club of Newton Highlands, Woman's Club of Woods Hole.
1918	Following club joined Federation: Massachusetts-Maine Daughters.
1919-1922	Mrs. George Minot Baker Federation president; redistricting plan creating fifteen districts approved.

Chronology

1919	Following clubs joined Federation: Hull Woman's Club, Newton Community Club.
1920	Following clubs joined Federation: Atlantic Women's Club, Bedford Woman's Community Club, Belmont Woman's Club, Canadian Women's Club, Cliftondale Woman's Club, Junior League of the Women's Italian Club, League of Women for Community Service, Inc. Newton Upper Falls Woman's Club, Saugus Woman's Club, Woman's Club of Easthampton, Woman's Club of the East Boston School Center.
1921	Following clubs joined Federation: Barre Woman's Club, Gloucester Woman's Club, Hingham Woman's Club, Kensington Park Study Club, Stow Woman's Association, West Springfield Woman's Club, Whitinsville Woman's Club.
1922-1924	Mrs. H. Gilbert Reynolds Federation president.
1922	First permanent headquarters established at 585 Boylston Street, Boston.
1922	Following clubs joined Federation: Barnstable Woman's Club, Inc., Monson Woman's Club, Orange Woman's Club, The Shawsheen Village Woman's Club.
1923	Following clubs joined Federation: Boston Eastern Star Woman's Club, Lunenburg Woman's Club, Onset Woman's Club, Inc., Orleans Woman's Club, Southampton Woman's Club, Timely Topics Club.
1924-1926	Mrs. Frederick G. Smith Federation president.
1924	Following clubs joined Federation: Braintree Point Woman's Club, Charlemont Woman's Club, Edgartown Woman's Club, Goodwill Auxiliary to Morgan Memorial, Holyoke Women's Club, Inc., Sandwich Woman's Club, Southwick Women's Club, South Yarmouth Woman's Club, Whalom Woman's Club, Williamsburg Women's Club.
1925	Following clubs joined Federation: Bay State Woman's Club, Deerfield Woman's Club, Shelburne Falls Woman's Club.
1926-1928	Mrs. Arthur D. Potter Federation president.
1926	Following clubs joined Federation: 9th District Presidents' Club, Auburn Woman's Club, Hopkinton Woman's Club, Italian Women's Club of Springfield, Stoughton Woman's Club, The Agawam Women's Club, The Centre Club, The Zenith Woman's Club of Winthop, Triad Club.
1927	Convention Hall at New Ocean House dedicated to Federation.

1927   Following clubs joined Federation: Braintree Junior Philergians, Cohasset Women's Club, Newell Woman's Club, The Harwich Woman's Club, The Northampton Woman's Club, Inc., Woman's Club of West Boylston.

1928-1930   Mrs. John V. Westfall Federation president.

1928   Following clubs joined Federation: East Freetown Woman's Club, Hopedale Community House Woman's Club, Marshfield Woman's Club, Methuen Women's Club, Somerset Woman's Club, Inc., The Fortnightly.

1929   Following clubs joined Federation: The Mothers' Club of Medford Hillside, The New England Hotel Women's Relief Association, Inc.

1930-1932   Mrs. Carl L. Schrader Federation president.

1930   State Forest presented 150 acres to State.

1930   Following clubs joined Federation: East Springfield Women's Club, Saugus M. M. Club.

1930-1931   Federation operated "Welfare Chest" for unemployed.

1931   Following clubs joined Federation: Junior Old and New of Malden, Linden Woman's Club (Linden Mothers' Club), Middleton Women's Club, Paxton Woman's Club, Revere Junior Woman's Club.

1932-1934   Mrs. Frank P. Bennett Federation president.

1932   Following clubs joined Federation: 5th District Presidents' Club, 7th District Presidents' Club, 8th District President's Club, 13th District Presidents' Club, The Directors' Club, Watch City Woman's Club (Jr.) (Waltham Junior Woman's Club), Woman's Community Club of Chilmark.

1933   Following clubs joined Federation: Junior Ladies' Library Association, Milton Junior Woman's Club, Inc., The Townsend Woman's Club, Wollaston Woman's Club, Juniors.

1934   Following clubs joined Federation: Greenwood Woman's Club, Hobbs Community Club, Junior Women's Club of Brockton, Rochester Woman's Club, Inc.

1934-1936   Mrs. Thomas J. Walker Federation president; club institute founded.

1935   Following clubs joined Federation: 1st District Presidents' Club, 14th District Presidents' Club, 15th District Presidents' Club, Junior Fortnightly Club of Sharon, North Andover Woman's Club, North Grafton Junior Woman's Club,

Templeton Woman's Club, Inc., The Junior New Century Club.

1936	Following clubs joined Federation: P. M. Club of Roslindale, Quincy Woman's Club Juniors, Roslindale Young Woman's Club, Woman's Club of Lynn, Inc.
1936-1938	Mrs. John H. Kimball Federation president.
1937	Following clubs joined Federation: Past Chairmen's Club, The Tuesday Club of Assonet, Massachusetts, Inc.
1938	Following clubs joined Federation: Greenwood Junior Woman's Club, Lynnfield Woman's Club, Mountain Lakes Woman's Club, Ramapogue Women's Club, The Community Service Club of West Newton, Wakefield Junior Woman's Club (Greenwood Junior Woman's Club).
1938-1940	Mrs. Henry W. Hildreth Federation president; "Come to New England" program undertaken.
1939	Following clubs joined Federation: 2nd District Past Presidents' Club, 10th District Presidents' Club.
1940	Following clubs joined Federation: Stoughton Woman's Club Juniors, Women's Association of the Massachusetts Osteopathic Hospital.
1940-1942	Mrs. David A. Westcott Federation president.
1940	Mrs. Herbert Foster proclaimed "Pioneer Clubwoman."
1941	Home Defense Committee formed; almost $100,000 defense bonds purchased by clubs.
1941-1945	World War II
1941	Following clubs joined Federation: 12th District Past Presidents' Club, Mattapoisett Woman's Club, West Springfield Junior Women's Club.
1942	Following clubs joined Federation: Agnes Carr Writers' Club, The Lake Pleasant Woman's Club.
1942-1944	Mrs. George L. Anderson Federation president; all clubs involved with work and projects in support of the war effort.
1944-1946	Mrs. Edwin Troland Federation president; Memorial Education Fund and Memorial Forest Fund established.
1944	Following club joined Federation: Sterling Woman's Club.
1945	Following clubs joined Federation: P. M. Division of Quincy Women's Club, The Continued Interest Club of Boston.
1946-1948	Mrs. Harvey E. Greenwood Federation president.
1946	Following clubs joined Federation: 3rd District Presidents'

Club, 6th District Presidents' Club, Massachusetts International Relations Club.

1947   Following clubs joined Federation: Wellesley Hills Junior Woman's Club, Westwood Woman's Club.

1948-1950   Mrs. A. Chesley York Federation president.

1948   Following clubs joined Federation: Feeding Hills Community Women's Club, Greater Lawrence Italian Women's Club, Women's Community Club of Magnolia.

1949   Following clubs joined Federation: Hyannis Junior Woman's Club, Ivy Circle of New Bedford (EDM).

1950-1952   Mrs. Lewis C. Stevens Federation president.

1950   Sudbury Memorial Forest dedicated; Evening Division created.

1950   Following clubs joined Federation: Boston Teachers' Club, Inc., Bourne Jr. Women's Club, Falmouth Junior Woman's Club (Junior Outlook Club of Falmouth), Granby P. M. Club, Junior Cabot Club, Milton P. M. Club (Milton Woman's Club, Evening Division), Old Colony P. M. Club, Somerset Woman's Club, Inc., P. M. Division, The Evening Division Club of Natick, The Natural Resources Club, The Oak Hill Park Woman's Club, The Ramapogue Junior Women's Club, Uxbridge Woman's Club, Wareham Junior Monday Club, Woman's Civic Club of Methuen.

1951   Following clubs joined Federation: Bridgewater P. M. Club (Evening Division of Ousamequin Club), Chaffins Woman's Club, Junior Woman's Club of Taunton, Marshfield Woman's Club, Evening Division, Inc., Oxford Woman's Club, Peninsula Women's Club, P. M. Club of Brockton, Rockland P. M. Weymouth P. M. Club.

1952-1954   Mrs. Ralph G. Swain Federation president; "Get Out the Vote" campaign resulted in 95 percent of electorate voting.

1952   Following clubs joined Federation: Harwich Junior Woman's Club, Inc., Newton Community Club, Inc., Evening Division, Resthaven Junior Club.

1953   Following clubs joined Federation: Daughters of Canada, Evening Club of Lynn, Inc., Music Lovers' Club of Boston, Westminster Woman's Club.

1954-1956   Mrs. David M. Small Federation president.

1954   Following clubs joined Federation: Dartmouth Woman's Club, Greek Ladies Philoptohos Society, Hingham Junior Woman's

Club, Montclair Women's Club, Reading Junior Woman's Club, Riverview Woman's Club of Hingham, The Chatterbox Club.

1955	Following clubs joined Federation: Braintree Women's Club, Fidamie Club, Lake Shore Women's Club, P. M. Club of Hingham.
1956-1958	Mrs. Kirke L. Alexander Federation president.
1956	Following clubs joined Federation: Dennis Women's Club, Holliston Woman's Club, P. M. Division, New Century Club.
1957	Following clubs joined Federation: Framingham Junior Woman's Club (Framingham Young Women's Club), Hampton Ponds Women's Club, Junior Woman's Club of Attleboro, The Club of Sohaywo.
1958-1960	Mrs. Earl R. Weidner Federation president.
1958	Following clubs joined Federation: Council Club, Sepia Hi-Fi Club of Boston, The Agawam Junior Women's Club.
1959	"Federation Night" of Boston Pops established.
1959	Following clubs joined Federation: The P. M. Club of Scituate, The Women's Service Club of Boston, Inc., Westwood Young Woman's Club.
1960-1962	Mrs. Charles E. Shepard Federation president; second volume of *Progress and Achievement* published.
1960	Following clubs joined Federation: Evening Division of the Taunton Woman's Club, Fieldbrook Young Women's Club of Stoughton, Valley Women's Club, Young Women's Evening Division of the Norwood Woman's Club.
1961	Following clubs joined Federation: Old Colony Junior Women's Club of South Weymoth, Sachem Young Woman's Club of East Bridgewater.
1962-1963	Mrs. Thomas L. Porter Federation president; Restoration of Clough-Langdon House.
1962	Following clubs joined Federation: Leicester Woman's Club, West Newton Woman's Club.
1963-1965	Mrs. Frederick J. Wood Federation president.
1963	Following clubs joined Federation: Dennis-Yarmouth Junior Woman's Club, GFWC Dennis Junior Women's Club, Harbor Women's Club, The Junior Woman's Club of Walpole, Wayland Woman's Club.
1964	Following clubs joined Federation: Evening Division Past Presidents' Club, The Lamplighters.

217

1965-1967	Mrs. Americo Chaves Federation president.
1965	Following clubs joined Federation: 4th District Presidents' Club, Marlboro Junior Woman's Club, Montague Junior Woman's Club, National Association of Railway Business Women, Nauset Junior Woman's Club (Orleans Junior Woman's Club), Suburban Club, Turners Falls Young Woman's Club.
1966	Following club joined Federation: Old Glory Club.
1967-1969	Mrs. Clarence F. Clark Federation president.
1967	Following clubs joined Federation: 11th District Presidents' Club, Beta Sigma Phi, Boston Area Council, The New Bedford Juniors.
1968	Following club joined Federation: Massachusetts State Committee of the American Mother's Committee, Inc.
1969-1971	Mrs. Raymond N. Peterson Federation president.
1969	Following clubs joined Federation: Junior Past Presidents' Club, Young Women's Club of Greenfield.
1970	Following clubs joined Federation: Amherst Community Women's Club (Jr.), Amherst Junior Woman's Club, Burlington Junior Woman's Club, Fine Arts League, Hanover Woman's Club Juniors, Harwich Women's Club, Evening Division, Mohawk Junior Woman's Club, Nonantum Women's Club, Sandwich Junior Woman's Club.
1971-1972	Mrs. Marshall W. Ross Federation president; Presidents' Fund established; *Blueprint for Action* implemented.
1971	Following club joined Federation: Pioneer Junior Woman's Club.
1972-1974	Mrs. Paul E. Congdon Federation president; "Touch and See Trail" developed at Laughing Brook.
1972	Following clubs joined Federation: Acton Junior Women's Club, Dartmouth Enrichment League (EDM), Meadows Junior Woman's Club, Inc.
1973	Following clubs joined Federation: Apple Valley Young Women's Club (Jr.), Athol Junior Woman's Club, Bellingham Jr. Woman's Club, Inc., Billerica Young Woman's Club, Poet's Seat Junior Woman's Club.
1974-1976	Mrs. Eugene G. Faucher Federation president; "Federation Focus", a legislative bulletin published.

1974	Following clubs joined Federation: Maynard Young Woman's Club, Milford Junior Woman's Club, Inc., Winchester Woman's Club, Juniors (Winchester Young Woman's Club).
1975	Following clubs joined Federation: Chelmsford Junior Woman's Club, Northboro Junior Woman's Club, Inc., Oak Tree League of Millis, Tewksbury Junior Woman's Club.
1976-1978	Mrs. John W. Holland Jr. Federation president.
1976	Following clubs joined Federation: Sassamanesh Junior Women's Club, Westford Junior Woman's Club, Weymouth Women's Club.
1977	Following clubs joined Federation: Chatham Junior Woman's Club, Hanson-Pembroke Women's Club, Wilbraham Junior Woman's Club.
1978-1980	Mrs. Edward C. Warner Federation president.
1979	Following club joined Federation: Dedham Junior Woman's Club, Inc.
1980-1982	Mrs. Garry R. Keessen Federation president; Headquarters building project begun.
1981	Following club joined Federation: New Bedford Woman's Club, Inc.
1982-1984	Mrs. F. William Ahearn Federation president; "Good Neighbor Award" given Federation by Channel 7 Priority One for its program on crime awareness and reduction.
1982	Following clubs joined Federation: Past Junior Officers Club, P. M. Club of Quincy.
1984-1986	Mrs. Theodore Billias Federation president; Family economics booklet published.
1984	Following club joined Federation: Women's Club of Melrose, Inc.
1985	Following clubs joined Federation: Auburn Junior Woman's Club, Junior Women's Club of Longmeadow.
1986-1988	Mrs. Royce E. Beatty Federation president; new history published; headquarters established at the Memorial Forest.
1986	Following club joined Federation: Tri-Community Junior Woman's Club.
1987	Following club joined Federation: Plymouth Woman's Club.

List of Illustrations

Julia Ward Howe (Mrs. Samuel G.) 3
May Alden Ward (Mrs. William G.) 5
Helen A. Whittier 6
May Alden Ward (Mrs. William G.) 7
Georgie A. Bacon 8
Minna Rawson Mulligan
 (Mrs. Henry Coolidge) 9
Florence T. Perkins
 (Mrs. George Winslow) 10
Claire H. Gurney (Mrs. Herbert J.) 11
Marion Chase Baker
 (Mrs. George Minot) 12
Grace Poole Reynolds
 (Mrs. H. G. Reynolds) 13
Mabel Johnson Smith
 (Mrs. Frederick Glazier) 14
Mary Pratt Potter
 (Mrs. Arthur Devens) 15
Isabel Packard Westfall
 (Mrs. John V.) 16
Maude Wallace Schrader
 (Mrs. Carl L.) 17
Irene Willard Bennett (Mrs. Frank P.) 18
Viola White Walker (Mrs. Thomas J.) 19
Maria Grey Kimball (Mrs. John H.) 20
Harriet C. S. Hildreth
 (Mrs. Henry W.) 21
Luella P. Westcott (Mrs. David A.) 22
Edith French Anderson
 (Mrs. George L.) 23
Ethel M. Troland (Mrs. Edwin) 24
Edna T. Greenwood (Mrs. Harvey E.) 25
Hortense S. York (Mrs. A. Chesley) 26
Lillian S. Stevens (Mrs. Lewis C.) 27
Ada W. Swain (Mrs. Ralph G.) 28
Esther Z. Small (Mrs. David M.) 29

Florence Alexander (Mrs. Kirke L.) 30
Natalie B. Weidner (Mrs. Earl R.) 31
Marcia E. Shepard (Mrs. Charles E.) 32
Lillian A. Porter (Mrs. Thomas L.) 33
Mary H. Wood (Mrs. Frederick J.) 34
Irene C. Chaves (Mrs. Americo) 35
Frances M. Clark (Mrs. Clarence F.) 36
Beatrice A. Peterson
 (Mrs. Raymond N.) 37
Eleanor B. Ross (Mrs. Marshall W.) 38
Helen C. Congdon (Mrs. Paul E.) 39
Catherine M. Faucher
 (Mrs. Eugene G.) 40
Ann L. Holland (Mrs. John W., Jr.) 41
Mary E. Warner (Mrs. Edward C.) 42
Annette M. Keessen (Mrs. Garry R.) 43
Bernice E. Ahearn (Mrs. F. William) 44
Penny Billias (Mrs. Theodore) 45
Nancy Beatty (Mrs. Royce E.) 46
Historic Jonathan Belcher House,
 Randolph 54
Ladies' Library Association
 Clubhouse, Randolph 55
Standish House, New Bedford 56
Whiton Hall, Dorchester 64
Dorchester Club Seal 64
Meetings of yesteryear 73
Bas relief plaque presented by
 Philergians of Braintree to
 Braintree High School 88
Rochester Woman's Clubhouse 90
Simeon Daggett mansion, Taunton 91
Somerset Woman's Clubhouse 92
Sippican Woman's Clubhouse 93
Milton Woman's Clubhouse 96
Belmont Woman's Clubhouse 98
Lancaster Woman's Clubhouse 104
First meeting house at Memorial
 Forest in Sudbury 117

List of Illustrations

Cover of the Memorial Education
Fund scrapbook of contributors,
designed by John Morrison 118
Abington Woman's Club Choral
Group at Cathedral in the
Pines, 1957 125
Parker Tavern, Reading 130
Bridge of Flowers, Shelburne Falls 140
Blind children on "Touch and See"
nature trail at Hale Reservation,
Westwood 142
Cathedral of the Pines, Rindge,
New Hampshire 144
Clough House, Boston 145
Logo of Priority One, WNEV-TV
award to the Federation 146
Present headquarters building,
Memorial Forest, Sudbury 147
General Federation of Women's Clubs
International headquarters,
Washington, D. C. 148

A day at the State House in 1982,
Boston 149
Talking Information Center (TIC) at
Liberty Plaza, Marshfield 150
Invitation to Bicentennial Anniversary
Ball, 1975 151
Dancing the minuet at Harwich
Bicentennial Anniversary Ball 151
Winning design for Federation
cup plate 152
Jericho House, Dennis 154
Hillside, home of the Quincy
Women's Club 156
Southborough club members admiring
afghans knitted for veterans 160
Souvenir stock crtificate used for
enrollment in president's project 181

INDEX

Index

Abington Woman's Club, 52, 53, 54, 87, 89, 121, 122, 124, 154, 189, 210

Adams, Hannah Woman's Club (see Hannah Adams Woman's Club)

Agawam Junior Women's Club, 139, 140, 181, 182, 183, 189, 217

Agawam Women's Club, 76, 134, 174, 189, 213

Ahearn, Bernice E. (Mrs. F. William), vii, x, 44, 62, 99, 149, 219

Aldrich, Elbert, 109, 176

Alexander, Marie Day, 15

Alexander, Mrs. Elisha, 82

Alexander, Florence (Mrs. Kirke L.), 30, 120, 139, 217

Amesbury — Elizabeth Whittier Club, 68, 100, 101, 130, 189, 210

Amherst Woman's Club, 76, 107, 108, 135, 175, 189, 209

Anderson, Edith French (Mrs. George L.), 23, 24, 116, 215

Andrews, Edith, 158

Apple Valley Young Women's Club, Hudson, 166, 169, 196, 218

Arlington Heights Study Club, 60, 189, 212

Arlington Woman's Club, 14, 60, 127, 189, 209

Ashland Historical Society, 57

Ashland Women's Club, 57, 95, 126, 159, 189, 210

Athol Woman's Club, 80, 112, 138, 179, 189, 211

Auburn Junior Woman's Club, 166, 174, 190, 219

Auburn Woman's Club, 171, 173, 190, 213

Bacon, Miss Georgie A., 6, 8, 51, 174, 211

Bagg, Mrs. Ernest, 79

Baker, Marion Chase (Mrs. George Minot), 12, 13, 83, 84, 212

Baldwinville Woman's Club, 169, 190, 210

Barclay, Miriam, 166

Barclay, Mrs. Robert, 130

Barre Woman's Club, 105, 106, 131, 170, 190, 213

Barron, Judge Jennie Loctman, 56

Bates, Katherine Lee, 12

Beatty, Nancy B. (Mrs. Royce E.), viii, ix, 46, 150, 174, 219

Bedford Woman's Community Club, 97, 127, 161, 162, 191, 213

Bellingham Junior Woman's Club, 160, 190, 218

Belmont Woman's Club, 97, 162, 190, 213

Bennett, Irene Willard (Mrs. Frank Pierce), 18, 85, 214

Bennett, Mrs. Warren, 180

Berlin Tuesday Club, 70, 74, 75, 103, 105, 107, 134, 167, 190, 210

Bersani, Ron, 45

Beveridge, Frank S., 42

Billias, Penny (Mrs. Theodore), 45, 149, 163, 219

Blanchard, Thelma, 166

Blackington, Mr. Alton Hall, 112

Booth, George F., 75

Boston City Federation of Organizations, 60, 98, 128, 190, 211

Boston Parliamentary Law Club, 66, 190, 212

Boston Women's Symphony Orchestra, 15, 84

Bott, Mrs. Homer, 101

Bourne Women's Club, 54, 87, 124, 154, 192, 212

Brackett, Dr. Jeffrey R., 54

Braintree Junior Philergians, 86, 89, 123, 124, 156, 192, 214
Braintree Point Woman's Club, 86, 87, 89, 90, 122, 123, 155, 192, 213
Braintree Women's Club, 121, 123, 192, 217
Brewster Woman's Club, 53, 89, 121, 124, 154, 157, 192, 212
Bridgewater Improvement Association, 58
Bridge of Flowers, 113, 139
Brockton Woman's Club (Woman's Club of Brockton), 52, 87, 91, 123, 193, 210
Brookline Woman's Club, 62, 193, 212
Bronson, Professor Charles P., 61
Brown, Mr. and Mrs. Dennison, 99
Buck, Mrs. Edgar J., 79
Burgess, Thornton W., 39, 154, 186
Burlington Junior Woman's Club, 193, 218

Cabot Club of Middleboro, The, 52, 53, 87, 89, 125, 156, 198, 210
Caldwell, Sarah, 159
Carlman, Beverly, 164
Carnegie, Andrew, 67
Centre Club, Lynnfield, 197, 213
Chaffins Woman's Club, 133, 167, 195, 216
Charlemont Study Club, 112
Charlemont Woman's Club, 80, 112, 179, 193, 213
Chatham Woman's Club, 53, 139, 193, 212
Chaves, Irene B. (Mrs. Americo), 35, 62, 142, 218
Chelsea Woman's Club, 193, 209
Chenowith, Mrs., 72
Chicopee Falls Woman's Club, 77, 108, 135, 193, 210
Churchill, Mrs. George B., 108

Clark, Frances M. (Mrs. Clarence F.), 36, 62, 143, 178, 179, 180, 218
Clarke, Mrs. James Freeman, 65
Clinton Women's Club, 72, 74, 106, 131, 167, 168, 169, 170, 171, 174, 193, 210
Clio Club of Ashburnham, 70, 105, 107, 132, 134, 167, 171, 173, 189, 211
Clough-Langdon House, 33, 34, 36, 37, 40, 43, 44, 99, 141, 142, 143, 148, 149, 165, 173, 185
Clover Club of Easton, 94, 95, 199, 211
Cobb, Eunice H. (Mother Cobb), 62
Cole, Mrs., 129
Community Club of Canton, 57, 95, 193, 212
Congdon, Helen C. (Mrs. Paul E.), 39, 143, 178, 218
Coolidge, Mabel, 165
Custer, Mrs. (General), 72
Crocker, Mrs. Emmons, 9

Danforth Junior Woman's Club, 94
Danvers Women's Association, 66, 163, 193, 209
Dartmouth Enrichment League, 152, 158, 193, 218
Daughters of Vermont, 26
Davis, Minerva, 175
Decker, Mrs. Sarah Platt, 6
Dedham Junior Woman's Club, Inc., 160, 193, 219
Del Castillo, Mrs. Nina, 102
Delphian Chapter, 110
Dennis Junior Women's Club, 152, 155, 194, 217
Dennis Women's Club, 121, 122, 194, 217
Dickinson, Mrs. Margaret, 135
Dix, Dorothy, 66
Dorchester Woman's Club, 62, 194, 209
Dukakis, Governor Michael, 158
Dwight, Mrs. William G., 79, 114

East Bridgewater Woman's Club (Woman's Club of East Bridgewater), 95, 159, 194, 212

East Freetown Woman's Club, 86, 194, 214

Eastman, Mrs. Maud C., 78

Edgartown Woman's Club, 87, 124, 155, 194, 213

Eighth District Presidents' Club, 100, 102, 131, 166

Eleventh District Presidents' Club, 104, 133

Elizabeth H. Whittier Club, Amesbury (see Amesbury — Elizabeth Whittier Club)

Elliott, Maude Howe, 56, 59

Emerson, B. K., 76

Epps, Miss Mary L., 80

Era Club of Boston, 50

Evening Division Club of Lynn, Inc., 129, 197, 216

Evening Division Club of Natick, 126, 161, 198, 216

Evening Division Past Presidents' Club, 66

Evensen, Phyllis, 166

Fairchild, Eloise Tower, 81

Falmouth Woman's Club, 87, 89, 90, 121, 124, 153, 194, 212

Farmer, Fannie, 56, 65, 68

Faucher, Catherine M. (Mrs. Eugene G.), 40, 62, 146, 165, 218

Federation Choral Society, 14

Federation Topics, 13, 19, 45

Fifth District Presidents' Club, 161

Fifteenth District Presidents' Club, 115

First District Presidents' Club, 86

Fitchburg Woman's Club, 72, 74, 106, 131, 132, 167, 170, 194, 209

Forbes, Mrs. J. Malcolm of Milton, 9

Ford, Henry, 26

Fortnightly Club of Leominster, 74, 75, 106, 132, 168, 169, 172, 196, 212

Fortnightly Club, Northfield, 110, 200, 214

Fortnightly, Winchester, 66, 67, 101, 164, 205, 219

Foster, Mrs. Herbert, 90

Fourteenth District Presidents' Club, 115, 141

Fourth District Presidents' Club, 161

Foxboro Woman's Club, 159, 194, 211

Framingham Girl's Club, 94

Framingham Women's Club, 94, 126, 194, 209

Framingham Young Women's Club, 194, 217

French, Mrs. Herbert F. (Anderson), see Edith French Anderson

Framingham Junior Woman's Club, 194, 217

Furcolo, Governor, 30

Gardner Woman's Club, 103, 107, 132, 133, 171, 195, 211

Garfield, James, 57

Gifford, Miss Chloe, 27

Gloucester Woman's Club, 100, 195, 213

Goddard, Miss Lucy, 65

Goddard, Professor R. H., 103

Granby P. M. Club, 135, 195, 216

Granby Woman's Club, 78, 108, 135, 175, 195, 211

Gray, Mrs. Ada Warner, 78

Grebenstein, Georgia, 165, 166

Greenwood, Edna T. (Mrs. Harvey E.), 25, 36, 117, 174, 215

Groton Woman's Club, 164, 195, 212

Guest, Edgar, 56

Gurney, Claire H. (Mrs. Herbert J.), 11, 55, 83, 212

Hale, Mrs. Eleanor, 79

Hampden County Progressive Club, 79

Hampden County Women's Club, 111

Hannah Adams Woman's Club of Medfield, 57, 197, 209

Hanover Woman's Club Juniors, 195, 218

Hartley, Raymond C., 122

Harvard Woman's Club, 72, 74, 75, 103, 133, 171, 195, 212

Harwich Junior Woman's Club, 121, 157, 195, 216
Harwich Woman's Club, 87, 89, 90, 154, 195, 214
Harwich Woman's Club, Evening Division, 152, 157, 195, 218
Headquarters, Federation (MSFWC), 13, 15, 17, 18, 24, 30, 45, 46, 117, 128, 151, 152, 174
Heckler, Congresswoman Margaret M., 40
Hildreth, Harriet C. S. (Mrs. Henry W.), 21, 85, 215
Hills, Mrs. Alice M. (Dwight L.), 107, 108
Hingham Woman's Club, 86, 195, 213
Holden Woman's Club, 75, 106, 131, 133, 167, 171, 172, 196, 212
Holland, Ann L. (Mrs. John W., Jr.), 41, 62, 146, 153, 165, 219
Holyoke, Mrs. Frank, 114
Holyoke Women's Club, Inc., 114, 184, 185, 196, 213
Home Economics Club, 78
Hopkinton Woman's Club, 94, 126, 160, 196, 213
Houghton, Audrey, 165
Howe, Julia Ward (Mrs. Samuel G.), 3, 9, 13, 33, 36, 50, 57, 59, 60, 65, 68, 72, 101, 108, 209
Howe, Dr. Samuel Gridley, 64
Hudson Woman's Club, 71, 73, 75, 76, 106, 132, 133, 168, 169, 170, 171, 196, 210
Hunt, Dr. Harriet K., 61, 62, 65
Hyannis Junior Woman's Club, 121, 124, 196, 216
Hyde Park Thought Club, 95, 196, 209

Ivy Circle of New Bedford, 121, 125, 155, 157, 199, 216

Jackson, Anita, vii, x
Jacobs, Mrs. Alice Taylor, 63
Jarvis, Amy, 158
Jenks, Rev. Dr., 62
Jolson, Al, 102
Junior Cabot Club of Middleboro, 121, 198, 216
Junior Ladies' Library Association of Randolph, 86, 201, 214
Junior Woman's Club of Newton Highlands, 94
Junior Fortnightly Club of Sharon, 126, 201, 214
Junior New Century of Needham, 95, 126, 198, 215
Junior Past Presidents' Club, 66
Junior Woman's Club of Bourne, 121, 192, 216
Junior Woman's Club of Taunton, 121, 203, 216
Junior Woman's Club of West Boylston, 105
Junior Women's Club of Longmeadow, 196, 219

Kallock, Mrs., 158
Kalmia Club of North Attleboro, 58, 159, 199, 210
Keessen, Annette M. (Mrs. Garry R.), 43, 148, 174, 219
Keller, Helen, 56
Kennedy, President John F., 34
Kennedy, Senator Edward, 167
Kensington Park Study Club, Arlington, 60, 189, 213
Kimball, Maria Grey (Mrs. John H.), 20, 85
King, Sharon, 42
Kosmos Club, Wakefield, 67, 100, 101, 130, 164, 165, 204, 210

Ladies' Association of the First Parish Church of Brighton, 209
Ladies' Library Association of Randolph, ix, 49, 52, 53, 54, 87, 89, 122, 123, 201, 209

Index

Ladies' Mission Club, 79
Ladies' Physiological Institute of Boston, ix, 49, 61, 191, 209
Lake Pleasant Woman's Club, 196, 215
Lancaster Current Topics Club, Inc., 71, 72, 75, 132, 166, 167, 168, 170, 196, 210
Larson, Mrs. Elinar T., 127
Lasselle, Betty (Mrs. Ralph E.), 166
Lawrence Woman's Club, 68, 102, 196, 209
Lederer, Judy, 183
Lee, Gerald Stanley, 76
Leicester Woman's Club, 71, 131, 166, 169, 172, 196, 217
Lindsey, Judge Ben, 61
Linkletter, Art, 36
Littleton Woman's Club, 67, 101, 102, 129, 196, 210
Livermore, Mrs. Mary, 65
Lothrop, Captain Thomas, 68
Lothrop Club of Beverly, 66, 67, 68, 101, 102, 128, 129, 164, 190, 209
Lowe, Alice, 158
Lunenburg Woman's Club, 73, 104, 105, 106, 167, 170, 172, 197, 213
Lynn Woman's Club, 100, 129, 163, 197, 210
Lynnfield Woman's Club, 100, 101, 164, 197, 215

MacAlster, Mrs. Fred S., 98
MacArthur Club, 132
MacCurdy, Eleanore (Mrs. Robert D.), vii, x
Magrane, Florence, vii, x, 166
Manchester Woman's Club, 197, 211
Mar, Solomon E., 125
Marlboro (Marlborough) Junior Woman's Club, 166, 167, 168, 197, 218
Marlborough Woman's Club, 197, 211
Marshfield Woman's Club, 123, 197, 214
Marshfield Woman's Club, Evening Division, 121, 153, 155, 197, 216
Massachusetts-Maine Daughters, 66, 191, 212
Mattapannock Woman's Club, 99, 202, 210
Mattapoisett Woman's Club, 87, 123, 153, 154, 197, 215

McCall, Mrs. Samuel, 61
McMann, Aina (Mrs. Earl D.), 163
Meadows Junior Woman's Club, Inc., 183, 184, 194, 218
Medford Junior Women's Club, 26, 130
Medford Women's Club, 26, 66, 100, 129, 130, 198, 209
Melrose Highlands Woman's Club, 164, 198, 210
Melrose Woman's Club, 164, 198, 209
Memorial Forest, x, 24, 25, 26, 28, 34, 37, 38, 40, 41, 45, 46, 99, 117, 119, 120, 143, 151, 152, 153, 164, 173, 174, 180, 215, 216, 219
Men's Country Club, 92
Merritt, Dr. Salome, 62
Merritt, President, 63
Metcalf, Conger, 159
Millbury Woman's Club, Inc., 70, 74, 103, 133, 167, 172, 198, 210
Milton Junior Woman's Club, 159, 198, 214
Milton P. M. Club, 159, 198, 216
Milton Woman's Club, 57, 58, 95, 126, 198, 210
Monday Club of Weymouth, 152, 205, 210
Moore, Mrs. Philip North, 7, 55
Muir, Mrs. J. Vernon, 128
Mulligan, Minna Rawson (Mrs. Henry Coolidge), 9, 51, 59, 211
Munroe, Mrs. William, 34

Nahant Woman's Club, 68, 100, 101, 102, 129, 163, 198, 209
Natick Woman's Club, 59, 160, 198, 209
Nauset Junior Woman's Club, Orleans, 152, 200, 218

229

Nautilus Club of Provincetown, 53, 89, 121, 122, 123, 157, 200, 211

New Bedford Woman's Club, 52, 53, 54, 55, 87, 157, 199, 219

New Century Club of Mansfield, 59, 95, 197, 211

New Century Club of Needham, 160, 198, 211

New England Conference, 8, 10, 13, 16, 26, 27, 32, 36, 39, 45, 51, 180

New England Women's Club, 4, 9, 49, 61, 63, 65, 162, 191, 209

Newton Centre Woman's Club, 59, 95, 199, 209

Ninth District Presidents' Club, 100, 101, 102, 129, 192, 213

Northampton Woman's Club, Inc., 110, 111, 137, 200, 214

Northboro (Northborough) Junior Woman's Club, Inc., 166, 169, 200, 219

Northborough Woman's Club, 70, 74, 105, 132, 134, 170, 200, 210

Norumbega Woman's Club, 65, 128, 193, 209

Norwood Woman's Club, 37, 58, 93, 200, 210

Nutting, Wallace, 102

Old and New of Malden, 66, 197, 209

Old Colony Club, 152, 202, 210

Old Colony P.M. Club of South Weymouth, 121, 202, 216

Old Colony Union Women's Club of Bourne, 53, 54, 87, 124, 154, 192, 212

Old Melrose Club, 66

Orange Woman's Club, 113, 139, 200, 213

Orleans Woman's Club, 86, 87, 89, 92, 122, 123, 124, 157, 158, 200, 213

Orlitzki, Mildred, vii, x

Osborne, Esther (Mrs. Raymond U.), 165

Ousamequin Club of Bridgewater, 58, 95, 126, 159, 193, 210

Outlook Club of Falmouth, 124, 194, 212

Oxford Woman's Club, 168, 200, 216

Palmer, Alice Freeman, 76

Past Chairmen's Club, 99, 163, 191, 215

Past Junior Officers Club, 66, 191, 219

Pauplis, Jeannette, vii, x

Paxton Woman's Club, 105, 131, 132, 173, 200, 214

Peabody, Elizabeth, 65

Peabody, Endicott, 68

Peabody, Mrs. Malcolm, 68

Peabody Woman's Club, 100, 101, 131, 200, 210

Pennybacker, Mrs. Percy, 9

Pepperell Woman's Club, The, 67, 101, 129, 164, 200, 211

Perkins, Florence T. (Mrs. George Winslow), 10, 51, 212

Peterson, Beatrice A. (Mrs. Raymond N.), 37, 99, 143, 218

Philergians of Braintree, The, 52, 53, 87, 89, 121, 122, 124, 155, 192, 210

Plymouth Woman's Club, 53, 200, 219

P. M. Club of Brockton, 121, 123, 124, 155, 193, 216

P. M. Club of Hingham, 121, 122, 123, 153, 155, 157, 158, 195, 217

Poole, Grace Morrison (Mrs. H. G. Reynolds), 13, 17, 84, 91, 213

Porter, Lillian A. (Mrs. Thomas L.), 33, 34, 141, 174, 217

Potter, Mary Pratt (Mrs. Arthur Devens), 15, 81, 84, 213

Presidents' Club of Massachusetts, 12, 66, 191, 212

Professional Women's Club, Inc., 66, 192, 211

Puerce, Ernest H., 67

Puma, Mrs. John J., 162

230

Quincy Women's Club, 53, 54, 92, 124, 155, 201, 211

Ramapogue Junior Women's Club, 137, 205, 216
Ramapogue Women's Club, 110, 136, 205, 215
Ramona Club, 76
Reading Junior Woman's Club, 130, 201, 217
Reading Woman's Club, 66, 67, 101, 102, 130, 164, 165, 166, 201, 209
Revere Women's Club, Inc., 66, 67, 163, 201, 210
Revil, Rita, vii, x
Reynolds, Dr. H. G., 13
Reynolds, Mrs. H. Gilbert (Grace), Morrison Poole, 13, 17, 84, 91, 213
Ripley, Mrs. Clara May, 62
Rochester Woman's Club, 86, 92, 121, 122, 124, 125, 155, 156, 201, 214
Rockland P. M. Club, 121, 123, 155, 201, 216
Rockland Woman's Club, 124, 201, 211
Rockport Woman's Club, 67, 68, 163, 201, 212
Roosevelt, Theodore, 79
Roslindale Woman's Club, 59, 201, 211
Ross, Eleanor B. (Mrs. Marshall W.), 38, 62, 143, 153, 218
Rowe, Olive M. E., 4, 50, 80, 210
Royston, Mrs. Katherine, 109
Ryder, Dr. Emily, 65

Salem Woman's Club, 129
Saltonstall, Governor Leverett, 99
Sandwich Junior Woman's Club, 152, 201, 218
Sandwich Woman's Club, 86, 87, 90, 122, 123, 124, 153, 154, 201, 213
Sargent, Governor Frank, 39
Scanlon, Mrs., 128
Schrader, Maude Wallace (Mrs. Carl L.), 17, 84, 214
Schweitzer, Dr. Albert, 62
Scoville, Mrs. George, 129

Second District Past Presidents' Club, 86, 192, 215
Severance, Mrs. Caroline, 64
Shaw, Miss Barbara E., 28
Shawsheen Village Woman's Club, Andover, The, 100, 102, 131, 189, 213
Shelburne Falls Woman's Club, 30, 113, 139, 202, 213
Shepard, Marcia E. (Mrs. Charles E.), vii, 32, 138, 141, 177, 178, 217
Shrewsbury Woman's Club, 75, 105, 131, 132, 134, 169, 171, 202, 211
Silsbee, Mrs. Alice M., 59
Sippican Woman's Club of Marion, 52, 53, 55, 92, 125, 154, 157, 158, 197, 211
Sixth District Presidents' Club, 99, 128, 192, 216
Small, Esther Z. (Mrs. David M.), 29, 120, 216
Smith, Mabel Johnson (Mrs. Frederick Glazier), 14, 84, 213
Smith, Mrs. J. Verrity, 99
Social Service League, 58
Somerset Woman's Club, 86, 92, 123, 124, 202, 214
Sorosis Club of New York, 70
Southampton Woman's Club, 78, 109, 111, 136, 176, 202, 213
Southborough Junior Woman's Club, 106
Southborough Woman's Club, 103, 105, 106, 107, 131, 133, 170, 172, 174, 202, 211
Southbridge Woman's Club, 70, 73, 75, 106, 131, 167, 202, 212
Southwick Women's Club, 109, 136, 176, 177, 202, 213
Sparhawk, Mrs., 67
Spencer Monday Club, 71, 104, 106, 168, 170, 172, 202, 209

Standish, Myles, 55
Sterling Woman's Club, 131, 132, 167, 168, 170, 172, 203, 215
Stevens, Lillian S. (Mrs. Lewis C.), 27, 31, 119, 174, 216
Stoneham Woman's Club, 66, 67, 100, 101, 128, 129, 164, 165, 166, 203, 210
Stoughton Woman's Club, 94, 160, 203, 213
Study Club, Whitinsville, 103
Sunderland Woman's Club, 81, 113, 139, 178, 179, 180, 203, 210
Swain, Ada W. (Mrs. Ralph G.), 28, 119, 120, 123, 216

Taft, William Howard, 56, 63
Talking Information Center, 43, 44, 45, 102, 149, 155, 157, 164, 173
Tatnuck Woman's Club of Worcester, 75, 105, 106, 132, 206, 212
Taunton Woman's Club, 53, 54, 87, 91, 125, 155, 157, 203, 211
Templeton, Louise, 165
Templeton, Lucille, 166
Templeton Woman's Club, Inc., 70, 72, 75, 103, 104, 107, 131, 169, 173, 203, 215
Tenth District Presidents' Club, 102, 192, 215
Third District Presidents' Club, 86, 192, 215
Thirteenth District Presidents' Club, 103, 192, 214
Towne, Mrs. William, 79
Townsend Monday Club, 106
Townsend Woman's Club, 106, 132, 167, 170, 203, 214
Tri-Community Junior Woman's Club, Southbridge, 166, 174, 202, 219
Troland, Ethel M. (Mrs. Edwin), 24, 36, 99, 116, 215

Trombley, Helene, 184
Tuesday Afternoon Club, 79
Tuesday Club of Assonet, The, 52, 53, 54, 87, 91, 125, 153, 156, 189, 215
Tuesday Club of Warren, 79, 111, 138, 177, 204, 210
Twelfth District Past Presidents' Club, 161, 192, 215
Tyler, John M., 76
Tyminski, Marian, 165

Upton Woman's Club, 74, 168, 169, 172, 174, 203, 211
Uxbridge Woman's Club, 133, 167, 203, 216

Village Improvement Society, 57, 74
Visiting Nurse Association, ix, 53, 58, 60, 65, 66, 74, 89, 92, 93, 95, 107, 108, 124, 132, 133, 159

Walker, Viola White (Mrs. Thomas J.), 19, 85, 174, 214
Walpole Health Center, 58, 95
Walpole Woman's Club, 57, 58, 95, 204, 209
Waltham Junior Woman's Club, 97, 204, 214
Waltham Woman's Club, 59, 96, 127, 204, 210
Ward, May Alden (Mrs. William G.), 5, 6, 7, 50, 210, 211
Wareham Junior Monday Club, 121, 204, 216
Wareham Junior Woman's Club, 89
Wareham Monday Club, 52, 53, 54, 87, 89, 122, 125, 157, 204, 211
Warner, Mary E. (Mrs. Edward C.), 42, 146, 148, 178, 180, 219
Washington, Booker T., 56, 68
Washington, George, 17, 18, 73
Watertown Woman's Club, 59, 60, 97, 127, 161, 204, 209
Webber, Florence, 97
Webber, Marion, 97
Webster Woman's Club, 106, 131, 204, 212
Weidner, Natalie B. (Mrs. Earl R.), 31, 120, 129, 217

Weld, Theodore, 57

West Concord Woman's Club, 59, 96, 193, 211

West Roxbury Woman's Club, 23, 204, 211

West Townsend Study Club, 106

Westborough Woman's Club, 71, 72, 106, 107, 133, 168, 169, 170, 171, 205, 212

Westcott, Luella P. (Mrs. David A.), 22, 86, 215

Western Massachusetts Women's Club, 111, 178, 203, 212

Westfall, Isabel Packard (Mrs. Azel A.), (Mrs. John V.), 16, 84, 214

Westminster Woman's Club, 133, 134, 171, 172, 205, 216

Weston, Harriet F. (Mrs. Richard G.), x

Westwood Woman's Club, 160, 205, 216

Weymouth P. M. Club, 121, 123, 124, 125, 205, 216

Weymouth Women's Club, 152, 155, 205, 219

White, Anna, 164

Whitinsville Library Club, 103

Whitinsville Woman's Club, 103, 106, 134, 173, 174, 205, 213

Whitman Woman's Club, 53, 92, 124, 153, 155, 205, 211

Whitmore, Mr., 81

Whittier, Helen A., 6, 50, 210

Whittier, John Greenleaf, 68

Wilbraham Junior Woman's Club, 184, 205, 219

Wilbraham Women's Club, 79, 112, 138, 178, 205, 211

Williamsburg Women's Club, 111, 205, 213

Wilmington Women's Club, 66, 67, 100, 101, 129, 205, 210

Wilson, Jessie, 56

Wilson, Mrs. Edmund I., 34

Wilson, Woodrow, 56

Winchendon Woman's Club, 74, 134, 168, 173, 205, 210

Winslow, Miss Helen, 6

Woburn Woman's Club, 66, 68, 100, 101, 165, 206, 209

Woman's Club of Brockton, 52, 87, 91, 193, 210

Woman's Club of East Bridgewater, 95, 194, 212

Woman's Club of Easthampton, 111, 194, 213

Woman's Club of Greenfield, 81, 139, 179, 195, 211

Woman's Club of Newton Highlands, 94, 95, 199, 212

Woman's Club of Shelburne Falls, 30, 113, 139, 202, 213

Woman's Club of West Boylston, 104, 105, 106, 107, 131, 132, 134, 168, 173, 204, 214

Women's Club of Melrose, Inc., 164, 198, 219

Women's Council of National Defense, 11

Women's Educational and Industrial Union, 7, 61

Women's Italian Club of Boston, Inc., 66, 162, 192, 212

Women's Municipal League, 114

Women's Service Club of Boston, Inc., 66, 192, 217

Wood, Mary H. (Mrs. Frederick J.), 33, 34, 141, 142, 217

Wood, William, 102

Worcester Woman's Club, 69, 70, 72, 74, 75, 134, 169, 171, 174, 206, 210

Worden, Mrs. H. Preston, 134

World Wide Study Club, 79

York, Hortense S. (Mrs. A. Chesley), 26, 100, 119, 129, 216

Young Women's Christian Association, 61, 117, 132

Young Women's Club of West Springfield, 110, 136

Young Women's Community Club, 54

Zakrzewska, Dr. Marie, 65

FROM THE PAST
TO THE FUTURE

has been published in a first edition
of fifteen hundred copies.
Designed by A. L. Morris,
the text was composed in Paladium
and printed by Sherwin/Dodge, Printers,
in Littleton, New Hampshire,
on Georgia-Pacific Natural Landmark Vellum.
The jacket and endleaves were printed on Curtis Tweedweave Text
and the binding, in James River Graphics Kivar,
was executed by New Hampshire Bindery
in Concord, New Hampshire.

Passed to be enacted

May 3. 1850

Approved.

A true copy: Witness

21. 1855. — Attest